Meaningful Game Design

This book provides readers with the tools and methods with which to create effective tabletop games. It covers the design and development process thoroughly, guiding readers through the necessary mechanics, messages, and motivations of games that must be understood in order to build successful tabletop games, including serious educational games for teaching or training.

Through a range of learning activities and methodologies, readers will develop an understanding of games and an appreciation for the creating and testing of game play whilst critically exploring the relationship between games, motivation, and learning. It includes chapters on design methodology, narrative, accessibility, play-testing, and more.

This book will be of great interest to students of game design and serious game design courses. It will also appeal to designers, educators, and hobbyists interested in designing and developing their own tabletop games, educational or otherwise.

Meaningful Game Design
The Methodology and Psychology
of Tabletop Games

Dr Devon Allcoat and Chris Evans

CRC Press
Taylor & Francis Group
Boca Raton London New York

CRC Press is an imprint of the
Taylor & Francis Group, an **informa** business

Designed cover image: Kim Watts

First edition published 2024
by CRC Press
2385 Executive Center Drive, Suite 320, Boca Raton, FL 33431

and by CRC Press
4 Park Square, Milton Park, Abingdon, Oxon, OX14 4RN

CRC Press is an imprint of Taylor & Francis Group, LLC

ISBN: 978-1-032-33403-5 (hbk)
ISBN: 978-1-032-33307-6 (pbk)
ISBN: 978-1-003-31951-1 (ebk)

DOI: 10.1201/9781003319511

Typeset in Times LT Std
by KnowledgeWorks Global Ltd.

Contents

              Kolb's Experiential Learning Cycle 20
              Learning Domains 21
              Bloom's Taxonomy 22

Chapter 4 Design Methodology 24

              Chris Evans

              Introduction 24
              What Problems Are We Trying to Solve? 24
              Types of Games 24
              Design Frameworks 25
                    Capability 26
                    Instructional Content 26
                    Intended Learning Outcomes 27
                    Game Attributes 27
                    Learning Activity 28
                    Reflection 29
                    Games Genre 29
                    Game Mechanics 29
                    Game Achievement 29
              The Design Process 29
                    Empathise Phase 30
                    Define Phase 31
                    Ideate Phase 31
                    Prototype Phase 32
                    Test (Playtest) Phase 32

Chapter 5 Accessibility 34

              Dr Devon Allcoat

              Why Accessibility? 34
                    Clarity 34
                    Increased Target Audience 36
              Protected Characteristics 36
              Eight Kinds of Accessibility 37
              Colour Blindness 38
              Visual Accessibility 40
                    Low Vision 40
                    Astigmatism and Double Vision 42
                    Simulator Sickness 42
              Cognitive 43
                    Attention 43
                    Intelligence 43
                    Information Processing 44

Chapter 11 Prototyping and Playtesting 132

Dr Devon Allcoat

Chapter 12 Taking Your Game to Market 142

Chris Evans

Chapter 13

Dr Lauren Schrock

Chapter 14

Dr Devon Allcoat

Acknowledgements

This book is something of a personal accomplishment, both for me and for Chris. However, just as our friends, family, and colleagues enrich our lives and support our efforts, this book wouldn't have happened without a strong, supportive community. I would like to take a moment to thank them for their contribution.

Thank you to Kim Watts, not only for your chapter, but for your incredible artwork and designs in the cover art and throughout the book. Your unfailing help and positive attitude, as well as your artistic skills, helped to bring this book to fruition.

To Lauren Schrock, thank you for your guest author chapter, and your contributions to our *Serious Tabletop Game Design and Development* module. Thank you to Alex Dixon, for your own work on our module, and for sharing the story of your crowdfunding journey for this book.

Thank you to my mother, Siân Allcoat, for your constant support and suggestions. Thanks also go more widely to mine and Chris' families for their kindness, sympathy, and patience during the writing process. Thank you to my rabbits, Remy and Jessie, for keeping me entertained during long writing sessions, and to my friends who provided guidance and feedback.

Finally, thank you to everyone who supported our endeavours, including Will Bateman from Taylor and Francis, who initially approached us to write this; Suzanne Turner, who shared advice on writing a textbook; Angela Clarke, who helped make sure I had time to write it; David Reynolds, whose interest and enthusiasm was always a joy; and you, reader, for supporting us by reading this book.

Dr Devon Allcoat

About the Authors

Dr Devon Allcoat develops and teaches courses and modules in game design and development at the University of Warwick, in the United Kingdom. Her expertise is in game design, pedagogy, human-technology interaction, virtual reality, and mixed reality, and she has previously worked in both the video game and board game industries. Her PhD in Psychology from the University of Warwick was awarded a Thesis Impact Prize for her doctoral research exploring the effects and applications of video games and virtual environments, particularly their cognitive effects and how they can be applied to education. In her current role, she continues to work on research projects examining technology, whilst collaborating with industry and utilising innovative teaching practices.

Chris Evans is the Head of Technology-Enhanced Learning at Warwick Manufacturing Group at the University of Warwick. In this role, he is responsible for the strategic development, coordination, and implementation of technology-enhanced learning policies and initiatives. With over 20 years' experience within lecturing, teacher training, and technology-enhanced learning, Chris has designed, implemented, and overseen numerous pedagogically driven game-based simulations within the tertiary learning sector. Chris also teaches game design at the University of Warwick and adopts a student-centric, interactive, and highly innovative approach to teaching and learning.

Kim Watts works as an e-Learning Multimedia Developer at Warwick Manufacturing Group at the University of Warwick. In her role, Kim supports academics to utilise both current and emerging technology within their teaching to create innovative, creative, and engaging learning content. Prior to Kim's current role, she worked in the private sector as a lead visual communications designer for an award-winning business innovation consultancy.

Dr Lauren Schrock is an Associate Professor at Warwick Manufacturing Group at the University of Warwick, where she teaches students how to successfully conduct independent research and write a dissertation. Since completing her PhD at Warwick Business School, Lauren's research has focused on transferrable skills education, the management of teaching and assessment for large classes, and student experience.

1 Introduction

Dr Devon Allcoat

WHAT IS A GAME?

Is a puzzle a game? Is a quiz a game? Where do you draw the boundary between an activity and a game? Each person may have a different definition of, or requirements for, a game. Maybe they expect to have rewards or prizes involved, or perhaps a certain challenge or difficulty level.

From the time that Huizinga (1938/1949) first explored the idea that games could be a field of study, various scholars and academics have attempted to define the concept of what a game actually is. The following list details some of those definitions in chronological order:

> A game is time-bound ... it has no contact with any reality outside of itself, and its performance is its own end. Further, it is sustained by the consciousness of being a pleasurable, even mirthful, relaxation from the strains of ordinary life.
>
> **Huizinga, 1938/1949, p. 13**

> To play a game is to engage in activity directed toward bringing about a specific state of affairs, using only means permitted by specific rules, where the means permitted by the rules are more limited in scope than they would be in the absence of the rules, and where the sole reason for accepting such limitation is to make possible such activity.
>
> **Suits, 1967, p. 148**

> [A] game is an exercise of voluntary control systems, in which there is a contest between powers, confined by rules in order to produce a disequilibrial outcome.
>
> **Avedon & Sutton-Smith, 1971, p. 405**

> A game is a form of recreation constituted by a set of rules that specify an object to be attained and the permissible means of attaining it.
>
> **Kelley, 1988, p. 50**

> A game is a form of art in which participants, termed players, make *decisions* in order to manage *resources* through *game tokens* in the pursuit of a *goal*.
>
> **Costikyan, 1994, p. 25**

> A game is a system in which players engage in an artificial conflict, defined by rules, that results in a quantifiable outcome.
>
> **Salen & Zimmerman, 2004, p. 80**

DOI: 10.1201/9781003319511-1

A game is any contest or effort (play) among adversaries or teammates (players) operating under constraints (rules and resources) for an objective (winning, victory, prestige, status, or pay-off). The exercise, or activity, should involve overt competition, or cooperation between the individuals or teams, who are competing against each other, or together (while jointly conquering circumstances) fighting the odds.

Klabbers, 2008, p. 28–29

A game is a problem-solving activity, approached with a playful attitude.

Schell, 2008, p. 37

Whist multiple of these definitions seem appropriate, despite all being different in terms of focus and terminology, some could be considered ambiguous or unsuitable. As you can see, these definitions typically do not dictate the mode of delivery. Digital games, tabletop games, or even sports can fit into these definitions, leaving a lot of things that can fall under the umbrella of the term "game".

Further to definitions in one or two sentences, some game theorists have suggested that games can be described by a list of criteria that all games must include. In his book *Les Jeux et les Hommes* (translated version: *Man, Play and Games*), Caillois (1961) defined a game/play as having the following characteristics:

- **Fun**: the activity is chosen for its light-hearted character.
- **Separate**: it is circumscribed in time and place.
- **Uncertain**: the outcome of the activity is unforeseeable.
- **Non-productive**: participation does not accomplish anything useful.
- **Governed by rules**: the activity has rules that are different from everyday life.
- **Fictitious**: it is accompanied by the awareness of a different reality.

Caillois expanded on Huizinga's work, critically appraising it and creating new knowledge in the study of play and game design. As criteria for games for learning however, the list above is somewhat problematic. In serious games, for example, the intended outcome may be predictable or foreseeable, and one would hope that a serious game would accomplish something useful.

Over the next 40 or so years, many scholars attempted to classify games using various definitions and criteria, but there was a more noticeable shift when game designers who were employed in game studies became involved. One such game designer is Juul (2005), who suggested that any game should consist of the following six criteria:

- A rule-based formal system.
- Variable and quantifiable outcomes.
- Different outcomes are assigned different values.
- The player exerts effort in order to influence the outcome.
- The player feels emotionally attached to the outcome.
- The consequences of the activity are optional and negotiable.

Indeed, most games fulfil these six requirements, though arguments may be made against purely luck-based games such as *Snakes and Ladders*. Clearly, there are a few key things games can be (Figure 1.1), so perhaps, instead, we should look at what they are not.

FIGURE 1.1   Games can take many forms.

So Where Does That Leave Us?

Ten definitions of "game" have been presented. This is only a sample; Stenros (2017) provides an overview looking at over 60 definitions and discussing the difficulty of defining games, and there are more definitions beyond those too. You can, of course, pick your own favourite definition, or have your own concepts and expectations. Looking at the 10 different definitions we have discussed (including those utilising criteria), let's consider the most common traits (Table 1.1).

TABLE 1.1

Common Traits and How Many Definitions Include Them

Traits Definition Inclusions

Traits	Definition Inclusions
Activity	4
Conflict/Competition	3
Goals/Objectives	5
Outcomes	4
Players	5
Recreation/Play	3
Rules	8
System	3

Some definitions define a game as an activity, others as a system (see Chapter 11 for explanation and discussion about systems). Half of the definitions mention the role of players; is it possible to have a game without players? Eight of the definitions discuss rules, the concept that games must have a set of constraints they are played within.

Fewer of the definitions specify the purpose, but those that do, discuss concepts such as recreation or play. However, for educational games their primary purpose is to teach. Furthermore, many games can be played professionally. In a sponsored tournament with prize money, for example, you could argue that the purpose is no longer recreation, but financial gain.

It's also important to think about the idea of conflict or competition. Given that single-player games and co-operative games exist, how can we say that a game is defined by conflict or competition? This is because the conflict or competition isn't necessarily against *other players*. It can also be against the game itself (such as what you can achieve within the confines of the rules), or yourself (such as improving your score).

Goals, objectives, and outcomes are also interesting concepts. Goals and objectives are often linked to endpoints – but does a game need to end to be a game? How about tabletop role-playing games, many of which take you through a story, but don't necessarily give you a specific goal to achieve. In these cases, often they players create their own objectives. A goal or objective is also not the same as an outcome. When comparing games to other mediums, one thing that stands out which isn't directly addressed in most of the definitions, is the idea of *interaction*. Unlike most books, film and television, you interact with the content of a game. This is what leads to different outcomes.

Considering the above, the following definition has been created:

A game is a system with rules facilitating competition, with players influencing outcomes through interaction, in pursuit of objectives.

WHAT DO WE MEAN BY "MEANINGFUL" GAME DESIGN?

SERIOUS GAMES

Firstly, it is important to consider the existing term "serious games". Clark Abt (1970) is generally deferred to as the originator of this term. He relates the idea to Jean Piaget's (Jennings, 1967) ruminations on how learning, knowledge, and intelligence are "born of action" and that we understand things by reinventing them. Abt suggests that this process of reinventing is the same as playing a game.

A serious game is a game designed for a primary purpose other than pure entertainment (Djaouti et al., 2009), so games centred around learning are commonly called serious games. Serious games are becoming particularly popular recently, and are being used in a wider range of environments, such as education, business, design, corporate training, healthcare, the military, management, public services, and more (Zeshan, 2020). However, the terminology is not consistent. Becker (2018), in an attempt to provide clarification and classification, included serious games as a part of a larger discipline which includes:

- Games
- Serious Games
- Games for Learning

- Game-Based Learning
- Game-Based Pedagogies
- Gamification

Becker (2018) discusses that gamification, serious games, and game-based learning have similar objectives in that they are designed to motivate. She states that the difference between gamification and game-based learning is that in gamification you apply game elements (leader boards, badges, achievements, and points are popular examples) to an existing non-gaming context, whereas in games for learning, you use existing games or specially developed games for learning. Becker also clarifies that the difference between game-based learning (or game-based pedagogy) and a serious game, is that game-based learning is a method or a way of learning, whereas a serious game is a product in which game-based learning is possible.

There are many examples of the use of existing games as educational tools, with a rule of thumb being that the more popular the game, the higher the likelihood that it will be adapted. The board game *Monopoly*, for example, has been used to teach accountancy (Shanklin & Ehlen, 2007), probability (Gazdula & Farr, 2020), diversity (Griffin & Jackson, 2011), and inequality (Ansoms & Geenen, 2012b).

Today, a serious game is commonly understood to be a game with a purpose beyond entertainment, particularly an educational component, or with some type of learning or training involved. It is worth noting that games which are designed primarily for entertainment can still be educational; they can still teach and be learnt from. Serious games are often considered to exist only as digital games used for purposes other than mere entertainment (Susi et al., 2007). The prefix "non-digital" or "analogue" is often applied to non-digital serious games, though this is not always the case, and for the purpose of this book, the term serious game applies to digital, non-digital, and hybrid serious games. This leaves us defining serious games as "A game with a purpose beyond pure entertainment, that is digital, analogue, or hybrid".

SIMULATIONS

Becker (2018) chose to include simulations within the serious game category, though sometimes simulations are seen as a separate category (Ahmed & Sutton, 2017). The Oxford English Dictionary provides the following definitions for the word "simulation".

1. a. The action or practice of simulating, with intent to deceive; false pretence, deceitful profession.
   b. Tendency to assume a form resembling that of something else; unconscious imitation.
2. A false assumption or display, a surface resemblance or imitation, *of* something.
3. The technique of imitating the behaviour of some situation or process (whether economic, military, mechanical, etc.) by means of a suitably analogous situation or apparatus, esp. for the purpose of study or personnel training. Frequently *attributive*.

The third definition is the most relevant for our purposes. There is some crossover with the concept of serious games providing education, learning, or training; more specifically, simulations more clearly imitate a scenario or process. Something can be both a simulation and a game, so for some products, as well as concepts and theories, these terms can be used interchangeably, particularly for education. Simulations can be digital or analogue, and some require no physical or digital elements at all.

Meaningful

The Oxford English Dictionary provides the following definitions for the word "meaningful".

1. a. Full of meaning or expression, significant; communicating something that is not explicitly or directly expressed.
   b. Having a serious, important, or recognisable quality or purpose.

The word "serious", as used by Abt (1970) in the term "serious games", makes an appearance here. Alongside this, however, are other expressions: "meaning", "expression", "significant", "important", "purpose", and a focus on communication. While some of these are covered in the definitions given for Abt's phrase, of particular note is the concept of communication. So, meaningful game design is about designing a game in a way that communicates something significant or purposeful through the medium of a game. By extension, a meaningful game is one which communicates something significant or purposeful. Finally, in our title, meaningful game design also alludes to the idea of the game design process itself being meaningful. So whilst we will use the term "serious games" in this book, as it is commonly used in the literature, the concepts we discuss can be applied to any type of meaningful game, educational or not.

Without constantly repeating dictionary definitions, the word significant could be substituted for serious, important, or other similar words, but regardless, it is still worth noting that what is considered significant, serious, or important will differ from person to person. Later in this book, we will discuss learning objectives, which is one method you can use to define the significant ideas or concepts you want to demonstrate.

SUMMARY

Overall, this should give you a better idea of what we mean by "Meaningful Game Design", as used in the title. This book will cover "serious games", as we have defined here, and simulations, considering both analogue and digital. We believe that good game design is good game design, whichever format it is delivered in, and regardless of what entertainment or educational purposes it may have. This book aims to deliver that strong foundation for good game design, no matter what you aim to create.

2 Serious Games

Chris Evans

INTRODUCTION

She had planned to make her subject today more interesting, more engaging, more game-like. Students liked games she decided, so this lesson was going to include a game.

> *"We're going to start with a test" the teacher said, silencing the room. "It will be in the form of a quiz, which you'll undertake in teams".*
>
> *"What will the test be on?" asked one of her students.*
>
> *"What you've learned so far, though you'll have to apply that knowledge in order to find the answers".*
>
> *She brought up a large timer on the whiteboard, setting it to 10 seconds.*
>
> *"You'll be timed out if you're too slow, giving the other teams a chance to steal".*
>
> *From behind her desk, she retrieved an oversized gameboard, holding it up for the class to see.*
>
> *"The game will be played on a giant game board, and you'll have tokens that represent your team" continued the Teacher.*
>
> *"Are we being assessed?" another student asked.*
>
> *"No, but there is a prize for the winning team" she said, producing a box of chocolates from under her desk.*

Even after almost a century of research, the definition of what constitutes a game is still a little unclear. At some point in the discussion above, the lesson crossed the line and became a game, though it is debatable when exactly that happened. Furthermore, was the lesson a game, or was it gamification, a serious game, a game for learning, game-based learning, or game-based pedagogy? Moreover, does it matter what names we use, just so long as the students learn effectively?

ARE SERIOUS GAMES EDUCATIONAL DIGITAL GAMES?

In recent times, serious games have gained popularity, and according to Zeshan (2020), the range of contexts in which they are being used is on the rise. As well as in education, serious games are increasingly used in the military, business, design, corporate training, healthcare, management, and public services.

DOI: 10.1201/9781003319511-2

Often, when we talk about games, we are exclusively referring to them in the digital context:

"You teach game design? Wow, I love computer games".

"Well, it's actually more theoretical...."

"Oh, so you teach programming?"

The same is true for serious games; though when the concept of a serious game was first defined, the term referred both to the pen and paper variety, and early serious games on mainframe computers (Abt, 1970), which were the state-of-the-art technology of the time. Since that time, various definitions have been proposed, some of which suggest that a serious game is purely digital, and others that leave it open to interpretation. For example, when Chen and Michael (2005, p. 21) defined serious games as "Games that do not have entertainment, enjoyment or fun as their primary purpose", they argued more the case that serious games were not just purely for education, rather than not just purely digital. Similarly, Becker (2018, p. 2) describes a serious game as "A game designed specifically with some learning goals in mind", leaving the interpretation open as to whether this definition of serious games refers to digital games or any type of game. To prevent any uncertainty, some researchers such as Laamarti et al. (2014) describe serious games as "*digital* serious games" in their overview of the genre, whilst others, such as us, describe non-digital serious games as serious tabletop games within our taught module. Whichever terminology is used, due to a majority that consider serious games to be digital, the responsibility should lie with the non-digital advocates to differentiate. However, when referring to serious games within this publication, the definitions described by Becker (2018) and Chen and Michael (2005) will apply, and we will consider the term serious games to include any type of serious game, differentiating only when necessary.

THE BENEFITS OF SERIOUS GAMES

Serious tabletop games in education can provide many benefits, but their adoption as a tool for teaching and learning is neither without risk of failure nor criticism. A colleague who was resistant to any form of games-based learning once told me that "Every minute that a student spends playing games is a minute lost of learning opportunity". People are predisposed to associate games with entertainment rather than with anything serious. The benefits of serious games must therefore provide enough compelling evidence to suggest otherwise.

BENEFIT 1: ENGAGEMENT

In educational terms, student engagement involves the psychological investment that students make in their learning (Newmann, 1992). However, Coates (2007) believes that student engagement is more nuanced than that. In his study on student engagement in higher education, Coates (2007) suggests that students have engagement styles, namely:

- **Collaborative**: students who lean towards social activities rather than the more cognitive modes of interaction.

- **Passive**: students who prefer not to get involved in any form of active participation, but that does not mean that they are not engaged in teaching and learning.
- **Independent**: students who want a high level of academic challenge, though not in a particularly social way.
- **Intense**: students who are both highly engaged in their academic study and enjoy active engagement with both peers and teaching staff.

We are a combination of all these traits, but will tend to favour one style over the others. Look at the list, which of these engagement styles would you want to be involved in when playing serious tabletop games in the classroom? Furthermore, which engagement style would you least want to play? The important takeaway here is that, if possible, the needs of all learners should be considered when designing games or introducing them into the curriculum. How does your game appeal to both passive and intense students? It does not have to, but as an educator, we make reasonable adjustments, and as a designer of serious games, demonstrating empathy with the learners' psychological needs can be a valuable quality.

Games have long been considered to be engaging activities, the argument being: why else would we play them? The question of why they are engaging has also been explored in some depth, though we can defer to Prensky (2001), who covers all bases when suggesting that games can be fun, involving, structured, motivating, interactive, adaptive, informative, exciting, creative, challenging, social, emotive, and appealing to our egos.

More than anything else, well-designed games are engaging, and the importance of engagement in education cannot be understated. It is of no surprise that the benefits of engagement figure prominently in many academic studies of educational games:

- Serious games "are engaging, enjoyable, challenging, and experiential", with the potential to change attitudes and behaviours (Safdari et al., 2016, p. 474).
- "Games are engaging and interactive; they offer a mechanism to learn beyond simple memorisation and encourage problem-solving with colleagues and peers" (Eidle et al., 2022, p. 1).
- "Math games are engaging, motivating, and fun for learners. They encourage conceptual thinking and problem-solving that deepen understanding of mathematical concepts" (Lipovsky & Brennan, 2022, p. 4).
- "Games are engaging because they address autonomy (the ability to make decisions), competence (the ability to do something successfully or efficiently), and relatedness (the state of being related or connected)" (Ishak et al., 2022, p. 4).

BENEFIT 2: IMMEDIATE FEEDBACK

Engagement in an activity can also lead to a condition called *flow* (Csikszentmihalyi, 1975) whereby a perceived balance between challenge and skills can result in a state of concentration or complete absorption with the activity at hand. To work effectively, flow requires a feedback loop, something to inform the learner of their progress. In a game environment, feedback is instantaneous, and in most, but not all cases, you know if you are winning or losing, and you know if you are making progress towards your goal, or falling behind. This constant monitoring and feedback acts as a motivational factor for learners.

Games, including serious games, frequently emphasise evaluating performance in areas where skills have already been honed. Assessment can encompass both quantitative and qualitative aspects, aiming to provide learners with feedback regarding the outcomes of their actions. In their study on what made serious games successful in enhancing learning, Ravyse et al. (2017) suggested that the feedback mechanisms of serious games ought to be depicted in two manners: (a) an in-game feedback experience employing a range of in-game reward mechanisms, and (b) through post-game debriefing and reflection sessions that elucidate the learning content, and position the game-based learning experience within a broader and more meaningful context.

In educational speak, games that focus on the post-game briefing may be mapped closely to Kolb's experiential reflective learning cycle (Kolb, 1984), which allows learners to review, examine, and evaluate their experiences within the game (refer to Chapter 3 for more information).

Hattie and Timperley (2007) acknowledged that whilst feedback was one of the most powerful influences on learning and achievement, the impact of the feedback can have both positive and negative effects on the learner. Most importantly, feedback must be fair. In the educational game *Oregon Trail*, for example, which exists as both a computer and a card game, you may suddenly and for no apparent reason die of dysentery. Learners naturally saw this feedback as unfair, although the game did achieve legendary status as a result.

Benefit 3: Active Learning and Social Learning

According to Bonwell (2000), active learning (also see Chapter 3) occurs when students participate in the learning, that is, they are actively doing something. Subsequently, whilst social engagement is not fundamental to facilitate student participation, cooperative learning can be described as the foundation for active learning (Johnson & Johnson, 2019). Active learning can take place anywhere where activities such as small-group work, role-play, simulations, and game-based learning can be effectively facilitated, either by an educator or by the students themselves. If done correctly, this form of learning is claimed to increase student interest and motivation and to build students critical thinking, problem-solving and social skills (Camilleri & Camilleri, 2017). Bandura (1977) argued that his social learning theory (known today as social cognitive theory) contributed to clarifying the process by which individuals acquire knowledge through observation, imitation, and modeling. This learning model implies that both environmental and cognitive factors significantly influence the acquisition of knowledge.

Games, at their best, are highly social, highly interactive experiences (Prensky, 2001), and active learning is enhanced through effective playing of serious board games (Yoon et al., 2014). Furthermore, studies focussing on the use of tabletop games for learning have reported a significant increase in student knowledge after playing the game (Cardinot & Fairfield, 2019), and increased motivation (Gonzalo-Iglesia et al., 2018), and concentration (Nakao, 2019) during the game.

For balance, it must be stated that playing serious tabletop games in a classroom environment is not always successful. Heikkilä et al. (2016) found board games no more effective in teaching Kanban management systems when compared with traditional teaching methods. They argued that the overheads, such as setting the game up and learning the rules, outweighed any benefits. Furthermore, the gameplay, which was considered to be engaging by the students, had the undesired effect of drawing the learner's attention away from the learning goals of the game.

That being said, academic learning objectives are not the only positive outcome that serious games can impart. In their survey of employers, Gruzdev et al. (2018) found that employers considered soft skills to be significant for business, whilst at the same time highlighting the lack of these skills in current university graduates to support their professional work. The interplay between active learning and soft skills has been well documented (Gruzdev et al., 2018), but can the same be said for playing serious games? The problem that we have is one of context; there are a multitude of factors that can impact upon the success of any intervention that utilises serious games in the classroom, and furthermore, there is so much variation within the choice of game that we play. For example, the social educational benefits of two students playing a high strategy game such as Chess could be less than what could be achieved by a group of five students playing a serious game which was adapted from a party game.

In their systematic literature review examining the different methods and procedures used to assess social learning outcomes of collaborative serious games, den Haan and van der Voort (2018) reported that the playing of games had an impact on relational learning (building working alliances), as well as cognitive learning. This should not be unexpected, as soft skills, which include communication, problem-solving, critical thinking, organisation, teamwork, leadership, and decision-making, can all be found in gameplay. Even when dispersed geographically, clusters of learners can cultivate skills in teamwork, leadership, coordination, and communication by engaging in interactions within online games (Riivari et al., 2021; Vlachopoulos & Makri, 2017).

These skills are in-demand, and according to scholars such as Minbaeva and Collings (2013) and Singh Dubey et al. (2022), the development of soft skills is more important than the development of technical skills when it comes to performing globally.

CONSTRUCTIVE ALIGNMENT

Constructive alignment, a principle proposed by Biggs and Tang (2011), directly addresses the intended **learning outcomes** by aligning them both with the **assessment** and with the teaching and learning **activities**. Subsequently, constructive alignment has been adopted as a tool to design curricula and its associated activities within tertiary academia. With the design of serious games, the activity may be considered to be the game. The assessment, which can be inside or outside of the game, can be influenced by the win/lose states of the game, and the learning outcomes often, but not always, are aligned with the learning outcomes of the course of study. When designing serious games, we recommend starting with learning outcomes in mind. What are the learners going to achieve by playing this game?

Constructive Alignment: Case Study

In a hypothetical scenario, a student wants to create a game that teaches binomial distribution. He explains that it is taught within one of his modules *Maths*, and that it is often seen as a challenging subject for students to grasp. The student began with the learning outcomes and selected the one that was most appropriate: *Know probability and distributions to present data.*

When designing the game, the student was then able to create an experience that met these learning outcomes, provided feedback mechanisms and assessment, and subsequently aligned with both the outcomes and the taught lessons.

The finished game, as shown in Figure 2.1, was available to play both online and as a board game, and featured enemy alien spaceships (that were represented by dice) and engaged in conflict through application of binomial distribution formula. To succeed in the game, the players needed to adopt strategies of cooperative teamplay along with the understanding of the probability and distributions that were required to defeat the aliens through the use of mathematics.

Binomial Disruption Game Information

The game is aimed at first-year university students studying Statistics or Maths, and specifically, the foundations of the binomial distribution and how to implement it.

The learning objectives for the game are based upon two specific learning outcomes, the first of which is taken directly from the module handbook, and therefore lends itself to the game being constructively aligned (Biggs & Tang, 2015). The second learning objective is around the soft skills that the players learn by collaborating and working together to defeat the invaders – learning binomial distribution by way of social constructivism (Vygotsky, 1978).

LEARNING OBJECTIVES

- Know probability and distributions to present data.
- Act independently and accept responsibility to interact effectively within a team, giving and receiving information and ideas.

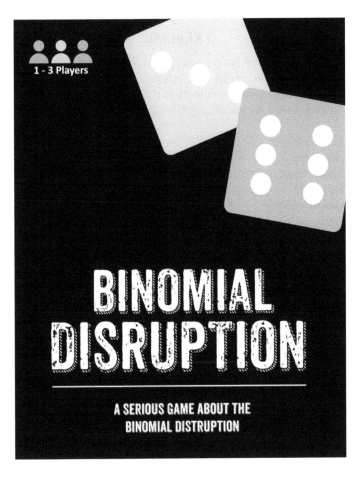

FIGURE 2.1   Binomial Disruption box design.

SUMMARY

Serious games are games that have been designed for a purpose other than that of pure entertainment, and with educational serious games, that purpose is learning. This is achieved using learning objectives that are intrinsically linked with the game's objectives, though not necessarily with the learning objectives of the associated course of study. Serious games are often used within the context of a wider teaching and learning objective, and as such are supported through periods of study and reflection that take place outside of the game. Within the game, the internal mechanisms of feedback loops act to reinforce learning, whilst the experiential aspects of gameplay keep the learner engaged in the subject material. Furthermore, the benefits of social learning allow students to learn through observation and collaborating and/or competing to achieve the game's objectives.

EXERCISE

Some "out of the box" tabletop games such as *Turing Machine* and *Cytosis* are designed to educate, whilst with others, such as *Wingspan* and *Twilight Struggle*, the learning is supplementary to the game.

But all games teach us something. Consider the following list of soft skills:

- Communication
- Leadership
- Critical thinking
- Teamwork
- Problem-solving
- Time management
- Decision-making
- Organisational skills
- Stress management
- Adaptability
- Conflict management
- Creativity
- Resourcefulness
- Persuasion
- Openness to criticism

Now think about your favourite game, or the one you have most recently played.

- Which of those soft skills are applied when playing that game?
- Can the use of soft skills within the game help develop those skills so they can be used outside of the game?

3 Psychology and Pedagogy

Dr Devon Allcoat

THE IMPORTANCE OF THEORY

This chapter will introduce a selection of theories and models that will be referenced elsewhere in this book. Theories underpin our understanding of how the world works, and how people work. This is why it is helpful to learn about and to understand theories related to your areas of interest and study. They inform us on core knowledge and can even be used to predict outcomes. This means that theories can be used to help determine the actions we should take, design of materials, including learning materials and how we should approach certain topics.

THE PLAYERS

TARGET AUDIENCE

Creating a game is of little benefit if nobody wants to play it. Therefore, there is a need to understand your target audience (Figure 3.1). Who are they, how many are there (how niche), and how do you reach them?

FIGURE 3.1 Game information (minimum age, number of players, and length of play) for your target audience.

DOI: 10.1201/9781003319511-3

There are many ways to categorise a target audience:

- Demographics (e.g. age, gender, occupation).
- Geographic (e.g. location).
- Psychographic (i.e. personality, values, interests).
- Behavioural (e.g. purchase habits, play patterns).

Of course, there are other stakeholders beyond the players (who are the primary consumers of the product), such as investors and colleagues. For a serious game, there are more potential stakeholders, such as teachers, facilitators, an organisation's administration and finance departments, and more. However, these stakeholders are of little relevance if there is no end consumer, so for now, let us focus on the players.

Bartle's Player Taxonomy

Bartle (1996) introduced classifications for the types of players who play multi-user dungeons (MUDs) or virtual worlds (Figure 3.2). These were typically games with multiple people playing online at the same time with elements of role-playing, player versus player, combat, and interactive fiction. Early MUDs were text-based, but now typically have visual graphics.

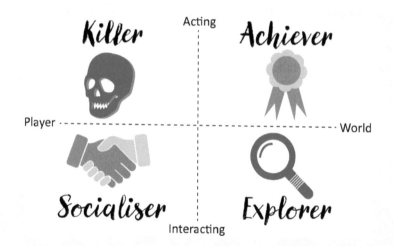

FIGURE 3.2   Bartle player types.

Bartle came up with his Player Taxonomy, also known as Bartle Player Types. This included a total of four types of players:

Killers
Killers get their sense of achievement from defeating other people, and other peoples' losses. They favour reputation and recognition and want to work out the best ways to apply their knowledge.

Achievers

Achievers enjoy doing the best they possibly can. They want to improve their power and status and achieve as much as they can through gameplay. Achievers want success through mastery of the game.

Socialisers

Socialisers prioritise the social experience of playing the game over the specific mechanics of gameplay. They are interested in gaining friends, contacts, and influence. To socialisers, the game itself acts as a background setting for their interests.

Explorers

Explorers want to discover. They want to gain knowledge and information, which they often enjoy sharing. Their main focus is to gain understanding and learn more about the game.

The four player classifications in Bartle's Taxonomy can easily be extended beyond MUDs. They can apply to not just other kinds of video games, but games in general, including tabletop games. Games will vary in appeal to the four player types. For example, player versus player combat-focused games will appeal more to killers than to socialisers. Games that are heavily story-based probably appeal most to explorers, and less so to achievers. Ideally, you want to appeal to multiple player types, not just one, to increase the target audience. However, it is also important to remember that although individuals can be classified by a questionnaire into one of these four categories, most individuals will have a combination of preferences and overlap the categories.

PLAYER MOTIVATION

Bartle's player types demonstrate how different types of players may have different driving factors and motivations for why they play. In addition to individual motivations, there are some general types of motivation, and motivational theories, that are helpful to understand.

EXTRINSIC MOTIVATION

Extrinsic motivation is a type of motivation that is based on external goals or rewards (or to avoid punishment). This can include being motivated by prizes or payment, gaining praise or approval, achieving good grades, or avoiding negative consequences.

INTRINSIC MOTIVATION

Intrinsic motivation, in contrast to extrinsic motivation, is not influenced by external rewards. Instead, it is an internal motivation to do an activity based on your inherent interest, personal reward or challenge, or satisfaction. There are a number of models specifically focused on the phenomenon of intrinsic motivation.

Self-Determination Theory

Self-determination theory (Deci & Ryan, 1985) suggests that outside of external influences and distractions, people are intrinsically motivated to achieve psychological growth when they feel that they have autonomy, competence, and relatedness. In this context, autonomy is referring to the feeling of having control over themselves. Competence is related to having and mastering the skills that they feel that they need. Finally, relatedness (or connection) refers to a sense of belonging.

Dan Pink's Motivation Model

Pink (2009) proposed a new intrinsic motivation model, which comprised Autonomy, Mastery, and Purpose. Two of the areas are clearly matched to Deci and Ryan's (1985) self-determination theory, Autonomy with the same name, and Mastery mirroring Competence. The final part of the triad (Figure 3.3) is now Purpose, which is about the desire to contribute to something larger than themselves. This model is specifically directed at working culture.

FIGURE 3.3   Dan Pink's motivation model.

LEARNING THEORIES AND MODELS

Psychology is the study of the mind and behaviour. The theories introduced to this point have been psychological theories (whether or not they originated from psychologists). Next, we will be focusing on learning and pedagogy. Pedagogy is all about teaching methods and practices. Pedagogy is typically informed by psychology and learning theories.

ACTIVE LEARNING

Active learning is any method of learning that allows students to actively participate in the learning process. Active learning activities can be individual or group activities, such as discussions, presentations, worksheets, case studies, and games (Figure 3.4). These types of activities help promote higher-order thinking skills, including application of knowledge, synthesis, and analysis. Active learning allows students to engage in deep learning, rather than surface learning, equipping students to be better able to apply and transfer knowledge.

FIGURE 3.4   Active learning.

Social Learning Theory

Social learning theory is linked to active learning. It is a theory proposed by Bandura (1977), a psychologist, that describes how behaviour is learnt through the process of observational learning, which comprised observation, imitation, and modelling. This learning model posits that both environmental and cognitive factors play an important role in knowledge acquisition. This is built on previous theories of classical conditioning (Pavlov, 1897; Watson, 1924; Watson & Rayner, 1920) and operant conditioning (Skinner, 1948, 1951, 1953; Thorndike, 1898).

Constructivism and Social Constructivism

Constructivism

Piaget, a developmental psychologist, pioneered the learning theory known as constructivism. This theory posits that learners construct new knowledge (in their minds) based on their experiences and prior knowledge (Piaget, 1964).

Teachers can facilitate constructivism in the classroom by creating learning opportunities for students, allowing the students the opportunity to utilise their own experience to construct their own understanding. This could be through various activities such as discussions and debates, self-guided learning, case studies, and other interactive techniques. Constructivism typically leads students to have freedom of interpretation, as they each experience the knowledge provided to them differently. Constructivism is all about building new ideas and concepts based on your own discoveries.

Vygotsky's Theory of Cognitive Development

Vygotsky's theories place importance on the fundamental role of social interaction in the development of cognition. His Cognitive Development Theory (Vygotsky, 1967) argued that our cognitive abilities are constructed, like constructivism, but specifically they are socially guided. This theory is not specific to learning, but general to all cognitive development, including attention, memory, and problem-solving, as well as learning. This theory came to be developed into social constructivism.

Social Constructivism

Social constructivism specifies that knowledge develops through collaborative learning, from how people interact with individuals and society. This, therefore, goes beyond constructivism, as it suggests that we do not just create our own knowledge through individual experience, but also through social experience and learning from others' experiences. In practice, this means that students not only learn from the teachers, but also from their peers. Group work and peer-to-peer feedback are great examples of tools to use for learning that are supported by the social constructivism theory. This also makes games particularly well-suited to education as per social constructivism, as games are typically played by groups in social environments, and players build experiences together.

KOLB'S EXPERIENTIAL LEARNING CYCLE

Kolb's experiential reflective learning cycle (Kolb, 1984) is a process which allows learners to review, examine, and evaluate their experiences. The four sections of this process can be seen in Figure 3.5.

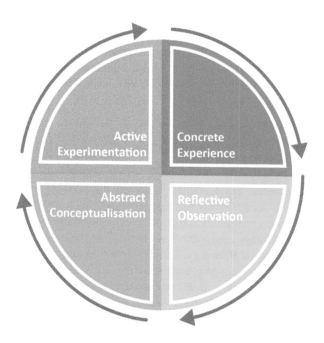

FIGURE 3.5   Kolb's experiential learning cycle. (From Kolb, 1984.)

Concrete Experience

Concrete experience is what it suggests, where you gain experience by engaging with an activity or task. This also links to concepts like active learning and constructivism, as concrete experience requires interactivity to acquire new knowledge. With games, this step may be completed by simply playing the game.

Reflective Observation

The reflective observation stage is where the learner is able to think about their experiences. This gives the students the opportunity to reflect on their understanding compared to their actual experiences. This stage can include the opportunity for discussion, such as asking questions and the sharing of different points of view. In the context of a game, this could be discussing how they felt about the game and their experience of playing it.

Abstract Conceptualisation

The next stage, abstract conceptualisation, is taking that reflection and applying it to generate new ideas, or modifying their understanding based on their new experiences. Having played a game and reflected on how it went, you may, at this stage, think about what you could do differently next time, and what new potential strategies you have learnt.

Active Experimentation

The final stage, active experimentation, is where the learner experiments with their ideas and tries new approaches and strategies based on their new understanding. This is when you play the game next time, and have the opportunity to implement these new ideas and strategies.

LEARNING DOMAINS

The theory of learning domains (Bloom et al., 1956) includes three domains: the psychomotor domain, the affective domain, and the cognitive domain. The cognitive domain has been the primary focus of most traditional education.

A similar pedagogic model is the hand, heart, and head model (alternatively called hand, heart, and mind). This is a holistic approach initially presented by Orr (1992) but later expanded to its current form by Sipos et al. (2008). This approach considers engagement (hands), implicit knowledge/relational knowing (heart), and critical reflection (head). It clearly maps onto Bloom's three learning domains, as seen in Figure 3.6.

FIGURE 3.6   Learning domains mapped to the hand, heart, and head model.

Bloom's Taxonomy

Bloom's Taxonomy follows on from Bloom's domains of learning, demonstrating a hierarchy of learning which suggests that there is not simply one way in which information is processed and learnt. The cognitive domain hierarchy has been the primary focus of work in education. The hierarchy consists of six stages of cognitive processes, from simplest to most complex: remember, understand, apply, analyse, evaluate, and create. The revised Bloom's Taxonomy (Bloom et al., 1956; see also Anderson et al. (2001)) can be seen in Figure 3.7.

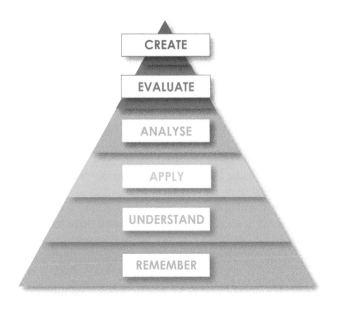

FIGURE 3.7   Bloom's Taxonomy.

It is suggested that these different cognitive types of learning use different processes, and as such, different education methods and approaches are more applicable to some levels of learning, which are equally more applicable to some subjects than others. For example, debates can be used to engage students for critical thinking (Camp & Schnader, 2010), but may not be as suitable for learning specific facts and figures, such as for mathematics.

SUMMARY

Psychology and pedagogy are both vast areas of study. This chapter has given an introduction to a few key psychology theories to consider when thinking about game design as a whole, and tabletop game design in particular. Understanding your target audience and your players' motivations will help you to design a game that meets their needs. This chapter has also covered pedagogic theories that can be applied to serious game design. These cover how people learn best, so that understanding can be applied to the design of teaching materials, including serious games. In particular, education can be applied through interactivity, social collaboration, and thoughtful reflection, across various aspects of learning.

4 Design Methodology

Chris Evans

INTRODUCTION

Designing a game is simple right? You might start with a game that you like and adapt it to make it your own. Alternatively, you might consider mechanics, dynamics, and aesthetics that you enjoy from several games and combine them in a way that creates something new. Game design can be influenced by playing and understanding how other games work, what makes them fun, and considering how they can be made better.

WHAT PROBLEMS ARE WE TRYING TO SOLVE?

Serious games are distinct in that they should include meaningful learning outcomes that are closely aligned with the learning outcomes of a lesson, a module, or a course. For example, an Undergraduate module in Business Studies might have a particular learning outcome which states that by the end of the module, the students should "Understand key concepts in core components of business studies: accounting, foundations of organisational behaviour, business strategy and marketing". How might a tabletop game be adapted to teach this; how might this subject be taught more interactively? A traditional classroom-based approach might be to use flash cards that explain these key concepts, and with the inclusion of game mechanics such as role playing, deck building, drafting, and traitors, the concept of a game will begin to emerge.

Starting with the learning outcomes usually, but not always, creates a solid foundation for serious game design. An alternative approach is to adapt an existing game as a way of teaching a particular concept, or subject.

Whether you construct the game to the learning or vice versa, the learning outcomes should always be considered. Students should be motivated to learn, and in Dan Pink's model of motivation (Pink, 2009), purpose, the desire to do something that has meaning and is important, is one of the three key pillars.

TYPES OF GAMES

Every game is different and what constitutes a fun experience will differ from player to player. Take the board game *Monopoly*, for example, a polarising game that represents both the best and the worst in board games, depending on your point of view. There are several causal factors that may influence a player's gaming preference, but in the case of *Monopoly*, this differentiation can be somewhat aligned with the diversity of player experience; that is, the inexperienced board gamer will be more inclined to enjoy *Monopoly*, whilst a player with more experience of a range of alternative board games will tend to dismiss it.

DOI: 10.1201/9781003319511-4

Monopoly is not a bad game, but it does have its drawbacks. It relies heavily on luck, and it was initially designed as a serious game, originally invented by Lizzie Magie so as not to be fun, but rather to promote Henry George's economic theory (Ansoms & Geenen, 2012). The stress and sense of injustice that one might feel whilst playing the game is deliberate.

Broadly speaking, board games can fall into three distinct categories: American-style board games, Eurogames, and Party games. *Monopoly* is an American-style board game, a game that encourages direct conflict between players, and has a significant degree of luck. They are often easy to learn and teach, and their familiarity as classic board games has resulted in a substantial number of adaptations to teach subjects as diverse as financial accounting (Shanklin & Ehlen, 2007) through to poverty and inequality (Ansoms & Geenen, 2012).

In contrast to American-style board games, Eurogames, or Euro-Style games, tend to be more strategic and have indirect player interaction. Games such as *Carcassone* and *Ticket to Ride* are good examples that have been adapted as serious games to teach geographic concepts (Mewborne & Mitchell, 2019) and graph theory and probability (Witter & Lyford, 2020), respectively.

Party games are games that are designed to be fun for players who enjoy the social element of playing games. These games are usually designed to be uncomplicated, quick, and fun, and together with their capacity to support teams of players, make good candidates for adaptation as serious games. The classic game of charades, for example, is often adapted to teach English (Halimah & Basri, 2017; Putri & Alhusna, 2021; Rahmah & Astutik, 2020).

DESIGN FRAMEWORKS

A significant number of serious games have been created in the past two decades, exhibiting differing levels of achievement. Until fairly recently, substantiating assertions that a particular game aligns with the learner's needs and/or anticipations has posed challenges. Design frameworks differ in the design of games that are purely for fun, and for serious games designed for learning in that the design of a serious game tends to take a more scientific and structured approach, or at least it probably should.

Yusoff et al.'s (2009) conceptual framework for serious games (Figure 4.1) acts as both a design tool and a checklist in the design of serious games, and whilst all elements do not have to be included, they should at least be considered.

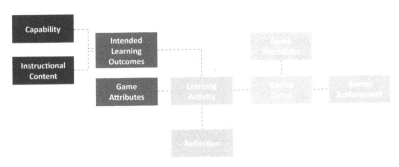

FIGURE 4.1   A conceptual framework for serious games (Yusoff et al., 2009).

The conceptual framework was developed in response to the lack of clear standards and guidelines that existed in the design of serious games, and especially to address the question of whether a particular serious game met the needs of the learner. The framework, which considers both digital and analogue serious games, consists of the nine elements in Figure 4.1, which will now be expanded on.

Capability

Capability pertains to the cognitive (intellectual), psychomotor (physical), and affective (emotional) proficiencies that learners are intended to cultivate through game participation. Bloom's Taxonomy (Chapter 3) is a well-known learning model that operates hierarchically, classifying learning objectives into different levels of intricacy, spanning from fundamental knowledge and comprehension to advanced evaluation and creation. So, for example, on the quiz show *University Challenge,* the contestants are just recalling knowledge; they are not learning anything new. Contrast this with the quiz show *Only Connect,* where the contestants arguably employ all levels of Bloom's Taxonomy to find the correct answer.

Unlike traditional learning, games can have the capability to exploit the psychomotor and affective domains. The psychomotor domain includes the capabilities such as manipulating physical objects, precision, and well-timed, fluid execution. The game Jenga is a good example where all three of these attributes are used. Games of dexterity, mimicry, role playing, and real time action, for example, could allow players to learn within this domain. These types of serious games are often used within business training courses to create meaningful memorable experiences to develop soft skills such as teamwork, problem-solving, and leadership. Escape rooms are another example that have recently been reimagined for education in subjects as diverse as programming (Lopez-Pernas et al., 2019), physics (Vörös & Sárközi, 2017), and medical education (Guckian et al., 2020).

According to Brett and Smith (2003), a growing body of evidence substantiates the assertion that humans are innately emotional. Moreover, these emotions and affective advancements significantly influence human growth and conduct, yielding both positive and negative outcomes that education often fails to adequately recognise. The affective domain pertains to the emotions evoked by an experience, and the corresponding skills encompass the ability to recognise, embrace, and appreciate fitting attitudes and perspectives. Games in general tend to stimulate feelings associated with the affective domain, though certain design decisions may positively or negatively impact the effect. For example, in the board game *Pandemic*, players are given roles such as the Medic or the Researcher. This simple mechanic instils value and status upon these players whilst encouraging wider interaction with other players.

Instructional Content

The instructional content refers to the material that learners are meant to acquire, encompassing resources like manuals, PowerPoint slides, e-Learning materials, scripts, and any other educational content. Furthermore, it is in the effective delivery of this content where the most successful learning occurs.

Efficient educational and instructional materials should achieve the subsequent objectives:

- Impart knowledge to learners without inundating them.
- Maintain student engagement.
- Offer simplicity of comprehension.
- Be tailored to the appropriate level for the intended audience.
- Communicate succinctly and directly.

However, when creating an educational game, it may not always be practical to include this content within the game itself. In order to include instructional content, it may be necessary to embed the game within the wider context of a more formal lesson and to build in opportunities for reflection outside of the game, as discussed previously.

Intended Learning Outcomes

Learning outcomes represent the achievements aimed for through engagement with the serious game, and they should originate from the learning objectives specified in the syllabus. An intended learning outcome is the consequence of combining capability (the proficiency to perform a task) with subject matter. For instance, learners might be expected to remember an important date, or apply a formula to solve a specific mathematical problem. Taxonomies of educational objectives are harnessed to formulate learning outcomes, occasionally encompassing learner abilities sourced from the psychomotor and affective domains, in addition to the cognitive domain.

For example, medical students undertake rigorous training in both the classroom and medical facilities. In a study that introduced medical simulations and games, Al-Elq (2010) suggested that the acquisition of clinical skills through a deliberate practice produced more positive outcomes when compared to the traditional apprentice style of learning.

Game Attributes

As proposed by Yusoff et al. (2009), the game attributes of serious games encompass the elements that facilitate learning and engagement. These attributes are formulated through the synthesis of critical thinking derived from the examination of behaviorist, cognitive, constructivist, educationalist, and neuroscience viewpoints in the literature. These attributes comprise:

- **Incremental learning** is the incremental introduction of learning activities to support the learning materials. This process allows learning outcomes to be addressed gradually, as opposed to all at once.
- **Linearity** describes how the game arranges the learning activities, and the degree to which an engaged learner can fashion their own sequences. For example, to provide the learners with meaningful choices within the game.

- **Attention span** is how long a learner is engaged with the game. For example, waiting too long to do something, confusion as to what to do, or being bombarded with too much information may all negatively impact upon cognitive processing and short-term memory.
- **Scaffolding** provides the support and help given by the game during the learning activities. Examples may include building upon prior learning, or recourse to additional help, if required.
- **Transfer of learned skills** is the support provided by the game to enhance the application of previously learned knowledge to other game levels.
- **Interaction** is the extent to which the learner responds or engages with the game activities. Do they have meaningful choices they can make? Do they receive effective feedback on these choices?
- **Learner control** describes the extent to which the learner can direct their learning activities within the game. This relates to agency.
- **Rewards** can be intrinsic or extrinsic, and are included in a game to encourage the learner and to maintain a high level of motivation.
- **Situated and authentic learning** in serious games involves a gaming environment or world that can be fantastical or reflective of industry, and in which a learner can relate their learning to their needs and interests in the outside world.
- **Accommodating the learner's styles** is about providing the learner with choices when playing the game, or even before they play. For example, some prefer to read the rules of a board game to understand how to play, whereas others will watch a video, and others will like to have the game explained to them.

LEARNING ACTIVITY

The learning activity is the activity designed to maintain the learner's engagement and facilitate learning within the game environment. Decades of research substantiate the perspective that the learner's engagement with the activity, and the resulting outcomes, hold significance for the learning process (Beetham & Sharpe, 2013). The degree of deep engagement or immersion experienced by the learner relies on how effectively these activities are delivered. Gilbert and Gale (2007) suggest a number of methods for constructing learning activities, taking into account intended learning outcomes.

To illustrate this point, if a learner is required to remember a concept, the learning activities would encompass presenting an instance of the concept and prompting the learner to provide its name, followed by providing feedback on the response. The activity should include learning materials that are suitable and stimulating for the learner aiming to achieve competence slightly beyond their current level. A significant portion of game designers invest substantial effort into refining this aspect of "gameplay" to ensure the game's success (Yusoff et al., 2009).

REFLECTION

Reflection is where the learner thinks about the purpose of the learning activities that have been undertaken and decides the strategy to apply during the next activity. Reflection can take place both within the game and after the activity has been completed. Opportunities for reflection can be built into the game by offering reflection activities such as a discussion of the errors made by the learner, as well as some corrective suggestions.

GAMES GENRE

Game genre is the type, theme, or category (such as described in *BoardGameGeek*) of the game played. The range of genres is diverse and in a serious board game should be given careful consideration. For example, a zombie-themed game may be appropriate in a serious game designed to be played outside of class, but could be considered trivial if included within the lesson. Students are motivated by solving real-world problems (Lombardi & Oblinger, 2007) and thus authentic themes or genres can be beneficial to the learning process.

GAME MECHANICS

Game mechanics, including rules, outline the specifics of the game. For instance, if the game falls under the Worker Placement strategy genre, it might necessitate game mechanics related to resource management and territory control. Yusoff et al. (2009) suggest that creating an enhanced game tailored to a specific learning style, target audience, or desired outcomes involves the learning activities and necessary instructional content shaping the choice of appropriate game mechanics.

GAME ACHIEVEMENT

Game achievement, on the other hand, pertains to the extent of learner success in engaging with these games. In the realm of serious games, much like traditional board games, this achievement can manifest in various manners such as game scores, the accumulation of resources or assets, or the time taken to fulfill game objectives. Beyond offering informative and motivational advantages, these rewards could also function as a means of evaluating the learner. The feedback from game achievements could lead to modifications in learning activities. The game achievement or score would reflect the level of learner understanding during gameplay, and if necessary, adjustments to learning activities should be made to suit the learner's aptitude (Yusoff et al., 2009).

THE DESIGN PROCESS

Having established the framework for the game, the next stage would be to design it, and perhaps the instinctive approach might be to start with a blank piece of paper and begin sketching out ideas, creating rudimentary cards and/or a game-board. However, with this approach, it is likely that things will be missed. The design process is a science as well as an art, and as such, over the last several decades, many design models have been developed to support this process. Once such model is design thinking, an iterative, non-linear process that seeks to understand the user of a product, challenge assumptions, and redefine problems, as shown in Figure 4.2 below.

To understand the complex and sometimes puzzling field of design practices, we must realise that they have been developed in response to a particular need (Dorst, 2011). The fundamental basis of design thinking is that the end user should be the driving force behind any decision that is made during the process. Opposed to the traditional approach that is focused on the end goal, design thinking is more human-centric and asks the question, what does the customer want and need?

In short, design thinking prizes the end user over a predetermined end goal. This leads to iterative problem-solving, also referred to as the design thinking process that consists of five stages: Empathise, Define, Ideate, Prototype, and Test.

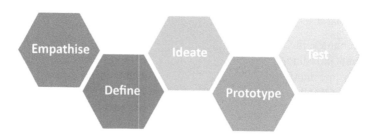

FIGURE 4.2   Design thinking (Plattner et al., 2012).

EMPATHISE PHASE

To understand what your customer needs are, you are going to have to communicate with them. The Empathise phase of design thinking is about researching your users' needs to gain an understanding of the challenges they face. Even if you are convinced that the game you have created is the answer to all their problems, if you have not established a dialogue, then you cannot possibly know that. We all come with our own preconceived notions and biases which we need to set aside to understand the needs and challenges others experience.

In serious game design, the user needs will differ; for example, teachers will want a product that is easy to deliver and that fulfils the needs of the curriculum, whereas students will want an engaging experience that benefits their learning in some way and is fun to play. Design thinking is especially helpful for problems that are not well defined; for example, you may identify a particular problem by talking to students and discovering a key concept within the curriculum that many struggle to understand. Would a game help to bridge this gap?

Tools that help in the Empathise stage include:

- First-hand interviews
- Questionnaires
- Empathy maps

DEFINE PHASE

In the Define stage, you will organise the information you have gathered during the Empathise stage. You will then analyse your observations to define the core problems you have identified up to this point and summarise them within a problem statement (Figure 4.3).

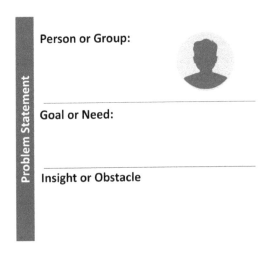

FIGURE 4.3   Example problem statement.

So, for example, in an Undergraduate Maths programme you may discover that a sizeable number of students struggle to understand a particular concept such as binomial distribution and that there are very few practical elements to this part of the course. This is your problem statement and your justification in staging an intervention by creating a game that actively teaches binomial distribution.

IDEATE PHASE

Using the information that you collected in the first two phases, you can now start and develop solutions for the problem statement you have identified. There are a number of steps that you can take to ideate, and oftentimes it involves brainstorming as many varied and diverse ideas as possible before whittling them down to a few options. Below are some suggested approaches that you might take in this phase:

- Make a list of the games (or mechanics) that you enjoy, as well as why you like them.
- Generate ideas quickly; no idea should be considered trivial.
- Allow yourself to generate a wide variety of ideas without having the define them.
- When you have enough ideas, go around, and ask questions to further clarify why these ideas may be considered.
- Consider if any of the games, or their mechanics could be adapted to make a serious game.
- Enable team members to express their preferences by providing them with a specific quantity of stickers or dots, allowing them to place them beside their preferred ideas.

PROTOTYPE PHASE

In this phase, you identify the best practical solutions for the problems you have found before creating a low-cost prototype and investigate possibilities. A prototype (see Chapter 11) can be defined as a preliminary version or model of all or a part of a system before full commitment is made to develop it (Smith, 1991), and it can be rudimentary and incomplete, as long as it is playable.

TEST (PLAYTEST) PHASE

By conducting playtesting (Chapter 11), you initiate the testing of your prototypes with a subset of end users. This is the phase where the process frequently transforms into an iterative one, as the findings you uncover often have the potential to loop back to the definition or ideation phase. This can be the result of negative (or positive) feedback, confusion with the rules, or the game not meeting its intended learning objectives.

Designing a game is different than designing other learning materials for many reasons, but perhaps the most significant addition is the need to playtest. Is the game fun? Is it balanced? Is it complete? Did the playtesters learn what you intended for them to learn?

Playtesting is how you understand whether your game is actually playable and that it functions the way you intended, as a game and as a learning solution. Furthermore, when you eventually reach the point where the game is as good as it can be and requires no more refinements, this is when you should carry out "blind" playtesting, which is the same as playtesting, but does not involve the designers in any way.

Playtesting is not something you do once or twice, and this is where the design thinking models work best. On the first playtest, there will be numerous things that will need to be changed based upon the user feedback, and for game design, the playtesting phase may also be considered to be starting the process again at the Empathise phase. Based upon this user feedback you will revisit the Define phase and define new problems and re-evaluate old ones. This will enable you to effectively amend the process and then it is back to playtesting. This is an iterative process that ends only when the game is as good as you can make it.

SUMMARY

Design frameworks enable the game designer to have an overview of all the components and attributes that are required for making a game, as well as the interconnections between those attributes. When creating a serious game, a design framework will also include opportunities for learning, feedback, and reflection.

Design methodology differs in that it describes the process which a designer will follow to create a game. Following an appropriate methodology when creating a game will help you to scrutinise any problems that the design may have before it is manufactured and available for the end user. There are many examples of design methodology, but an iterative design thinking approach maps particularly well to the processes involved in creating a board game.

5 Accessibility

Dr Devon Allcoat

WHY ACCESSIBILITY?

Perhaps this is the chapter you are most excited to see, or perhaps you plan to skim read it. Perhaps you are already a champion for accessibility, inclusivity, diversity, and equality. These topics are certainly being more widely discussed and considered in the world today. There are a significant variety of very good moral, ethical, and social reasons behind this. This book is not here to educate on these, important though they are. However, there are other reasons for why good design is accessible and inclusive.

CLARITY

For design to be accessible, it needs clarity. In particular, clarity of wording and visu-alisation using images in the rulebook (Figure 5.1). If a player reads the rulebook, and cannot understand the rules, or they are ambiguous, then your rulebook is not truly accessible, and therefore, the game is not truly accessible to its audience. This can lead to a number of unintentional effects.

1. Your players might suffer from *rulebook fatigue*: tired of reading, and even re-reading, the rulebook, sometimes to the extent that they never get around to actually playing the game. This can also happen when a rulebook is sim-ply too long, and is therefore inaccessible not due to its complexity, but its length. Essentially, the time and energy costs are too high.
2. Another possibility is *rulebook frustration*, wherein a player gets frustrated with the complexity or inaccessibility of the rulebook, and hands it off to someone else, be it someone else in the group, or outsourcing to online resources.
3. Misinterpretation. Sometimes, a player reads through the rulebook, starts to play the game, but has misinterpreted a rule. This could be due to vague wording, or a lack of clarity of intention (i.e., understanding what the game's designers intended). This can lead to the game being played incorrectly. If it is the other players first time playing the game, this can lead to them being taught to play the wrong way, and they may then teach others that way. It can become a snowball effect. Ultimately, if the game is not being played as intended, this can significantly affect game balance, game difficulty, and player satisfaction.
4. Missing information. What if a scenario occurs, and there are no rules for it? Or, if it is not clear which rules apply? This can also cause frustration

DOI: 10.1201/9781003319511-5

and can lead to some of the same consequences as above. Players may seek help from others and may end up needing to create house rules (unofficial changes or additions to the rules), which can again cause it to be played not as intended.

5. Difficult to find information. A rulebook that does not have an accessible layout can cause irritation during gameplay. Perhaps a rare scenario has occurred, and therefore the players need to clarify a rule. When players are in the middle of gameplay, they typically do not want to take a lot of time out to look up a rule, as it often causes play to be suspended, which can cause frustration for the players. If the rulebook is not well laid out, finding information takes much longer.

6. Clarity of intention is also applicable to cards in a game: because the written information on the card may inform the player about how it works, how it might interact with other cards in the game, etc.

FIGURE 5.1　Rulebook.

Accessible and inclusive design requires clarity from the designers and can also add clarity for the players. Visuals are particularly important for this; for example, using images in a rulebook to visualise information, such as game set-up, or using icons as well as colours to make the distinction between cards or game pieces clearer (helping with unusual/poor lighting conditions, or colour blindness).

Increased Target Audience

The more inclusive and accessible your product is, the more people that can engage with it. The more people that can engage with it, the more people will buy it. For games that involve multiple players, a purchase may be dependent not just on accessibility to the purchaser, but also the individuals they would be playing with. If, for example, one of the group members is colour blind, it might mean none of the groups are willing to purchase a game which excludes one of the players. For serious games, corporate games, or simulations, it means that the game needs to be accessible to all students or staff members. If it is not, it could mean losing a huge potential source of income and sales, depending on how many sites and people the potential organisation has.

Even if the features that are not accessible and inclusive are not apparent pre-purchase, and therefore, do not prevent purchases in the first instance, they can lead to problems in the future. Namely, unhappy customers (or, more broadly, stakeholders). This can manifest itself in returns, bad reviews, and even to diminished interest in your future offerings. Unhappy customers are certainly not the ideal! Dissatisfied stakeholders can be problematic in other ways, and this can depend on what type of stakeholder they are. For example, an investor may withdraw current or future funding.

PROTECTED CHARACTERISTICS

The Equality Act (2010) outlines the following protected characteristics:

- Age
- Disability
- Race
- Religion or Belief
- Sex
- Gender Reassignment
- Sexual Orientation
- Marriage and Civil Partnership
- Pregnancy and Maternity

The Equality Act (2010) is an Act of Parliament of the United Kingdom, which legally protects people from discrimination in the workplace and in wider society.

This is not to be confused with the Equality Act from the US, which is a (currently proposed) bill that includes protection against discrimination based on sex, sexual orientation, and gender identity, as well as expanding existing civil rights for other groups. Whilst the Equality Act (2010) is not specifically related to game design, it is a useful guideline for some of the areas to consider when thinking about accessibility and inclusivity. Many of these will be relevant to the "Representation" section of this chapter, whilst physical impairments and cognitive impairments have their own dedicated sections. Note that other countries may have their own sets of customs and expectations, and game designers should consider these if the game is aimed at an international audience.

EIGHT KINDS OF ACCESSIBILITY

Heron et al. (2018) created a toolkit to evaluate the accessibility of tabletop games, used for the "Accessibility Teardowns" on the website Meeple Like Us (Meeple Like Us, n.d). They included seven key sections: visual accessibility, cognitive accessibility, emotional accessibility, physical accessibility, communication, socio-economic accessibility, and intersectional accessibility. Our updated framework adapted from this includes eight different areas of accessibility to consider when designing a game:

- **Colour Blindness**: relating to all types of colour blindness.
- **Visual Accessibility**: relating to blindness and visual impairment.
- **Cognitive Accessibility**: relating to issues of fluid and crystallised intelligence, attention, and information processing.
- **Memory**: relating to issues of short-term memory, working memory, long-term memory, or sensory memory.
- **Emotional Accessibility**: relating to issues of emotions such as anger and despair.
- **Physical Accessibility**: relating to fine-grained and gross motor skills.
- **Communication**: relating to issues of hearing, of talking, of reading, and of expression.
- **Representation**: relating to issues of representation, inclusion, diversity, and intersectionality of these.

Seeing all these different areas of accessibility and inclusivity may be quite intimidating. Realistically, the vast majority of games simply cannot cater to every individual. Those who struggle with fine motor skills typically would not choose to play a dexterity game. That does not mean that you cannot design a dexterity game.

Whilst recognising that you cannot be all things to all people, it is always worthwhile to look at what changes can be made in a way that maintains the core principles of the game whilst being as accessible as possible or, ideally, designing with these in mind from the start.

COLOUR BLINDNESS

"Colour blindness (colour vision deficiency, or CVD) affects approximately 1 in 12 men (8%) and 1 in 200 women in the world. In Britain this means that there are approximately 3 million colour blind people (about 4.5% of the entire population), most of whom are male" (Colour Blind Awareness, 2022).

There are multiple different types of colour blindness (see Figure 5.2).

- **Trichromacy**: using all three types of light cones; normal colour vision.
- **Anomalous Trichromacy**: one cone is slightly out of alignment.
  - **Protanomaly**: a reduced sensitivity to red light.
  - **Deuteranomaly**: a reduced sensitivity to green light (most common).
  - **Tritanomaly**: a reduced sensitivity to blue light (extremely rare).
- **Dichromacy**: only two types of cones, also with three variations: **Protanopia, Deuteranopia, Tritanopia**.
- **Monochromacy (achromatopsia)**: seeing in black and white; an extremely rare condition.

There are a wide variety of games that are simply not playable for people with colour blindness, at least not independently. Two examples include *Sagrada* and *Qwirkle*; in both of these, you are required to be able to distinguish between the colours in order to play the game successfully. Gameplay hinges entirely on using the right colours at the right time. That is not to say, of course, that these are bad games. They are successful games with many fans, but for the colour blind community, they are inaccessible.

Some games, which started as inaccessible for individuals with colour blindness, have brought out new versions or expansions which are more appropriate for colour blind individuals. For example, *Century: Spice World* has yellow, brown, green, and red cubes. For some types of colour blindness, as many as three of these colours are indistinguishable from each other (brown, green, and red). They later released the *Golem Edition*, which used a much more colour blind-friendly palette of yellow, light blue, hot pink, and dark green.

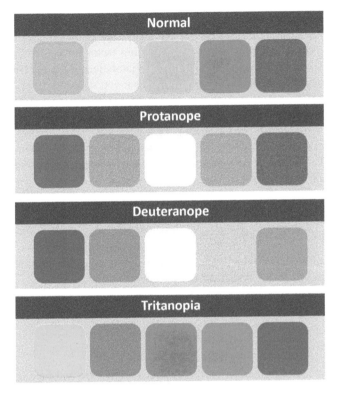

FIGURE 5.2   A visual mock-up of how the "normal" colours would look to someone with protanope, deuteranope, and tritanope colour blindness.

However, there are examples of games which through expansions have gone from colour blind friendly to *not* colour blind friendly. *Scythe* had a relatively accessible colour palette of yellow, red, dark blue, white, and black for player pieces. The expansion added purple and green, which then made it less accessible.

There are plenty of games that got it right from the get-go. *Sushi Roll* has colourful dice, that are lovely to look at, but the colours do not affect gameplay. Each colour of dice has its own unique symbols, so even if you cannot see what colour dice it is, you can see the symbols that are on it, and these are not repeated across different colours.

7 Wonders has different coloured cards, which are helpful to quickly distinguish each different card type, but again are not necessary, because each type has its own symbol to differentiate it. *Ticket to Ride* is another example. Gaining cards of a specific colour allows you to place game pieces (usually trains) on the respective colour on the gameboard. Again, the colour is useful to quickly differentiate the different paths and spaces, but not a requirement, as each colour has its own unique icon.

There is a distinctive thread that links these examples together: icons and symbols. Whenever colour is used in a gameplay-relevant way, the simple addition of an icon or symbol specific to that colour, or the type of object, can immediately make the game accessible to people with all types of colour blindness, even monochromacy.

This would not necessarily work for every different gameplay type; for example, the aforementioned *Qwirkle* utilises both shape and colour in the gameplay, so a shape could not be easily integrated as a distinguishing factor for colour. Alternatively, different types of lines may be useful differentiators (e.g. dotted, dashed, or solid lines). If icons or symbols are not appropriate, but you still want to make the game colour blind friendly, you can run the colours through a colour blindness simulator. These will typically allow you to simulate the three main forms of colour blindness (some do not simulate monochromacy). That way, you can see which colours are indistinguishable for each colour blindness type, so that you can find an appropriate palette. This would ideally be done for the playtest stage, and again at the early manufacturing stage to test the samples of any physical components, before mass production begins.

VISUAL ACCESSIBILITY

The effects of colour blindness are clear and significant, and although it is a recognised subject, it is not consistently translated into game design. However, even less commonly considered, but nonetheless important, are other visual accessibility issues that have different challenges, possibly with their own unique solutions.

Low Vision

Low vision includes blindness, partial blindness, and a limited field of view. Each of these has distinct impacts on a player. Some games do have specific versions for those who are blind or visually impaired. These include *Braille Monopoly, Braille Scrabble* and *Braille Bananagrams*, braille playing cards, adapted chess and checkers sets, and more. Whilst braille or other physical adaptations may not be an easy or cheap inclusion, or a solution for all visual impairments, it is an option that should not be forgotten. For example, chess is adapted by having bumps on the back of the pieces, as well as spaces being raised, so that white and black pieces on the board are differentiated. For other games, tactile dice are also an accessible option.

6pt 8pt 12pt 18pt 24pt 32pt

FIGURE 5.3   For low-vision visual impairments, design aspects to think about include the minimum text size.

For low vision or visual impairments, design aspects to think about include minimum text size, font types, and the choice of text colour in combination with background colours. Text that is not tiny is typically appreciated by the majority of people anyway, not just those with significant visual impairments, but it can be a make or break for those who do (Figure 5.3). When text that is important to gameplay is too small, it can make the game simply unplayable for some people. This is especially relevant when the text is meant to be "hidden" from the other players, so you cannot just have someone else read out its content without it impacting gameplay.

Font types are also important (Figure 5.4). Perhaps you want to choose a "hand-written letter" style of font. It could be thematic or give character to the visual design. But how readable is it? How much text will need to be in that font? A few words in a fancy font may be acceptable, but what about a huge block of text that you have to put extra effort into reading? Not ideal!

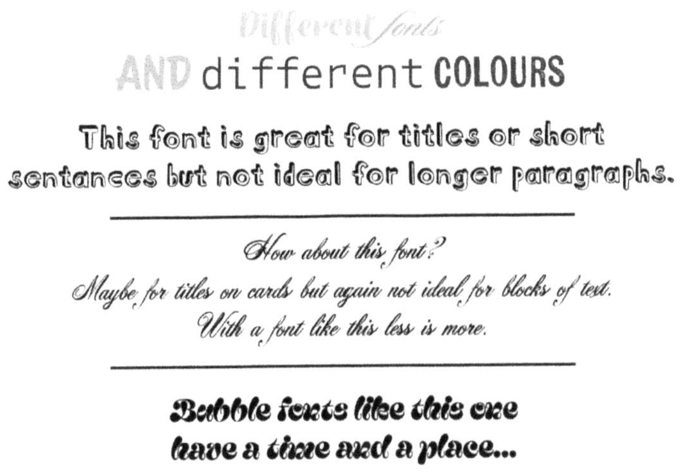

Different fonts

AND different COLOURS

This font is great for titles or short sentences but not ideal for longer paragraphs.

How about this font?
Maybe for titles on cards but again not ideal for blocks of text.
With a font like this less is more.

Bubble fonts like this one
have a time and a place...

FIGURE 5.4   Examples of different font types.

Finally, selecting appropriate colours is important even outside of colour blind-ness. Someone with perfect vision will still struggle to read something when the colours of the font and background are not appropriately distinct or if they inter-act poorly (Figure 5.5). A lack of contrast can make reading harder, whether it is between different colours, or shades of the same colour. Even if the perfect colour palette for your game is red and green, using a green font on a red background is not necessarily a good idea. Arthur and Passini (1992) created a formula for calculating the contrast between two colours, with a suggested optimal contrast value that is a useful guideline.

If an element of the game dictates that a certain colour combination is neces-sary, consider using outlines or highlights to better distinguish text and background colours that have insufficient contrast.

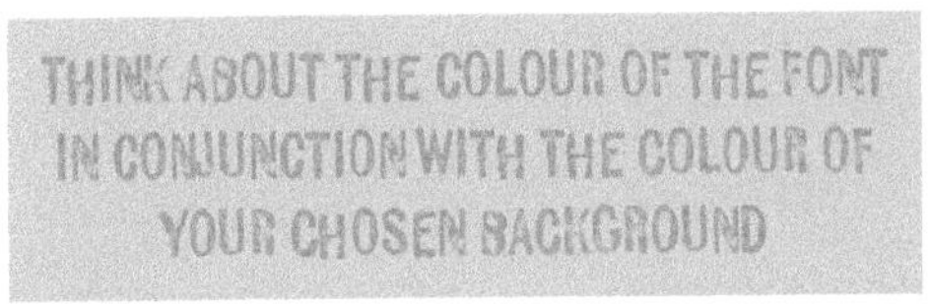

THINK ABOUT THE COLOUR OF THE FONT
IN CONJUNCTION WITH THE COLOUR OF
YOUR CHOSEN BACKGROUND

FIGURE 5.5   Consider the contrast between the font and background colours.

ASTIGMATISM AND DOUBLE VISION

Astigmatism (an imperfection in the curvature of the eye's cornea or lens) can cause blurred vision, double vision, difficulty focusing on printed text and lines, eye strain, headaches, and so on. All of these can impact gameplay experience, for both analogue and digital components.

Approximately, one in three people are affected by astigmatism to some degree (Lazarus, 2021).

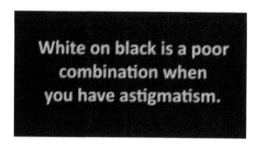

FIGURE 5.6   Astigmatism and double vision.

Although it is true that having a combination of black and white as text and background colour is the highest contrast combination, it is problematic for astigmatism, causing double vision or a visual blurring effect (see Figure 5.6). Instead, try dark grey instead of black (see Figure 5.7).

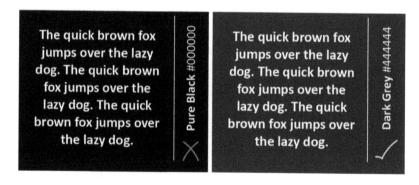

FIGURE 5.7   White text on a black background versus a dark grey background.

SIMULATOR SICKNESS

Simulator (or simulation) sickness is a form of motion sickness linked to interaction with a simulated environment. Symptoms include:

- Lethargy
- Nausea

- Vomiting
- Sweating
- Headaches
- Uneasiness
- Drowsiness
- Disorientation
- Ocular Motor Disturbances

Simulator sickness is specifically relevant for digital interfaces. Reducing or eliminating simulator sickness is important – it is an unpleasant feeling; therefore, it will decrease the users' enjoyment of the game if they suffer from it. Whilst there are things that the user can do to reduce simulator sickness (such as being in a well-lit and temperate room and taking regular breaks), good design will also help reduce simulator sickness. Be careful of motion effects (such as rotation or acceleration), low frames per second, and lag.

COGNITIVE

ATTENTION

Attention span is how much time someone can concentrate on a task for, before they become distracted. It varies from person to person, and from task to task. Attention span can be affected by not only the type of task, but also variables such as age, general state of mind, and a variety of clinical diagnoses (such as ADHD, anxiety, or depression), as well as sensory processing. If the game design demands too much from the players' attention span, it can adversely impact their experience of the game, and how playable it is for them. This can include overlooking details, difficulty following what is happening, organisation concerns, impatience, and more. All of these can make for a more negative experience and impression of the game.

Visual attention is also a factor to be aware of, especially for digital games. Visual attention is the cognitive process of selecting and processing important information in a visual scene. How much we are aware of, how quickly we identify some things and filter others out, and which objects draw our attention most in a scene (such as movement, colours, shapes and more) are all part of visual attention. Understanding visual attention helps in the design of visuals to draw attention to the important information, whilst not overcrowding a visual scene or having distracting objects in it.

INTELLIGENCE

Many different types of intelligence have been identified and defined, including emotional intelligence (EQ). Emotion and social skills will be explored in later sections of this chapter. Another common conceptualisation of intelligence is the idea of *fluid intelligence* and *crystallised intelligence*. Fluid intelligence encompasses basic reasoning processes and other mental activities, and does not significantly depend on prior learning. Crystallised intelligence, however, is specifically resulting from prior experience, including learned knowledge and procedures.

A pure entertainment game typically primarily utilises fluid intelligence. In this case, accessibility is dependent on the difficulty of the mental activities. For example, what level of processing do you need in order to participate successfully? This is often represented in a game through the "minimum age" rating, which suggests at what age a typical individual will have the appropriate processing and information retention abilities to play the game. Of course, this is a somewhat limiting and imprecise measure, as there are many individual differences and other factors involved in fluid intelligence, not just age, but nonetheless, it is helpful as an indication.

A game that is educational in nature, or a game such as a quiz game, may have a much more significant focus on a specific subset of crystallised intelligence. Inevitably, this will make the game less accessible, as it is best suited to individuals with that subset of knowledge. However, this is entirely dependent on the target audience and the purpose of the game, but it is helpful to clearly communicate which audience it is aimed at.

INFORMATION PROCESSING

Information processing relates to attention, intelligence, and other factors. Questions to consider as part of this include: How much information needs to be processed to play the game? How quickly do you need to process information? This also links into the next section about memory. Overall, be aware that the more information that needs to be processed, and the more quickly this needs to happen, the less accessible the game will be.

MEMORY

Memory, which is one aspect of cognition, is important, so it is worth looking at in more detail, with focus being on four categories of memory: sensory memory, short-term memory, working memory, and long-term memory.

SENSORY MEMORY

Sensory memory is essentially the input from all of the senses. It has a large capacity, but for a brief duration, resulting in most of the information being lost through "decay" (Figure 5.8). If your attention is focused on something from one of the sensory stores, then it will be transferred to short-term memory. This is useful to know from a design perspective to recognise that information is not significantly processed in a conscious capacity until attention is focused on it. If there is a lot of distracting sensory information, this could make a game less accessible.

FIGURE 5.8   Memory.

SHORT-TERM MEMORY

Short-term memory is the second part of Atkinson and Shiffrin's (1968) Multi-Store Model of Memory (after sensory memory), and it is what it says on the tin. Information only stays in your short-term memory for a very brief period of time, typically believed to be in the range of seconds, not minutes. Short-term memory has limited capacity (theorised to be 7 items plus or minus 2) as well as a limited duration. There is relatively little, if any, processing at this stage. Not everything from your short-term memory will make it to your long-term memory, but repetition and rehearsal will improve this. In particular, for accessibility, it is important to recognise the limited capacity of short-term memory, and that not everything makes it into long-term memory. The more players need to remember for the game, the more repetition this may require.

WORKING MEMORY

Working memory, unlike short-term memory, involves processing information as well as retaining it. The working memory model (Baddeley & Hitch, 1974) replaces short-term memory with working memory. Others differentiate between them and utilise both (Aben et al., 2012). As with short-term memory, working memory has limited capacity, the theory being that learning and complex reasoning use up capacity in order to process information. Again, this is important for the context of accessibility as the more information that needs to be processed at any given time, the less accessible it is, particularly for those who have limited or impaired memory capabilities.

Long-term memory is the final stage of both the multi-store model and the working memory model. This can last anywhere from a few minutes to years. It comprises both implicit and explicit memory. Explicit memory is basic information that is purposefully and easily stored and accessed, or articulated. Implicit memory is knowledge you unconsciously have, including procedural memories for basic tasks (like riding a bicycle or brushing your teeth). It is possible for long-term memory to be impaired, which can impact someone's ability to play games that need this (such as quiz games that rely on explicit memory).

EMOTIONAL ACCESSIBILITY

Creating emotion is frequently desirable – it can have a positive impact, it can help create a lasting impression, and it can certainly be linked to fun and enjoyment. However, not all emotions are positive ones, and whilst a sprinkling of some negative emotions can be of relevance to the overall experience of playing a game, this is an area that is important to be mindful of.

Tension, either from the difficulty of the game itself or from the tension it can create between players, creates stress. Stress can be motivating (Lazarus et al., 1952), but it can also negatively affect your attention, working memory, and decision-making (LeBlanc, 2009). It is also typically not very pleasant and can have negative physical effects.

Emotions can enhance your memory (Tyng et al., 2017), which can help improve learning and create lasting memories of an experience, but negative emotions do this too – you could be creating a lasting memory for a player of how much they dislike something (including the game), or how upset or angry they became. Overall, some tension may be appropriate, but caution should be exercised since this should be balanced.

PHYSICAL ACCESSIBILITY

DEXTERITY AND FINE MOTOR SKILLS

Games that require dexterity and fine motor skills (Figure 5.9) will simply not be playable for some individuals. Anyone who experiences tremors, has limited hand-eye coordination, or has other physical factors that cause a reduction in mobility or dexterity, will almost certainly have difficulty in playing games that require these skills. There is a large genre of dexterity games that simply would not be suitable for these individuals. However, games that do not have complex dexterity demands as part of the gameplay mechanics can certainly be made more user-friendly.

Does your game have worker placement? Or does it require moving any components around? If so, consider:

- The size, shape, and quantity of the components – are there small, "fiddly" components? Are they flat against the surface? Are there lots of them?
- How easy are they to pick up and handle, how dexterous do you need to be? Can you slide them over the edge of a table, or do you need them to be in a certain orientation to pick them up?

- How precise do you need to be when placing them – how large is the designated space on the board, or the card? If digital, do you need to get within a certain range in order for the object to snap into place?

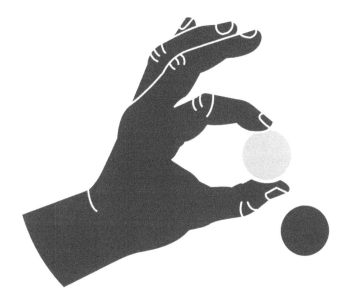

FIGURE 5.9   Dexterity/motor skills.

GROSS MOTOR SKILLS

Gross motor skills are those that require large movements using your whole body. Do you need to move between different spaces (e.g. *Two Rooms and a Boom*)? Perhaps you need to undertake various physical activities (e.g. *Don't Get Got*)? Or maybe you need to conceal items, or even pick up and carry a large, heavy, or unwieldy game box. These kinds of activities are where gross motor skills come into play. Think about whether they are a requirement or not, and how demanding they are to complete.

COMMUNICATION

Do your players need to be able to communicate with each other, or does the game communicate with the player? If so, the following may be relevant.

HEARING

Hearing loss is important to consider when designing a game. Does your game require communication with other players? Do they communicate verbally? Does your game use a digital audio experience?

There are silent, non-communication co-operative games like *The Mind*, in which hearing impairments would not affect gameplay. However, many co-operative games require communication between players, commonly verbal or auditory. For example, games like *Werewolf* or *Mafia* rely entirely on communication – including when to have your eyes open or closed, and debating on who to vote out of the game. If a player is unable to receive or give these instructions, or join in on a debate, they are unable to actively participate in the game. Even a single-player game may have communication issues for those with hearing impairments. In particular, when there are digital audio instructions.

SOCIAL

There are a variety of disabilities related to learning and social skills. These can impact on an individual's ability to interpret social cues, the environment, or other people's behaviour. Outside of disabilities, there are a variety of individual differences, such as mental health or personality that could impact social interactions and communication. Of course, if you are designing a social deduction game (see Chapter 6), it is unlikely that you can meet all of these differences. It does not mean that there is not a market for social deduction games; however, they will not suit everyone; some people simply will not enjoy games which require high levels of social interaction.

LANGUAGE

Similar to hearing concerns, a relevant questions is: do the players need to be able to communicate with each other (Figure 5.10)? Additionally, do the players need specific communication skills in order to understand or play the game? Every game will need to communicate some kind of goals and/or rules, and rulebooks are typically language-dependent. However, there are games that are language-independent outside of the rulebook. Games that do not have text on the game material are commonly considered to be language-independent. Numbers would also be commonly considered language-independent, though there are of course languages that use different writing systems for numerals. However, some games which do not have written text outside of the rulebook still involve communicating with other players, so there is normally a need for all the players to speak the same language. For example, *Dixit* has no words on the cards; it is purely pictorial, but the players need to be able to verbally communicate a concept with each other in each round. *Dobble*, which is similarly picture-based, could be played with each user using a different language, though as a caveat, there would be a certain level of trust required amongst players that the word shouted out is for a symbol on the card (that said, the speed at which *Dobble* is typically played often means that this applies, regardless of the language used). Truly language-independent games do not require players to speak the same language because they do not necessitate verbal communication during gameplay if they already know the rules (e.g. *Carcassonne*, *Splendor*, *Ticket to Ride*).

FIGURE 5.10   Language and communication.

There is also the question of translation versus localisation. Translation directly converts text from one language to another, whilst localisation also incorporates cultural and contextual changes. Which of these is more appropriate is entirely dependent on the content of the game.

Of course, language goes beyond language dependence and language independence. Even if all players speak the same language, the accessibility of the language can be affected by the complexity of the vocabulary and the type of language used, such as slang and jargon, uncommon acronyms, and "inappropriate" language. Generally, it is considered best to avoid slang and jargon, keep things simple, and any acronyms should be clearly explained.

Reading ability is also an important consideration. Not only in relation to vocabulary, but other aspects of the reading process, such as reading speed. The time it takes to read an excerpt of text, either to yourself or even out loud, differs from person to person. The capacity for reading, including attention span, as discussed earlier, also impacts the accessibility. A game that requires a lot of reading generally makes it less accessible, and sometimes less appealing since it slows down the pace of play. It is always useful to consider this, especially when comparing first time players to those who know the game well, or players with reading-related cognitive impairments compared to fast readers.

REPRESENTATION

Representation is important and again, not just for moral, ethical, or social reasons. Representation helps the players with immersion. The more immersed they are in the game, the better the player experience and the more invested they are. One of the reasons representation helps with immersion is through the concept of ownership (Peck & Shu, 2015; Pierce et al., 2003). Ownership in this context is referring not to legal ownership, but to psychological ownership. The concept is simply that "you feel that something is yours". Psychological ownership can lead to increased motivation (Pickford et al., 2016). In the workplace, this psychological ownership has even been shown to increase job satisfaction (Jakada et al., 2021). If a player's character is represented by a basic meeple, that can create a sense of ownership (even just by touching it – Peck & Shu, 2009), especially so if it is their favourite colour; it can feel as though it belongs to them and represents them. When player characters are more complex in design, a player may end up with one that they do not feel they have much ownership over because it does not represent them very well. This could be because the character is dissimilar to them in terms of physical appearance (be it gender, hair colour, race, age, etc.) or has different personality characteristics, but the end result could be that they are less invested in the character's outcome than they would be otherwise. In fact, research has shown that there are benefits and increased user acceptance of having avatars that match a player's skin tone (Herrera & Bailenson, 2021) and gender (Schwind et al., 2017). Diversity in available characters can also include non-visual aspects, such as character names.

Representation in a game could be as simple as cover art, such as the game *Fog of Love*, which provides different cover art, including LGBTQUA+ couples, and another with representation of a wheelchair user. Having representation of the varied individuals that exist in this world is only one part of the conversation, and it is important to avoid tokenism. Equally important is to avoid misrepresentation. Misrepresentation can include negative stereotypes, typecasting, and other problematic portrayals.

Decolonising design is one way to move away from misrepresentation. Today, decolonisation represents recognition of how societal ideology was imposed on colonies, and how this has framed perspectives that are perpetuated even now. Essentially, decolonisation is about recognising other cultures and adopting a wider viewpoint.

Another way to move away from misrepresentation is through diversity. Whilst decolonising is about changing the way things are looked at and thought about, diversity is about bringing a range of different voices to the table, including different social and ethnic backgrounds, genders and sexual orientations, etc. This can be done during initial design stages, but also through playtesting, a very important stage of game design which is covered in Chapter 11.

SUMMARY

In this chapter, we have covered a vast array of areas to consider when thinking about accessibility and inclusivity. It is important to recognise that you cannot design a game that is perfectly accessible to every individual, and their unique characteristics and preferences. However, that should not stop you from making your game design as accessible as possible within the constraints of the type of game you are creating and what resources are available to you. To help you do this, we have included some of the ways that you can make your game more accessible for each of the accessibility areas.

EXERCISE

Choose any game you like. Rate it on each of the eight kinds of accessibility.

- How did it do?
- What adaptations could be made to improve the accessibility?

6 Game Categories and Mechanics

Chris Evans

THE KEY COMPONENTS OF SERIOUS GAMES

Games are made up of different components, not just the physical parts such as a board, cards, and player tokens, but other structural elements that we cannot necessarily see when we play the game, but nevertheless are fundamental to make the game play as it does.

According to Prensky (2001), all games require six structural factors:

1. Rules
2. Goals and Objectives
3. Outcomes and Feedback
4. Conflict/Competition/Challenge/Opposition
5. Interaction
6. Representation or Story

Apart from these structural aspects, crucial design elements contribute to engagement and differentiate a quality game from a subpar or average one.

In his model, Prensky (2001) included all elements that create a good game and, with the inclusion of outcomes and feedback, has also ticked the serious games box. Furthermore, these elements have been incorporated within the conceptual framework for serious games (Yusoff et al., 2009) that provides structure when designing a serious game.

WHAT MAKES A GOOD GAME?

There are many elements that need to come together to create a good game; many of these themes are discussed in other chapters of this book, but in 1997, *Next Generation* magazine (Next Generation, 1997) asked this exact question, and the answers that it arrived at do not seem out of place when applied to a modern board game:

- **Good game design is balanced**: balance ensures that players perceive the game as both challenging and equitable, avoiding extremes of being excessively difficult or overly easy at any juncture.
- **Good game design is creative**: creative here meaning the opposite of formulaic. Good games are not merely clones of other games but add something original.

DOI: 10.1201/9781003319511-6

- **Good game design is focused**: focus is understanding what it is that makes your game fun and providing the player with as much of it as possible.
- **Good game design has character**: it is a game's depth and richness. Both the character and the characters in a game, if fully developed, are what is memorable.
- **Good game design has tension**: every good game does it in its own way, such as in chess when you play a risky move, or in poker when you are bluffing. The classic way is to make the player care about the goal of the game, and then make it hard to achieve.
- **Good game design has energy**: this comes from things like movement, momentum, and pacing.

WHAT MAKES A GOOD SERIOUS GAME?

A good serious game is a good game that has the key elements of learning and play integrated (Egenfeldt-Nielsen, 2011). What this means is that for the player/learner to succeed in the game, they will also need to master the learning goals behind the game.

BOARD GAME GENRES

It can be challenging to categorise games. Many games can exist in multiple genres, whilst others require a genre to themselves. In lieu of any official guide, the following board game genres are mapped to the subdomains on the BoardGameGeek website (BoardGameGeek, 2023a). Each genre will be discussed briefly and explored within the context of serious games.

ABSTRACT GAMES

An abstract game is a strategy game that minimises luck and does not rely on a theme. Ang (2006) defined games as having two layers, a narrative and an abstract, and whilst most games contain elements of both an abstract game has only the abstract. Most abstract games will conform to the strictest definition of having a game board, cards, and/or tiles in which there is no hidden information, no non-deterministic elements (uncertainty), and usually two players or teams taking alternating turns.

In abstract games, popular mechanics include pattern matching, game theory, pattern recognition, problem solving, and victory points. Like that of *Chess*, the games will sometimes have a loose theme that will be represented within the design and the gameplay.

Abstract games can be further categorised as follows:

Chess-**like Games** – whose educational benefits have been explored in some detail by Gobet and Campitelli (2006). *Chess*-like games are symmetrical, competitive board games between two players involving playing pieces that are often representative of the hostile factions involved.

Blockade Games – for example, *Hare and Hounds* (Michaelsen, 2015). These involve moving your pieces to block your opponent from having any move they can make.

Paper-and-Pencil Games – this category of games has enjoyed a renaissance in recent years with the popularity of *roll and write* games. An example is *Noughts and Crosses* (Gardner, 1989). Educators such as Dietrich (2019) have taken advantage of this popularity, developing games such as *Chem&Roll*, a roll and write game that illustrates chemical engineering and the contact process.

"N-in-a-Row" – games in this category entail positioning or shifting game pieces on a board with the objective of forming a configuration of a specific number of your pieces in a straight line. *Connect Four* stands as a well-liked example of such a game.

Connection Games – a type of strategy game in which players attempt to complete a specific type of connection with their pieces. In his 2005 book, *Connection Games: Variations on a Theme*, Browne (2005) explores this category in detail, exploring the mathematical theory behind the games.

Non-Combinatorial Abstract Games – unlike most abstract games, these include hidden information or setup, random elements, or simultaneous movement. Games like *Boggle* (Fauziah et al., 2018), *Cribbage* (Samoray, 2002), *Scrabble* (Kobzeva, 2015), and *Mafia* (Wan Norhaidi et al., 2019) are in this category. It is worth noting that all these games have been used or adapted for teaching and learning.

FAMILY GAMES

A Family game is unsurprisingly a game that can be played by a family or a group of friends. These games tend to be light strategy games that are quick to play, have similar levels of luck and skill, and have a low complexity rating (<2.5). Games in this category include *Carcassonne* (1.9), *Catan* (2.30), *Wingspan* (2.45), *Ticket to Ride* (1.85), and *King of Tokyo* (1.49). Due to their low complexity, popularity, and fun, these games are often adapted to create serious games and the papers associated with these provide excellent case studies for inspiration. For example, in their adaptation of *Catan* (Illingworth & Wake, 2019), they include authentic and thoughtful adaptations that highlight the dangers of global warming.

THEMATIC GAMES

Thematic games, sometimes referred to as American-style board games, contain a strong theme which drives the overall game experience, creating a dramatic narrative like a book or movie. In *The Art of Game Design*, Schell (2008) suggests that most game themes are experience-based, and the goal of how this is designed and implemented is to deliver an essential experience to the player.

Thematic games often feature player elimination as a natural result of the elevated levels of direct player-to-player conflict (Rogerson et al., 2018). A thematic game is typically built around its central dramatic theme, with its rules and mechanics designed to portray it. Such themes often revolve around battles or clashes between good and evil, featuring protagonists and antagonists. Themes like science fiction and fantasy are frequently encountered.

With serious games, the theme may be a means to convey authenticity, such as a business setting in a business simulation, or a warehouse theme within a logistics game. Other times, the theme may be a layer of fantasy that is used to make the game more memorable.

Clarke et al. (2017) set a good example of thematic design when creating a framework for an escape room experience around research methods. After identifying the participants' needs and the learning objectives, they set about creating a compelling and immersive theme. They wanted to utilise mechanical devices for the puzzles and therefore designed the game around a Steampunk theme, which was consistent with the game's artefacts. Moreover, in order to enhance the theme's engagement and infuse a richer experience, the prototype was additionally rooted in the fictional narrative of *The Island of Dr. Moreau*, a story which revolves around the contentious subject of animal testing – an area that harmonizes thematically with research methodologies.

In creating their escape room, Clarke et al.'s (2017) framework focused strongly on the authenticity of the thematic experience by embedding the challenges and game narrative into the environment, also referred to as Jenkin's concept of Narrative Architecture (Nicholson, 2016).

PARTY GAMES

Party games are designed to foster social interaction, often characterised by uncomplicated setups and straightforward rules. They are well-suited for accommodating sizable groups and can be played within a brief timeframe. For all these reasons, party games and their mechanics are often used as the foundation for the creation of a serious tabletop game. Examples of serious adaptations of party games include:

Cards Against Humanity – To enhance engineering students' comprehension of ethical concerns within their field (Burkey & Young, 2017), the main objective of creating and engaging in this game was to introduce students to the subject of Ethics in Engineering. The intention was to evoke pre-existing knowledge and identify biases regarding predicaments that underscore engineers' involvement in ethical choices. The game utilises cards containing ethical scenarios relevant to engineering, diverging from the original question deck of Cards Against Humanity.

Secret Hitler – To educate about the history of Nazism (Lanicek et al., 2020), *Secret Hitler* presents a tense game of political intrigue and betrayal, set in 1930s Germany. In this game, players assume the roles of either liberals or fascists, working together to spread mistrust and elect Hitler. The liberals, however, must uncover and thwart the Secret Hitler before it's too late. The game effectively illustrates the influence of groupthink – how a group of intelligent individuals can make erroneous choices. When framed within the context of the historical events surrounding the ascent of Nazism, the game offers an opportunity for constructive discussion and deliberation.

Codenames – To teach and train civil engineering students (Sousa, 2020). The authors developed the game to teach mobility management by maintaining the rules of *Codenames* but replacing the cards with subject-specific terms devised by the students. Sousa (2020) rationalised that games foster face-to-face interaction, collaboration, and furthermore that the materiality of the game could amplify learning (Xu et al., 2011). Additionally, compared with a digital game, a physical game would be easier to modify to address the objectives of a serious game.

Pictionary – To help students review course material (Peterson, 2017). The aim of Pictionary is to guess what the active player, who is drawing words from a list of cards, is drawing. Designed for classroom play, in this version students have a minute to visualise microbiology-related words for their team to guess. The game was designed to help students make connections between terms and concepts, visualise these concepts, and promote positive group dynamics.

All tabletop games have the potential to create positive learning environments, but those with social interaction at their core, for example, party games, are particularly well suited to optimising the benefits of social constructivist learning theories (Vygotsky, 1997). This includes:

- Promoting student agency.
- Developing advanced skills such as critical thinking, analysis, evaluation, and creation.
- Promoting diverse viewpoints.
- Encouraging students to reflect, evaluate their work, and identify intermediary skills to acquire based on their needs.

STRATEGY GAMES

Games where a player's skills are the predominant determining factor in game outcomes are called strategy games. The evidence as to how much skill is required for a game to be described as strategic is inconclusive. *Chess*, for example, is certainly a strategy game, but is *The Game of Life* a strategy game? BoardGameGeek categorises it as such. Some strategy games can be solved, and others include reasonably high elements of chance. Strategy games encompass both abstract games, characterised by artificial rules and minimal to no thematic elements, and simulations (including wargames), which feature rules designed to replicate and recreate real or fictional situations.

Strategy games tend to be more problematic to set up and play within a classroom environment due to their more complex set of rules and accompanying game components. With digital games, there is a need to understand what to do, but the mechanics and maths are handled by the computer. Learning complicated rules in a new game takes time away from the gameplay and can be tedious (Xu et al., 2011), however, conversations and interactions among players support the learning process collaboratively and, if time allows, can be incorporated into the gameplay.

WARGAMES

According to Dunnigan (2000), wargames are strategy games in which two or more players command opposing forces in a realistic simulation of an armed conflict. Moreover, many wargames encompass political and strategic decisions that replicate themes from history, fantasy, the near-future, or even science fiction.

Priestley and Lambshead (2016) argue that fantasy wargames stretch the definition of wargaming by representing fictional or anachronistic armaments, but suggest that they may still be called wargames if they resemble the players' interpretation of real warfare.

Wargames can be played for fun as a recreational activity, often in a competitive context, whereas professional wargames are used by the military as a serious tool for training or research. Wargames are popular amongst history students, but sometimes the mechanics and themes of these games are used to create learning games in unexpected subject areas. For example, Hershkovitz (2019) argued the case for wargames to be incorporated into corporate training by clarifying the similarities and the analogical relationship between the fields of war and business. Another use was investigated by Haggman (2019) who suggested that wargames could be used in cybersecurity education. Haggman (2019) suggested that with its rich pedagogic history, the use of wargames would provide a unique approach to teaching about this global problem within a domain that is traditionally delivered in a digital format.

TABLETOP GAME GENRES

It is recognised that the above list is not exhaustive, and there are more genres and subgenres. Whilst it is not practical to cover all of them in this book, in this section, we will highlight a few more notable genres of broader tabletop games, which are in addition to the board game genres from BoardGameGeek (2023a) discussed above.

STORYTELLING GAMES

Storytelling games have become more common in recent years, appealing to a player's sense of narrative games. Games such as *Above and Below, Sherlock Holmes Consulting Detective,* and the *Seventh Continent* are games where the embedded narrative tells the story to the players as they play as characters in the story. Legacy games are similar, though tend to be built on the solid construction of the mechanics of an existing popular game. In these cases, the story is added to create a new twist to an existing game. Stories are classically linear, so to create a sense of agency, these types of games reveal the stories in chunks, and due to the choices that you make, you may never experience some of these chunks. If there were no consequences to the choices you make, then it would not be a game, it would be a story.

Then there is the other type of storytelling game, the ones where the players tell their own story. Games such as *Snake Oil, Debatable,* and *Big Idea* allow the player to devise a short story and pitch their idea to the other players. This is a form of emergent narrative, the extended version of which is more common in role-playing games.

ESCAPE ROOM GAMES

Whilst puzzles have fascinated humankind for millennia, it has only been in the last 20 years that these puzzles have been combined in ingenious ways to create escape rooms. Making their way from the computer screen to the real-life escape room, and then to the tabletop, escape room experiences are now so popular as to be afforded a genre to themselves. Game series such as *Exit* and *Unlock!* are the most popular, with the players collaborating to solve a series of puzzles within a set time (usually an hour). Not being as grounded as their real-life counterparts allows more scope to transport the players to fantastic worlds such as castles and space stations, appealing to a sense of fantasy. Serious escape room games tend to work better with the sciences due to the relatedness of puzzles to science subjects.

LEGACY GAMES

A legacy game is a tabletop board game where over many game sessions, the story, player characters, and mechanics are permanently altered due to the embedded and emergent narratives (see Chapter 7). In these games, the decisions that the players make in one game sitting will have consequences in future games. Popular games such as *Risk, Pandemic,* and *Betrayal at House on the Hill* all have legacy versions available, whereas games such as *The King's Dilemma* and *Gloomhaven* have been designed from the outset as legacy games.

ROLE-PLAYING GAMES

A role-playing game is a game in which the players assume the roles of characters in a fictional setting, with the most famous being *Dungeons & Dragons*. This genre of game can be played on a tabletop, online, or in the real world, through discussions and actions. In both cases, there is a games master who controls both the narrative and any in-game character or creature that the players interact with. Role-playing games deal with themes of teamwork and overcoming conflict, and as such make good serious team-building games, albeit with a less fantastical narrative. Serious role-playing games exist as real-life simulations that can be played on the tabletop, in real-life, or in a combination of both.

DECKBUILDERS

Deckbuilding is a genre of game in which players aim to improve their hand by playing and drawing cards. For example, in the popular medieval-themed game *Dominion*, players start with an identical set of cards but can buy cards from the centre of the table to improve their hand to score victory points. A deconstruction of *Dominion* reveals multiple mechanics at play that provide players with many strategic choices.

TCGS

TCGs or trading card games such as *Magic: The Gathering* or *Pokémon* allow players to collect highly personalised sets of cards that can be used for trade or conflict. Alongside deck building and card drafting, this genre has the potential for designing a serious game in which formulas could be created through trade. This is an interesting area of study in serious games due to the dynamics that develop within a learning environment.

EUROGAMES

A Eurogame is a German-style tabletop game that favours skill over chance, strategy over conflict, and less player interaction. In *Catan* and *Carcassonne*, for example, players tend to play their own game by outmanoeuvring the other players rather than trying to destroy them as you might in an American-style game such as *Risk*. There are some interesting mechanics that we can extract from Eurogames that convert well to serious tabletop games. For example, the worker placement mechanic, representative of scarcity of resources, might translate well to subjects such as economics or business. Similarly, auctions work well in serious games due in part to the fact that auctions exist in the real world, but also because of the energy that a bidding war can create within a learning environment.

DEXTERITY GAMES

Commercial tabletop dexterity games include classics such as *Jenga, Subbuteo*, and *Crokinole*. Dexterity games are also often used for corporate training events: build the tallest tower out of straws or Lego, drop an egg from the greatest height without breaking it, the barter jigsaw puzzle game, etc. These games are designed to teach soft skills such as collaboration, communication, and leadership, but dexterity games also exploit skills found in the psychomotor domain of learning such as coordination and motor skills.

THE MECHANICS OF SERIOUS GAMES

Anyone familiar with the website BoardGameGeek will probably know that there is a section included that contains the mechanics of a game (BoardGameGeek, 2023b). Here, there is a list of almost 200 mechanics that are included within tabletop games, everything from *Acting* through to *Zone of Control*.

However, according to Schell (2008), game mechanics are much more than that; he argues that they are the core of what a game truly is. "They are the interactions and relationships that remain when all of the aesthetics, technology, and story are stripped away" (Schell, 2008, p. 130). In other words, for tabletop games, mechanics are everything other than the aesthetics, story, and any technology that may support the game and its associated teaching and learning. For learning games, outcomes may be included as an element that is not necessarily contained within the game, though the means of achieving those outcomes mostly are.

Schell (2008) organises game mechanics into seven categories: (1) Space, (2) Time, (3) Objects, (4) Actions, (5) Rules, (6) Skills, and (7) Chance.

This categorisation works well for serious tabletop games with the methods for meeting any specific learning objectives contained within these seven categories. In the remaining portion of this chapter, we will delve deeper into these seven categories, examining them with greater scrutiny and analysis. The aim is to provide a comprehensive understanding of each category, shedding light on their intricacies and significance with regards to game design.

MECHANIC 1: SPACE

Schell (2008) describes the space in which a game is played as the *Magic Circle* (Huizinga, 1950). Theses spaces:

1. Are either discrete or continuous.
2. Have a number of dimensions.
3. Have bounded areas that may or may not be connected.

If you consider the game *Chess*, for example, there are 64 *discrete* squares in which pieces can be positioned. The game itself is played over two dimensions (even though the pieces are three-dimensional) and the squares are bound together and connected to their adjacent squares. Of course, anyone who has seen enough Star Trek episodes will realise that *Chess* can also be played over three dimensions, with the oldest known version dating back to 1907 (Pritchard, 2007), and furthermore, with the thousands of *Chess* variants in existence, there are also several one-dimensional versions that are played along a single row of the board (Pritchard, 2007).

A game can also have zero dimensions. For example, the classic debating game, *Would You Rather...* can be played as an icebreaker, with the ridiculous questions substituted for subject-specific questions, for example:

> Would you rather.... Be a superhero with the power to alter the charge of things, or the force of things?

These questions can still be fun, and they can get students thinking and arguing their theories of why one of these things is better than the other.

MECHANIC 2: TIME

As with space, time in games can be discrete or continuous, that is, time can represent a *discrete* turn in a game, or it could be represented by a *continuous* ticking clock as you may find in an escape room activity. Furthermore, there are many games where time is not a limiting factor, but it is still a meaningful factor. For example, a game of *Dungeons & Dragons* may continue for many hours with no perceivable end in sight, until eventually, one or more of the players is too tired to continue playing. This is true for serious games, with classroom-based games bounded by the time the teacher allows, and for games played outside of the classroom, the stamina or inclinations of the players may be the limiting factor.

In games we can alter time as, other than escape rooms and a few other notable exceptions, very few games are played in real time. Even games that have the *real-time* mechanic such as *Captain Sonar* are unrepresentative and unrealistic if we were to consider that the distances covered by the opposing submarines could take place in minutes.

When designing games, the time that a game takes to play is a key factor to gather feedback on from playtesting. Schell (2008) suggests that instead of simply asking if the game is too short or too long, consider the following stretch questions if appropriate:

- What is it that determines the length of my gameplay activities?
- Are my players frustrated because the game ends too early? How can I change that?
- Are my players bored because the game goes on too long? How can I change that?
- Would countdown timers make my gameplay more exciting?
- Time limits can irritate players. Would I better off without time limits?
- Would a hierarchy of time-based structures help my game? For example, several short rounds that together comprise a larger round?

MECHANIC 3: OBJECTS

Games have objects and in board games these are usually referred to as the game components such as a board, tokens (meeples, miniatures, pawns, standees), counters, cards, dice, rules, player cards, character sheets, coins, cubes, tiles, and timers.

Objects have attributes, so a King in *Chess*, for example, has attributes that determine how that piece looks and moves (it has a cross at the top and it can normally move one space on the board in any direction).

Objects also have states, so in the case of the King, it can be free to move, in check, and in check mate.

Although players should be aware of the objects, their attributes, and their possible states, games also contain secrets not always revealed to all of them. This is often because of playing or drawing cards (card games are inherently games of hidden information whereas board games are inherently games of manoeuvre and location (Pulsipher, 2012)), but can also be because of game narrative or player actions.

MECHANIC 4: ACTIONS

Schell (2008) describes actions as the verbs of the game, what players can do in a game, which he divides into two categories. In the examples below, for familiarity purposes, the board game *Monopoly* is used to demonstrate the differences between these actions:

Basic Actions – Roll the Dice, Move your Token, Draw a Card, Pay a Fine, Collect a Reward.
Strategic Actions – Purchase a Property, Develop some Houses, Pay a £10 Fine or take a Chance.

Depending upon which variant of the game you play, compared with most games, the strategic decisions that you make within *Monopoly* are less frequent. Taken to the extreme, in *Chess*, for example, where unless you have only one move available (such as being forced to move out of check), all moves are regarded as strategic or dynamic (Hunicke et al., 2004), though the action of physically moving the piece may be considered a basic action.

Actions Equals Mechanics

Actions are at the heart of mechanics, so much so that most of the mechanics that can be found on BoardGameGeek's extensive list are actions, or can be reworded as such: action drafting, acting, area movement, kill steal, follow, worker placement, storytelling, take that, voting, tile placement, and so on. For the rest of this section on actions, several often-used mechanics will be explored in more detail and in relation to their appropriateness for serious games.

Dice Rolling – Whether to move or to resolve a conflict or situation, dice rolling is the most often used method to introduce randomness into a game. This randomness, however, can be mitigated by adding more dice, allowing players to adapt strategy. Games like *Catan* use this in the setup and gameplay. By using two dice, as shown in Figure 6.1, numbers closer to the mean are more likely to be rolled and are therefore more favourable.

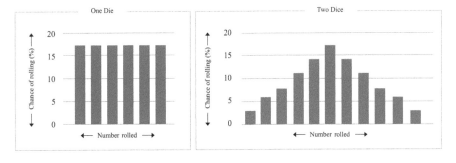

FIGURE 6.1   Odds of rolling a specific number with one or two dice.

Randomness serves as a method for representing unpredictability. In mathematics, a deterministic function is one in which the result can be foreseen with absolute certainty when the input is known. In contrast, for a random function, even if the input is known, the outcome cannot be entirely foreseen. Instead, the outcome can solely be described as a probability distribution; it might have a higher likelihood of assuming one value over another, but there's no complete certainty regarding the specific value it will assume.

It could be argued that serious games should have less randomness, and more fun games should have more. Good game design may, for example, allow players to mitigate randomness; however, one of the single most disliked mechanics in modern board gaming is the pure "roll to move" mechanic.

The evolution of board games has seen a movement away from this mechanic, and oftentimes movement takes place through a series of logically interconnecting lines (such as in the game *Pandemic*), or by simply moving your token to the space required in a single move (such as the *worker placement* mechanic in games such as *Agricola*).

Auctioning and Bidding – auction mechanics are often seen in business and economics simulations and games. However, the auction mechanic can be used as a primary or secondary mechanic to add elements of risk, suspense, and uncertainty to any subject – for example, Olano et al. (2014) created a cybersecurity game that affords players the opportunity to acquire energy units at an auction and can choose to encrypt their bids to gain an advantage. Furthermore, and keeping with the theme of cybersecurity, opposing players can eavesdrop on the bid and steal the energy units if successful at encryption.

Variable Player Powers – One element of games that is considered good design is in its characters (Prensky, 2001), and by providing players with a unique set of skills, you impart status and encourage teamwork. The *Pandemic* board game (Anania et al., 2016) with its variable player powers has been used to study teamwork, where powers are decided at the start of the game by assigning roles such as Engineer, Researcher, Scientist, and so on. In other games, such as *King of Tokyo*, players make strategic choices using the *open card drafting* mechanic to level up their creature.

In *Pandemic*, which is a collaborative game, and *King of Tokyo*, in which the player's base powers are equal, balancing the game is not so much of a problem. Using the variable player power from the start in competitive games, however, can cause unbalance, which should be avoided, mitigated, or at least understood. For example, a serious game that has the objective of teaching students the concept of competitive advantage would be more effective if the students were assigned different business models from which to make their bids.

Open (Card) Drafting – In modern games, it is usually preferred over drawing blind from a deck of cards. Open drafting presents the players with meaningful choices, which is seen as one of the main objectives both in game design (Salen & Zimmerman, 2005) and in serious game design (Nicholson, 2015). Furthermore, as randomness is reduced, skill is increased, which in a serious game reduces the risk of it being seen to be unfair (Prensky, 2001). The theory of the importance of choice is represented in both Deci and Ryan's Self-Determination Theory and Dan Pink's motivational model as Autonomy (Deci & Ryan, 1985; Pink, 2009; Ryan & Deci, 2000).

Cooperative Play – Most of us work in teams and cooperative play is a great mechanic for improving soft skills (Azizan et al., 2018) such as teamwork, leadership, and problem solving within any subject area. One tactic, often used in a classroom, is to pit teams against each other to create a competitive element to cooperative games. In their study on student interaction of competitive versus collaborative games, Creighton and Szymkowiak (2014) perhaps unsurprisingly found that playing a cooperative game within a classroom setting resulted in more learner interaction when compared to the playing of a competitive game.

Take That – This mechanic refers to the competitive manoeuvres that directly attack an opponent's progress towards victory, but do not directly eliminate any characters or components representing the opponent. It is a fun mechanic, especially for the Bartle player type *Killers* (Bartle, 1996). Nevertheless, designers should be sensitive to the potential negative effect on player's emotional accessibility. In their accessibility teardown of *Monopoly* (which indirectly employs this mechanic), Heron et al. (2018) suggested that playing *Monopoly* with players who are bad losers is not recommended.

Push Your Luck – Risk-taking adds elements of risk and suspense, linking to aspects of the game pleasure taxonomy such as challenge, discovery, and submission (Hunicke et al., 2004). The simplicity and success of the game *Codenames*, for example, demonstrates the effectiveness of this mechanic, and its adaptability as a serious game has already been discussed earlier in this chapter (Sousa, 2020). The push your luck mechanic demonstrates a particular proficiency in assisting the memory storage process, primarily due to the potential release of dopamine linked with risk-taking (Bransford et al., 2000; Jovanovic et al., 2008). Moreover, given its effective resemblance to gambling – a recognized trigger of dopamine release – the mechanic's capacity to positively influence retention can be further amplified (Rigoli et al., 2016; Shizgal & Arvanitogiannis, 2003).

Pattern Building (Recognition) – With this mechanic, players must configure game components in sophisticated patterns to score or trigger actions. This is a popular mechanic for science-based subjects, particularly Mathematics, which has been called the science of patterns (Oliveri, 1997; Steen, 1988). From a player's perspective, the pattern mechanic appeals to lovers of challenge, expression, and (often) sensation (Hunicke et al., 2004). Popular games in this category include *Shifting Stones, Hive,* and *Azul.*

Social Deduction – This is a fun party game mechanic, which is typically characterised by games in which a group of players tries to deduce which players have been secretly assigned to a stereotypically bad/evil/traitor faction such as spies, criminals, or mythical creatures. Games such as *Werewolf, Mafia*, and *Blood on the Clocktower* are extremely popular games that use this mechanic, and furthermore, popular shows such as *The Traitors* and *The Mole* use this same mechanic very effectively to create compelling reality television. The downside to creating a serious game around this core mechanic is that it just doesn't lend itself naturally to most subject areas. Studies in using this mechanic tend to focus on more equivocal areas of study such as in the prediction of persuasion strategies (Lai et al., 2022), learning to deceive (Aitchison et al., 2021), and communication theory.

Worker Placement – A stylised form of action drafting, players take turns choosing where to place tokens in order to trigger an action from a range of options. This is a heavily skill-based and thus highly effective serious mechanic. Players have a real sense of autonomy, mastery, and (with learning objectives) purpose (Pink, 2012) with this mechanic, which should appeal most to achievers (Bartle, 1996).

The worker placement mechanic imposes a scarcity or restriction of choices and resources on players and, therefore, would be particularly suited within subject areas that might be relevant. Examples include sales and marketing, business, or economics. However, the strategic nature of this mechanic gives it wider appeal in serious gaming. For example, to understand the overall operation of data centres, Lopes (2014) created a worker placement-designed game to provide an environment for reflection and concept learning for his computer science students.

Mechanic 5: Rules

According to Schell (2008), the rules are the most fundamental mechanic as they define all the other mechanics. Furthermore, in serious games, rules should include additional elements such as:

- The overall (learning) goal.
- The learning outcomes and how to achieve them.
- Suggested lessons that this game would be associated with.

- Opportunities and resources to provide further information and facilitate any reflection on learning.
- If this is a classroom activity, then a condensed lesson plan to structure the game.
- Roles and duties within the game, including an explanation of the role of the teacher/facilitator (if relevant).

PARLETT'S RULE ANALYSIS

In his analysis of rules involved with gameplay, Parlett (2005) suggested that games have both explicit and implicit rules, in other words, rules written down (or can be verbalised) and implied. Parlett (2005) breaks down the rules of a game further, as shown in Figure 6.2.

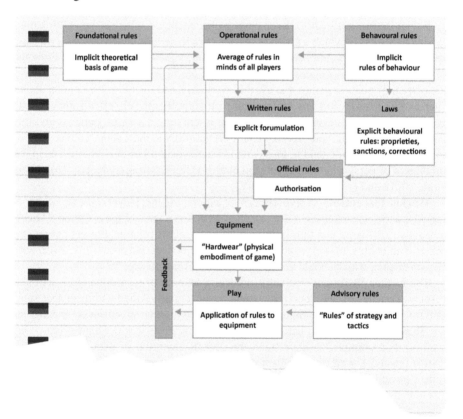

FIGURE 6.2   Parlett's Rule analysis model. (From Parlett, 2005.)

Considering each of these subsets, in turn:

- **Operational Rules** explain how to play the game.
- **Foundational Rules** are the structure of the game. For example, the operational rules might say, "The player should roll a six-sided die and collect

that many power chips". The foundational rules would be more abstract: "The player's power value is increased by a random number from 1 to 6" (Schell, 2008, p. 145).

- **Behavioural Rules** are good sportsmanship rules.
- **Written Rules** are the rules that come with the game.
- **Laws** are only applicable for tournament games.
- **Official Rules** are written rules merged with laws. Saying "check" in *Chess*, for example, is an example where this has happened in the past.
- **Advisory Rules** are rules of strategy, the D (Dynamics) in the MDA model (Hunicke et al., 2004).

The Most Important Rule

The most important rule of any game is its objective, which is usually achieved following a series of goals. Objectives and goals must be stated clearly within the rules. It must be noted that game objectives often, but not always, differ from learning objectives. If the game has constructional alignment (Biggs & Tang, 2015), then some similarities between game objectives and learning objectives would be expected.

MECHANIC 6: CHANCE

Terminology

There is a lot of talk about luck in games: "You were lucky that you threw an eight and landed on Go, and not on Mayfair with my hotel". It is true that it was lucky, but as a player, you must prepare for, and deal with, uncertainty. You work out what the chances are of landing on a mortgage-inducing property and make decisions based upon those risks. Ultimately though, at least with the game *Monopoly*, your fate is decided by both the randomness of the dice and any cards that you may pick up on your travels around the board. Modern board games, however, do not eliminate randomness, but rather they turn it into an important strategic detail, namely probability (Bartolucci et al., 2019). Randomness, chance, probability, uncertainty, and luck all have their place at the gaming table, in the correct context:

- **Randomness**: Lacking a pattern or principle of organisation. Unpredictability; the throw of one die.
- **Chance**: A possibility of something happening; I have a one in six chance of throwing a six.
- **Probability**: The extent to which something is likely to happen; like chance, the probability of me throwing a six in one in six.
- **Uncertainty**: The state of being uncertain; I am uncertain as to what number I will roll.
- **Luck**: Chance considered as a force that causes good or bad things to happen; I was unlucky I threw a one.

Uncertainty

If we have learned anything from the COVID-19 pandemic, we know that uncertainty is not always a good thing. We do not wish to be uncertain about our health or the health of our loved ones, or to be uncertain about the potential loss of earnings, or of our jobs. But whilst individuals, businesses, or governments try to reduce uncertainty, the reality is that we live in an uncertain and conditional universe, and we must deal with uncertainty all the time.

Games are no different, though they do differ from other forms of media. If you are watching a movie or reading a book for the first time, you may be uncertain as to what happens next, but if you were to watch it a second time, the same storylines will unfold, and the ending will be the same. Games differ in that by degrees, and within the rules the uncertainty persists.

In his book *Uncertainty in Games*, Costikyan (2013) argued that in designing games, a certain degree of uncertainty is essential, and went as far to suggest that if there is no uncertainty, then it is not a game. Costikyan's argument appears flawed when considering skill-intensive games such as *Chess*, or when faced with a puzzle that needs to be solved. However, Costikyan considers this by breaking uncertainty down into four elements as shown in Figure 6.3 (Costikyan, 2013).

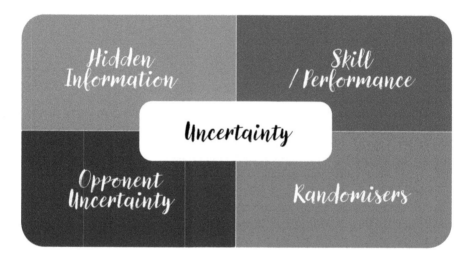

FIGURE 6.3   Elements of uncertainty in games. (From Costikyan, 2013.)

In the case of puzzles, the uncertainty is in one's own skill and performance at solving the puzzle. *Chess* is also reliant on one's own skill and performance as a player, but also the uncertainty represented by the player's opponent.

Input Randomness and Output Randomness

An important distinction to be made by game designers is in the context of input and output randomness. According to Burgun (2014), input randomness is randomness of context that informs the player before they make their decision, which would include the random setup of a *Catan* board, card drafting in *King of Tokyo*, and to a lesser extent, paying a £10 fine or taking a chance in *Monopoly*. Output randomness, however, is randomness that occurs after the player has decided what to do, including rolling to move or to engage in combat, or drawing a card from a shuffled deck. Input randomness stresses skill, whilst output randomness favours luck.

Solver's Uncertainty

Until recently, solver's uncertainty was rare in tabletop games, with the game *Cluedo* being an early exception. The reason is that most tabletop games are algorithmic, rather than instantial, meaning that the game's "content" is algorithmically generated by the nature of its system, and not a set of predesigned elements that are less interesting on second exposure (Costikyan, 2013). This analogy can be somewhat comparable to the concept devised by Juul (2002) whereby games can be classified as games of emergence (simple rules combining, leading to variation) and games of progression (serially introduced challenges). However, there are outliers in the tabletop world that in recent years have become more common. Subsequently, narrative-based board games, escape room games, legacy games, and role-playing games all tend to be games of progression.

Finally, before moving to skill, it is worth noting that chance and skill are not opposites; for example, games can contain a lot of chance and a lot of skill, or conversely virtually no chance or skill:

- Low Luck, Low Skill e.g. *Noughts and Crosses.*
- Low Luck, High Skill e.g. *Chess.*
- High Luck, Low Skill e.g. *Snakes and Ladders.*
- High Luck, High Skill e.g. *Poker.*

MECHANIC 7: SKILL

According to Larkey et al. (1997), skill is the extent to which a player, properly motivated, can perform the mandated mental or physical behaviours for success in a specific game. For the sake of inclusion, with the addition of the affective domain, our definition of skill now reads:

> Skill is the extent to which a player, properly motivated, can perform the mandated mental, physical, and social behaviours for success in a specific game.

The majority of games demand a combination of diverse abilities from the participants. When designing a game, it's valuable to compile a list of the proficiencies your game necessitates, These proficiencies can then be categorised into three primary groups:

1. **Physical Skills:** these include skills involving strength, dexterity, coordination, and physical endurance.
   For serious games, physical skills are represented within the psychomotor domain (Simpson, 1972) and consist of:
   i. **Imitation**: observing and repeating the behaviour of someone else.
   ii. **Manipulation**: the ability to perform certain actions by memory or following instructions.

    iii. **Precision**: involves honing and becoming more accurate. It entails executing a skill with a high level of exactitude.

    iv. **Articulation**: coordinating and adapting a series of actions to achieve harmony and internal consistency.

    v. **Naturalisation**: high-level performance becomes second-nature or natural (e.g. playing the piano at mastery level).

2. **Mental Skills:** these include the skills of memory, observation, and puzzle solving.

    For serious games, mental skills are represented in the cognitive domain (Bloom et al., 1956) as follows:

    i. **Knowledge**: recall data or information. For example, a quiz game.

    ii. **Comprehension**: to understand the meaning of something, translation, and interpretation of instructions and problems. Use one's own words to state a problem. For example, the card game *Taboo*.

    iii. **Application**: use a concept or formula in a new situation. For example, any maths-based serious game.

    iv. **Analysis**: separates material or concepts into component parts so that its organisational structure may be understood. For example, deconstructing a game.

    v. **Synthesis**: builds a structure, pattern, or concept from diverse elements. Put parts together to form something new, with an emphasis on creating a new meaning or structure. For example, creating a new board game using ideas and mechanics from other games.

    vi. **Evaluation**: make judgements about the value of things. For example, evaluating all the mechanics of the board game *Scythe*, and determining which is the least necessary when creating a serious version of the game.

3. **Social Skills:** these include, among other things, reading an opponent and coordinating with teammates.

    For serious games, physical skills are represented within the affective domain (Krathwohl, 2002):

    i. **Receiving Phenomena**: being aware, listening, focused attention.

    ii. **Responds to Phenomena**: active participation from the learners.

    iii. **Valuing**: the value that one attaches to a particular object, phenomenon, or behaviour.

    iv. **Organisation**: prioritises values through contrasting them, resolving any conflicts, and creating a new unique value system.

    v. **Internalises Values**: has a value system that controls their behaviour.

Game Balance

Much like the concept of game design, the interpretation of game balance differs among various designers and developers. Nevertheless, there is a consensus that game balance manifests in some manner across all types of games. Game balance constitutes a facet of game design that can be characterized as a mathematical algorithmic representation of the integrated numerical values, mechanics, and their interrelationships. Game balance involves the adjusting of values to create a user experience that may be considered fair to all players. The objectives of balancing a game are to optimise the players' perception and experience.

The Importance of Turn Order

Games often provide an advantage to the player going first, although this is not always the case. For example, games where each player has the same number of moves can provide advantages to the player going last. Bowls and curling are good examples in sports where there is a strong advantage to playing second. In various games, whether digital or board-based, a skilled designer possesses the ability to address any initial player advantage. Consider *Catan*, for instance, where players take turns to place two settlements at the outset. Starting first might provide an inherent benefit as it allows a player to secure prime spots on the board. However, an ingenious mechanism comes into play by reversing the order of resource allocation when placing the second settlement, wherein the last player goes first. Despite this clever mechanic substantially enhancing game balance, an examination of tournament play indicated a slight advantage for both the first and fourth players in a four-player game (Nagal, 2021).

Generally, the advantage is with the player who goes first. This advantage may be marginal, as with a zero-skill game such as *Snakes and Ladders*, moderate with a game of luck and skill such as *Monopoly*, or significant, as with a skill-based game like *Chess*.

Snakes and Ladders

Since the odds of moving to any square are independent of any previous game history, *Snakes and Ladders* can be represented exactly as an absorbing Markov chain (Althoen et al., 1993). As shown in Table 6.1, in a standard board of *Snakes and Ladders* a player will need an average of 39.2 dice rolls to move from the starting point to square 100. A two-player game is expected to end in 47.76 moves with a 50.9% chance of winning for the first player (Audet, 2012). These calculations rely on a modification where rolling a six does not grant an extra turn, and the player needs to roll the exact number to reach square 100. If the roll goes beyond 100, the player's token remains stationary.

TABLE 6.1

Probabilities and Expectations in the Game of *Snakes and Ladders* for Two Players

Percentage Chance of Winning *Snakes and Ladders*

Player 1	Player 2
50.9	49.1

Source: Audet (2012).

Monopoly

If there is an advantage to going first in a two-player game, then it would be reasonable to assume that the disadvantages would increase for subsequent players in games of three or more players. In the game *Monopoly*, for example, the chance of a player establishing their first *Monopoly* was calculated by Gruska (2012).

TABLE 6.2

Percentage Chance of Creating a Monopoly Naturally

| | Percentage Chance of Achieving First Monopoly | | | | | |
	Player 1	Player 2	Player 3	Player 4	Player 5	Player 6
2 Players	53.5	46.5	–	–	–	–
3 Players	37.2	33.1	29.6	–	–	–
4 Players	29.0	26.2	23.4	21.3	–	–
5 Players	24.1	21.8	19.6	18.0	16.5	–
6 Players	20.7	18.8	17.2	15.8	14.3	13.2

Source: Gruska (2012).

Whilst the percentages as shown in Table 6.2 should not be conflated with the chance of winning the game, there is certainly a correlation. Players going last in this case would be disadvantaged the most, and in serious games, this could be problematic. The main problem with *Monopoly* is in resource depletion, rather than being in last position on the board. The rule of being unable to purchase on the first circuit does little to mitigate this as in the law of averages, the player is still a dice roll behind their competitors.

Chess

In the game of *Chess*, there is a consensus among players and theorists that the player who makes the first move (White) has an inherent advantage (Brams & Ismail, 2021; Ribeiro et al., 2013). Furthermore, *Chess* can be moderately to severely unbalanced depending upon the skill of the players. In decisive tournament games, for example, as shown in Table 6.3, white on average beats Black 55% of the time, but for elite players, the winning percentage for White is 64%. This discrepancy can be mitigated with each player playing an equal number of games with both White and Black, but oftentimes this is not possible.

TABLE 6.3

Fairer Chess: A Reversal of Two Opening Moves in Chess Creates Balance between White and Black

Percentage Chance of Winning "Decisive" *Chess* (Where There Must Be a Winner)		
	White	Black
Good players	55	45
Elite Players	64	38

Source: Brams and Ismail (2021).

Even with the thousands of variations of *Chess* available, changing the rules of this ancient game to be the accepted standard would be challenging to say the least, even if this resulted in a fairer game. Nevertheless, some have tried. In their recent paper, Brams and Ismail (2021) suggested that a simple reversal of two opening moves (Balanced Alternation) resulted in greater balance, and more recently, Anbarci and Ismail (2022) explored the use of artificial intelligence (AI)-powered mechanisms as judges in the event of a drawn game.

Sometimes however, balance is simply not possible, or, as in the case of many serious games, even desirable. One problem that often arises from imbalance is in the emergence of a runaway leader who simply cannot be caught. With little or no chance of winning, the fun of the gameplay for the other players is negatively impacted upon, and in game design, this is something that should be avoided. Rather than attempting to adjust or eliminate existing mechanics, some game designers have introduced new ones that provide losing players with opportunities to catch up. These mechanics are commonly referred to as "*catch the leader*" mechanics.

Catch the Leader

The "*catch the leader*" mechanic is an interesting concept as it inherently unbalances the game by introducing advantages to players that are behind, or alternatively, disadvantaging players that are ahead. The game *Monopoly* is often cited as one that needs a catch-up mechanic. For example, if we were to plot interest (in the game) over time using an interest curve (Schell, 2008), we would see a difference in players' enjoyment as illustrated in Figure 6.4. Interest curves are discussed in more detail in Chapter 7.

In the graph below, the clear diversion of players 1 and 2 represents the point on the interest curve where player 2 realises that they have no hope of winning.

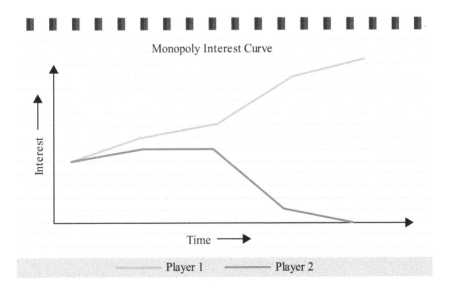

FIGURE 6.4   Monopoly interest curve.

There are many examples of *catch the leader* in board games, and mostly they comprise subtle bonuses or penalties that enable a degree of levelling up that prevents runaway winners but does not eliminate the benefits of good gameplay.

Examples of the *catch the leader* mechanic in board games include:

- *Dominion* – as players collect victory cards, the efficiency of future turns is negatively impacted upon.
- *Charterstone* – played as a campaign, the game provides advantages to losing players at the end of a game.
- *The Quacks of Quedlinburg* – employs a catch-up mechanic between rounds to prevent runaway leaders.
- *Power Grid* – As plants are purchased, more efficient plants become available, so by purchasing early, you are potentially allowing others access to superior equipment.

SUMMARY

Game mechanics are the rules, structures, actions, challenges, goals, and outcomes through which games are played. With board games, mechanics are enabled by the components and, in turn, the mechanics enable player strategy. Some mechanics favour luck and others skill. We have also learned that certain mechanics are more effective when creating serious games. Game mechanics influence game balance, which we have learned is challenging, though possible to achieve. Game theory-based games, for example, are inherently balanced, as are certain games that involve simultaneous play. Finally, game mechanics, and by association, games, feature across all three domains of learning and allow us, as game designers, to improve our learners' social skills, physical skills, and of course, mental skills.

EXERCISE

A teacher asking a student a question is a fundamental method of active learning, but could we turn this form of enquiry into a game?

Think about game mechanics in terms of space, time, objects, actions, rules, skills, and chance.

Which are the most applicable within a classroom setting to turn a Q&A session into a game?

How would this be achieved?

7 Narrative

Dr Devon Allcoat

WHY NARRATIVE AND STORYTELLING?

Firstly, this chapter needs to start with a caveat: narrative is *not* a prerequisite of a tabletop game. Over the course of the chapter, we will look at the benefits that narrative can bring to a game, but that does not mean that a game has to have narrative in order to be considered a good game.

Why might we want to use narrative in a game, or a serious game? Many people have spoken on the benefits of narrative:

- "Narrative contextualises abstract concepts and provides a scaffold for the transfer of knowledge within specific contexts and environments" (Fiore et al., 2007, p. 35).
- "Within narrative psychology, narrative has been proposed as a way of understanding cognition" (Bruner, 2002, p. 52).
- "Telling stories is a means for making sense of everyday experience" (Shank, 2006, p. 713).
- "Stories fulfil a profound human need to grasp the patterns of living – not merely as an intellectual exercise, but within a very personal, emotional experience" (McKee, 1997, p. 12).

EXERCISE

Narratives and storytelling are most commonly associated with...

- Literature
- Films/TV
- Video Games

What are some of your favourite stories? Could they be told in a tabletop game format?

NARRATIVE TERMINOLOGY

"Narrative" is often used synonymously with "story". However, here we will use a more nuanced definition. Narrative is the communication of story materials to an individual, and their experience of it. Ultimately, narrative is about what happens in the game or simulation, and the players experience. Part of narrative is the experiences that the players create through their thoughts and actions, something which is unique to interactive forms of media, such as games.

DOI: 10.1201/9781003319511-7

SETTING

The setting is all about the world (or universe) that the game takes place in. This includes all of the aspects of "world building" that have taken place, i.e., everything that went into constructing the world, including history, geography, laws, technology or magic, and much more.

BACKSTORY/BACKGROUND

The backstory can be used to help "set the scene" of the game. It may include some information from the setting, but it will mostly focus on the historic events leading up to the start of the player's journey, explaining the environment that they are arriving into.

STORY

The story is what happens, the actions and events. So, what is the difference between story and narrative? Two different people can tell the same story in two different ways, i.e., there will be two narratives describing the same story. In the context of narrative in a game, the story can be separated from the game mechanics, and told independently. The story covers all aspects of the story arc (also known as the narrative arc).

THE STORY/NARRATIVE ARC

Stories, across all mediums, typically follow the same basic elements of a story arc.

Exposition
Exposition is the introduction to the story. This is directly linked to the backstory/background, but also typically includes the introduction of any characters.

Rising Action
This is what sets your story in motion, something that creates a situation that stimulates action.

Climax
The climax is the primary point of conflict you have been working towards throughout the story. Typically, this will require important decisions or choices, and will include the convergence of various interactions and events up until this point.

Falling Action
Falling action is the result, or the fallout, after the climax. We have now got past the primary point of conflict, and it is "wrapping up".

Resolution

The resolution is the end of your story, the endpoint of any interactions, and you can see how the environment has changed from where it began.

FLAVOUR TEXT

The term flavour text is specific to games. It is commonly associated with card games such as *Magic: The Gathering*, but is also used more widely in the tabletop and video game industries. It refers to text which is not related to the mechanics of the game, but instead provides story detail. Flavour text can also be used to provide educational information. For example, in *Wingspan*, each bird card has flavour text with facts about the bird represented on the card.

DIGITAL GAME TERMS

Cutscenes

Cutscenes are story events which the player cannot control; these are typically triggered by reaching a certain location or point in the story and, for the duration of the cutscene, players usually cannot control their characters. Many cutscenes are prerendered, and can look cinematic in style compared to standard gameplay visuals.

In-Game Artefacts

Digital games use in-game artefacts, game objects the player can interact with, to add to the story and experience. These can be documents, images, 3D modelled objects, audio files, and more. Similar to flavour text, they typically provide story detail or more world building information. They can sometimes also be used to deliver hints that help with the gameplay. In-game artefacts can be particularly useful to provide additional educational information, facts, or figures. The *Assassin's Creed* video games provide a variety of in-game documents, some of which are about the game world, and some of which include historical information.

Non-Playable Characters (NPCs)

NPCs are exactly what they sound like. They are characters that the players do not have control over. NPCs act independently, and often have specific roles assigned to them.

TYPES OF NARRATIVE

LeBlanc (2000) proposed two types of narrative in games: embedded narrative and emergent narrative.

EMBEDDED NARRATIVE

Embedded narrative is the narrative that has been designed by the creators of the game. Storytelling games, role-playing games, legacy games, escape room games, and simulations are all genres that more easily lend themselves to embedded narrative.

TABLE 7.1

Levels of Theme and Narrative Interaction

Abstract	Minimal Theme	Moderate Theme	Strong Theme	Narrative Theme
Just rules and components	Thin theme irrelevant to gameplay	Identifiable theme within some of the mechanics	Mechanics devised to fit the theme	Thematic storyline that plays like a movie or a book
e.g. *Connect Four, Draughts*	e.g. *Chess, Hangman*	e.g. *Catan, Monopoly*	e.g. *Pandemic, Battle of Gettysburg*	e.g. *Stuffed Fables, Mega Games*

Theme and Narrative

Games can be discussed in terms of their *theme*. Both the mechanics and narrative can be linked to this theme at varying levels (Table 7.1). Ultimately, the primary purpose of a game is to create an enjoyable interactive experience for the players, unlike a book or a film, which is a passive experience. Given this, it makes sense that writing for a game should take into account that interaction. In practice, this means linking the writing to the gameplay, such as tying together the narrative with the theme. Using the tools games provide, such as the mechanics, in order to strengthen the narrative, can be particularly beneficial.

EMERGENT NARRATIVE

Emergent narrative, in contrast to embedded narrative, does not come from the game creators; instead, it comes from the players themselves. It is the players' own experiences and the sequence of events during the game. This includes how they think about their actions, and the consequences of these on the story, and even their interaction with other players.

BASIC PLOTS

Robert A. Heinlein (1947) said that there are two basic ways to write science fiction – you can write about gadgets or about people. When writing about people, he suggested that there are three basic plots:

- "Boy-meets-girl" is any story where the major dramatic question involves romance.
- "The Little Tailor" is any story about a protagonist who goes from zero to hero (or vice versa).
- "The man-who-learned-better", a story about a protagonist who learns or changes their perspective.

Kurt Vonnegut also suggests similar basic story plots, which he maps onto a graph (see Kurt Vonnegut Shape of Stories, 2018; O'Donnell, 2020). These six plots can be visualised as simple shapes, rising on the vertical "G-I" axis (standing for "good fortune" and "ill fortune") for good health and happiness, and falling for despair, poverty, and the like. These shapes are drawn as the narrative changes over the course of the story (see Figure 7.1). You will see alignment here between Vonnegut's and Heinlein's plots. Booker (2004) also suggested seven plots, which generally align across both Vonnegut's and Heinlein's plots.

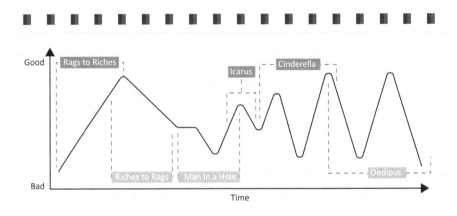

FIGURE 7.1   Vonnegut's six basic stories.

- **Rags to Riches**: a rise in fortune over time.
- **Riches to Rags**: a fall in fortune over time.
- **Man in a Hole**: an initial fall in fortune, followed by a rise.
- **Icarus**: an initial rise in fortune, followed by a fall.
- **Cinderella**: an initial rise in fortune, halted by a turn of events causing a fall, followed by a rise ending in grand success.
- **Oedipus**: an initial fall in fortune, with a change in fortune causing a rise, but ultimately once again falling to the depths for an unhappy ending.

HOW DOES NARRATIVE BENEFIT GAMES

Effective use of narrative helps the player feel more involved and more immersed in a game. Not only does it provide context and meaning, but it helps the player understand what is required of them. Unlike narrative presented through other formats or mediums, games can benefit from the player being a part of the story.

Narrative and Flow

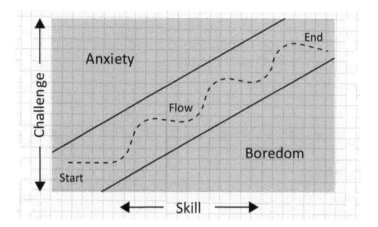

FIGURE 7.2   The flow model. (From Csikszentmihalyi, 1975.)

As discussed in Chapter 2, to achieve "flow", a balance between challenge and skills must be met (Figure 7.2). Conditions for flow also include clear goals and clear and immediate feedback. In order to meet these conditions, narrative can be employed:

- A well-paced narrative can support a steady increase in challenges over time, to match the player's increasing skills. This allows for a good balance between the challenges of the activities, and the players' understanding.
- Narrative can be used to dictate the primary player objectives, as well as tasks and activities, enabling flow by directing attention to clear objectives.
- Narrative demonstrates to the players what the consequences of their actions are. This allows for good interim feedback and appropriate adjustments (feedback loop).

Interest Curves

Narrative can also act as a reward for the players. Schell (2008, p. 247) stated that "the quality of an entertainment experience can be measured by the extent to which its unfolding sequence of events is able to hold a guest's interest", as demonstrated by interest curves, which visualise a player's interest over time (Figure 7.3). As events in the story are revealed, these become interim goals and/or rewards. Pacing is useful as part of the narrative, and for the flow of the game, keeping interest and engagement levels high by having the action spread out over time. This can be done by progressively introducing new or more complex events, or enemies or obstacles of increasing difficulty to keep the player engaged.

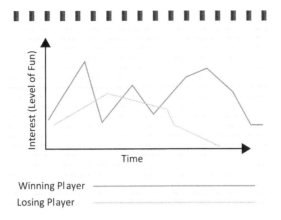

FIGURE 7.3   The interest curve. (From Schell, 2008)

This also works well for education; pacing the introduction of more complex concepts and information, and adding new opportunities for interaction at set intervals
can help to maintain interest, engagement, and learning. Narrative can also give the
situation, and the actions that the players are taking, an increased sense of authenticity. Simulations frequently use narrative in this way.

SIMULATIONS

Simulations were defined back in the introduction chapter. They are especially useful
for teaching and training and, as just discussed, narrative can be particularly beneficial
for the flow of learning and engagement across the course of a simulation. Following a
literature review, Lean et al. (2006) developed a typology of simulations (see Figure 7.4).

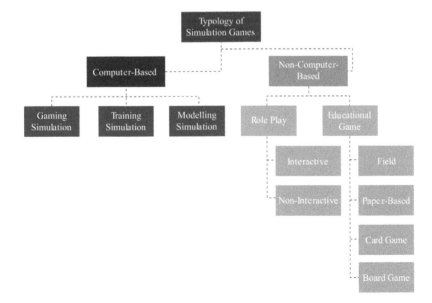

FIGURE 7.4   Typology of simulations. (From Lean et al., 2006.)

As you can see, there is a wide variety of simulation methodologies and types. Some will clearly lend themselves more easily to embedded narrative, such as role-play, but all have the capability for emergent narrative. All of these different types of simulations can involve learning and have educational value, which can be benefited by the use of narrative.

IMMERSION

Immersion is a state of being deeply involved with something. The individual is absorbed in what they are doing, or the environment they are in. This leads to the game world becoming their primary reality at that point in time. It has been related to Csikszentmihalyi's (1975) flow state and is also linked to the concept of suspension of disbelief.

A previously unpublished theory of immersion, initially proposed by Constantinescu et al. (2016), can be seen in Figure 7.5. This theory suggests that immersion is supported by three core components, one of which is narrative. The other two are agency (the feeling of control) and ownership (the feeling of being represented in the game environment).

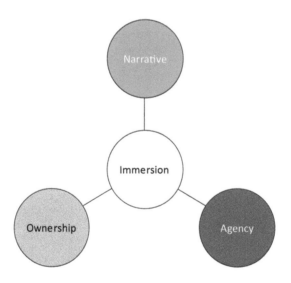

FIGURE 7.5   Theory of immersion.

This theory was initially proposed in relation to immersion in virtual reality, and ownership (see Chapter 5) in virtual reality was specifically linked to having an avatar that represented the player (which, for example, can be particularly effective when in a first-person viewpoint). This sense of ownership is also significant for games in other medias, as it helps the player to feel that they, as an individual, have a specific identity and purpose. Agency, having control of your actions, also relates to autonomy, the freedom to choose what you do, outside of external influences, which is a core part of motivational theories (as discussed in Chapter 3). Ownership and agency, combined with narrative, give that sense of being drawn into the game world, by being totally involved in the setting and your actions.

WHAT CONTRIBUTES TO NARRATIVE IN GAMES?

We have already looked at various levels of theme integration with narrative, but there are many other ways to increase narrative.

- The game represents something.
- The content is represented in the components.
- The rules and mechanics mirror the dynamics of the content they represent.
- Content and mechanics converge to create the game experience.
- The game events are related by causation.
- The player characters are unique and identifiable.
- Characters have goals and objectives and undergo change during play.
- Player strategies mirror character strategies.
- There is a degree of uncertainty, of revelation, such as found in storytelling.

SUMMARY

This chapter discussed narrative, the power it has, and how it can be incorporated into games. Narrative is not a requirement for a tabletop game. Many very good, very popular games are entirely abstract with little to no embedded narrative. However, even these games can create emergent narrative through gameplay and interaction with other players. Ultimately, whilst narrative is not a requirement, it can be a powerful tool to elevate the immersion, enjoyment, and emotional impact of a game. When using narrative, ideally it will reward the players, provide good pacing and engagement, and help to advance the game.

EXERCISE

List your top five favourite games.

- What type of narrative does each game have?
- Can you think of specific examples of emergent narrative from your time playing these?

8 Deconstructing a Game

Chris Evans

INTRODUCTION

The process of designing and developing serious games can pose challenges. To consistently create games that uphold both quality and educational standards, designers must enhance the efficiency and effectiveness of the development process. Throughout the past few decades, numerous guides, methodologies, and theories have been formulated to aid in the analysis, design, or dissection of games.

If we take the broader interpretation of deconstruction, which pertains to various loosely defined methods of comprehending the connection between text and meaning, then the deconstruction of a game could be seen as a collection of loosely defined strategies aimed at understanding the correlation between a game and its meaning. In plain English, and putting aside for one moment the subjective nature of fun, the deconstruction of games is an approach to understanding why games are fun.

It would be reasonable to assume that the process of deconstruction might start with the rules, but to suggest that games are defined by rules would be over-simplistic and would not account for the myriad of options and strategies that are available to the player. It is one thing to say that games are defined by their rules, and quite another to suggest that the activity of playing them is constituted or defined by these rules (del Castillo, 2017). Games are defined by their deep mechanics and complex systems of interaction (Consalvo & Paul, 2020), and games are also defined by the feelings that are evoked by the playing of these games. These feelings may be the "meaning" as to why these games are played. Furthermore, when considering serious games, the definition may be further expanded to include "purpose while maintaining a game context" (Gómez-Maureira et al., 2022, p. 3).

In this chapter, we will explore deconstruction of serious games through the game review lenses and the Mechanics-Dynamics-Aesthetics (MDA) model's design approach (Hunicke et al., 2004).

WHAT IS GAME DECONSTRUCTION?

According to Luton and Freeman (2021), deconstruction broadly refers to the application of rigorous, critical, and analytical analysis to a piece of media or art (such as a game), by breaking it down so its component parts and their interconnections can be better understood. *Deconstruction* does not mean that you tear something apart, at least not literally; instead, it means to break down or analyse something to discover its true significance. As game designers, we tend to do this anyway. We will play games that we like and think about how we can develop

DOI: 10.1201/9781003319511-8

elements such as the mechanics, the rules, the theme, and create something new. We are breaking the game down mentally, but not scientifically. Similarly, we will find "problems" with the rules of existing games we play and devise new ones that may be incorporated into the gameplay, and this is how new games are created.

Take card games, for example; there are countless versions available today, but most historians agree that the first card game was played in China more than 800 years ago (Sackson, 1981). The game evolved over the years, and continues to do so, as the components and rules were modified to meet various definitions of fun. Gambling games, as another example, often appeal to the player's senses of **challenge** and **fellowship**, whereas solitaire games are more about **submission** and **discovery**. These expressions of enjoyment stem from the classification of game pleasures proposed by LeBlanc (2004). The taxonomy recommends using a more precise language to describe fun, rather than relying on vague terms like "gameplay" and "fun." This taxonomy was incorporated into the MDA framework (Hunicke et al., 2004), which serves as an analytical tool for studying games. We will delve deeper into the MDA framework as a means to deconstruct games.

WHY DECONSTRUCT A GAME?

Before you even begin to deconstruct a game, you need to understand what you want to take from the process. When we analyse games, we try to understand what makes them fun to play; at least, that would be one of our primary objectives, though often a deconstruction is more interested in improving what does not work so well. Serious games are different in that we also need to understand that key learning outcomes can be achieved – which can occur within the game, but also within the learning that may encompass the game.

Fun in games is a result of gameplay, and that can be influenced by many factors. For example, in their deconstruction of the game *Candy Crush*, Varonis and Varonis (2015) found that it is crucial for each level to provide increasing challenges that motivate increased mastery, but do not frustrate a player to the point of quitting. Similarly, academic design that provides the opportunity for learners to achieve a sense of flow (Csikszentmihalyi, 1990) through the opportunity to identify goals, meet challenges, and receive feedback, may encourage them to persist even when they are working autonomously as with some online environments, or with playing an academic game.

GATHERING INFORMATION ABOUT A GAME

In her textbook on game analysis, Fernández-Vara (2019) suggests that when we look for context for our game, one of the first things that we want to find out is what has been written about the game already. Fernández-Vara (2019) suggests that in addition to the game (together with its box and its manual) game reviews, academic articles, press releases, developer talks and texts, and pre-existing theories might also be considered when analysing and deconstructing a game.

OVERVIEW OF POSSIBLE RESOURCES

Many sources are available to help us understand more about a particular game. The following sections discuss relevant frameworks and models that can support game deconstructions, namely:

- Gagne's Nine Events of Instructions
- The MDA Framework
- Elemental Tetrad
- The Design, Play, and Experience (DPE) Framework
- The Design, Dynamics, and Experience (DDE) Framework

Towards the end of this chapter, game reviews will be covered in detail due to their significance to game analysis and deconstruction. When analysing or deconstructing something, you are carrying out a detailed examination of its elements or structure. Writing a review follows a similar purpose, typically with the intention of being public-facing, and therefore appropriate for a wider audience.

MODELS USED TO CONSTRUCT A SERIOUS GAME

In education, we tend to construct things rather than deconstruct them. The closest we tend to come to deconstruction is when we reflect upon the merits of a lesson, an activity, or a game, or receive feedback, either from our peers or our students.

The design of educational games or activities tends to follow tried and tested educational models such as:

- **ADDIE – Analysis, Design, Development, Implementation, Evaluation**: the most well-known learning model used by instructional designers and training developers to create effective learning experiences. Its five-phase structure (Analysis, Design, Development, Implementation, and Evaluation) guides the creation of materials that effectively engage learners and align with objectives (Branson et al., 1975).
- **Gagne's Nine Events of Instructions**: examines cognitive processes learners undergo when presented with instructional stimuli. This model stresses optimising comprehension and retention through structured learning experiences. The nine events, from attention to retention, aid educators in aligning instruction methods to cognitive processing (Gagné, 1972).
- **Merrill's First Principles of Instruction**: a problem-solving design model. Its five components (activation, demonstration, application, integration, and facilitation) promote active engagement and practical skill development, with an aim to provide a meaningful learning experience (Merrill, 2002).
- **ARCS Model of Motivation (Attention, Relevance, Confidence, and Satisfaction)**: John Keller's ARCS Model of Motivation is an instructional design model that focuses on student motivation. Addressing Attention, Relevance, Confidence, and Satisfaction, educators create instruction capturing interest, boosting confidence, and offering rewards (Keller, 1987).

These instructional models collectively offer educators a range of approaches to design and deliver effective learning experiences, catering to different learning styles, contexts, and motivational needs.

Whilst these models are not particularly useful as a tool for deconstruction, they are useful as a means of both structuring the design of a serious game and in understanding the wider context in which a serious game sits.

For example, Gagne's Nine Events of Instructions suggest that a teacher can structure a lesson by:

1. Gaining attention.
2. Informing learners of objectives.
3. Stimulating recall of prior learning.
4. Presenting the content.
5. Providing learning guidance.
6. Eliciting performance.
7. Providing feedback.
8. Assessing performance.
9. Enhancing retention and transfer to the job.

A serious game played in the classroom would fall into one or more of these events, but all nine events would ideally be connected in some way to the game, the learning outcomes, and any assessment.

MECHANICS, DYNAMICS, AND AESTHETICS: A STRUCTURED APPROACH TO UNDERSTANDING GAMES

Until recently, there was no comprehensive model or framework that could help design or deconstruct a game. However, Hunicke et al. (2004) published *MDA: A Formal Approach to Game Design and Game Research*, an attempt to bridge the gap between game design and development. The model evolved from the concept that games were made up of rules, a system, and fun. Without due care, a deconstruction can become a mechanical process of breaking down a game's systems and function (Luton & Freeman, 2021). Using a more formalised approach to deconstruction is helpful in exploring not just how a game works on a functional level, but also why it works.

The MDA framework as illustrated in Figure 8.1 formalises these distinct components and establishes their design counterparts: Mechanics, Dynamics, and Aesthetics, represented in ascending order; that is, the mechanics influence the dynamics, which, in turn, influence the Aesthetics.

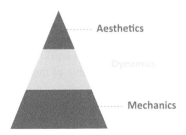

FIGURE 8.1   MDA: A formal approach to game design and game research. (From Hunicke et al., 2004.)

Mechanics include the various actions, behaviours, and control mechanisms that a player affects within the context of a particular game. These are the typical "dice roll" or "worker placement" type mechanics but may also include the rules of a game or actions on a game card.

Dynamics describes how the mechanics, acting on player input, can interact with other mechanics. Within the context of board games, players apply this strategy within the rules' boundaries. Dynamics work to create aesthetic experiences. For example, challenge is created by things like time pressure and opponent play (Hunicke et al., 2004).

Aesthetics describes the desirable emotional responses evoked in the player (the outputs) when they play the game. Hunicke et al. (2004) suggested that there were eight types of fun that could be enjoyed when playing a game:

1. **Sensation**: A game with a strong sensory character, and with board games this would usually indicate that a strong visual design such as Wingspan and Azul might help elicit this emotion.
2. **Fantasy**: A fictional game. Games create a fictional world, a reality that players can choose from. Serious games will often take place in simulated worlds that reflect real life.
3. **Narrative**: Games are drama. A game with a well-written narrative, with a well-defined character or world. Role-playing games are a good example of games that may result in this type of fun for players.
4. **Challenge**: A competitively minded game that inspires the thrill of competition and/or collaboration. It should be noted that it can also happen in a single-player game, where the fun comes from overcoming difficult challenges.
5. **Fellowship**: Play as a social framework. One aspect of gaming is for players to build social relationships with peers.
6. **Discovery**: Gaming is an uncharted territory. A game that inspires players to explore and discover new features.
7. **Expression**: As a game of self-discovery. Games that enable players to find ways to express themselves.
8. **Submission**: Gaming as a pastime. Games that focus on distracting players. This is generally the realm of computer games, though addictive serious non-digital games may invoke the submission pleasure as players strive to understand a concept or overcome a problem.

CRITICISMS OF THE MDA MODEL

Whilst the MDA framework is the most widely accepted approach to game design, it has recently been criticised for having several weaknesses in its practical implementation and theoretical design. The most notable of these are as follows:

1. Whilst Hunicke et al. (2004) use *Monopoly* as one of the games they analyse, and although they also mention some other non-digital games in their paper, they are working from a point of view shaped by their experience with digital games (Duarte, 2015).

2. It neglects many design aspects of games, focusing too much on game mechanics (Walk et al., 2017). Furthermore, according to Kramer (2015), durability, functionality, and the visual appeal of the materials contribute to the perceived value of a game.
3. It fails to provide a framework or even a coherent approach for narrative design (Cardona-Rivera et al., 2020; Walk et al., 2017).
4. It is not suitable for all types of games, including particularly serious games or any type of experience-oriented design (as opposed to functionality-oriented design) (Walk et al., 2017).
5. Game designers tend to reject a methodological or structured way of developing a game because it is widely believed within the field that one cannot survive without creativity (Xin, 2022).
6. It allows the game designer only indirect control over the dynamics and aesthetics of a game because it assumes that all the game's dynamics and aesthetics result from its mechanics (Winn, 2011).

OTHER DESIGN MODELS

ELEMENTAL TETRAD

In *The Art of Game Design*, Schell (2008) introduces a new conceptual framework used for game design, the elemental tetrad as shown in Figure 8.2. Building upon the work of Hunicke et al. (2004), and in response to the subsequent criticism, Schell (2008) suggested that games had closer relationships between the emotional aesthetics of a game and its mechanics, story, and technology.

Unfortunately, due to the greater importance that this model places on the use of technology, this model provides little benefit to the design and creation of tabletop games.

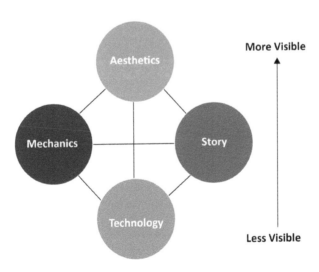

FIGURE 8.2   The elemental tetrad. (From Schell, 2008.)

THE DESIGN, PLAY, AND EXPERIENCE (DPE) FRAMEWORK

Winn (2011) argued that the existing approaches, such as MDA (Hunicke et al., 2004), did not consider serious games, that is, any learning element that games imparted upon the players. Winn introduced a new concept by expanding MDA into the Design, Play, and Experience (DPE) framework (see Figure 8.3), which depicts the relationship between the game designer and the player in the same way as MDA, but also translates additional design aspects into layers. Designed for serious games, the DPE approach proposes that such designs do not simply comprise gameplay mechanics, but also include pedagogical content to be learned, characters, settings, and narratives of the story to be told, and a user interface (Winn, 2011).

This would create an effective approach to understanding serious games; however, DPE also incorporates the underlying technology as a fundamental prerequisite for the creation of serious games, and for mediating between the DPE aspects of a game.

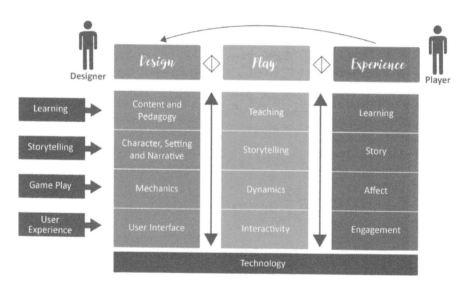

FIGURE 8.3   The Design, Play, and Experience (DPE) framework. (From Winn, 2011).

THE DESIGN, DYNAMICS, AND EXPERIENCE (DDE) FRAMEWORK

The DDE model closely resembles the MDA model, except the word aesthetics which has changed to experience, and mechanics is now design. Walk et al. (2017) argue that most mechanics are not actually mechanics, and the word *aesthetics* is just plain confusing.

Walk et al.'s (2017) main argument, however, was for the inclusion of a narrative design element within the copious detail included within the framework. Designed exclusively for the digital design market, the framework does not translate well for the design of tabletop games.

DECONSTRUCTING A GAME USING THE MDA APPROACH

As most readers will be familiar with the structure and gameplay of the board game *Monopoly*, we will use this for our deconstruction, and our first question should be "Why are we doing this, what are we trying to achieve?" In this deconstruction, we will evaluate *Monopoly* as it is a game that divides opinion. There is no disputing the success of the board game *Monopoly*; with over 275 million copies sold since its introduction in 1935, it is the fourth biggest selling board game ever (Johnson, 2018), and furthermore, its popularity is on the increase with its biggest year ever coming during the COVID-19 pandemic (Carter, 2021). Economists (McKenzie & Lee, 2019) suggest that the game's popularity is probably attributable in no small way to the fact that it taps into twin passions: to win and to acquire wealth (even play wealth), though fundamentally, playing *Monopoly* is a social experience that is made better by the friends you play with (Mitic, 2011).

Monopoly has evolved and diversified. On his gaming blog, Berlinger (2021) lists 3,697 versions on *Monopoly* that mostly adhere to the official rules, yet differ in theme and design. This appeals to a variety of definitions of fun as described in LeBlanc's taxonomy of game pleasures (LeBlanc et al., 2004), such as the creation of **fantasy** *Monopoly* worlds such as *Star Wars*, *Lord of the Rings*, and *Harry Potter*, or the **sensation** and **expression** evoked through use of tokens that you voted for to be in the game. Furthermore, Hasbro has addressed criticism of there being too much luck in the game by providing players with more strategic decisions and **challenges**, such as the addition of strategy dice as seen in tournament play (Heron, 2016). Hasbro refined the rules over the years to improve gameplay and timing.

As an "out of the box" serious game, *Monopoly* works to improve our cognitive abilities. As Baldassarre (2015) argues, playing any board games increases neuroplasticity, which allows us more ability to see things from different points of view and understand the causes and effects of behaviours and emotions. Furthermore, due to its universal appeal, *Monopoly* has become the "go to" board game when adapting a game to create a classroom activity (Ansoms & Geenen, 2012; Griffin & Jackson, 2011; Orbanes, 2002; Shanklin & Ehlen, 2007).

However, as with all games, there are some issues. Accessibility, which is excellent in many areas compared to other board games, can be problematic for emotional accessibility. According emotional accessibility issues with the game, Heron (2019) recommends that it is not a game for bad losers.

Even the manufacturer's Hasbro Games appear to have recognised the potential for emotional distress by releasing the *Sore Loser* edition which effectively includes a *"catch the leader"* mechanic. However, as ingenious as this mechanic might be, it exacerbates another common criticism of *Monopoly*, that is, the indeterminate length of time it takes to play. Famously, the length of time a game took to play was a major concern of Edward P. Parker, a former president of the then manufacturer's, Parker Brothers (Brandreth, 1985). Hasbro has taken steps to address this issue by amending the rules and to speed up the game, the rules clearly state:

> If the player lands on an unowned property, whether street, railroad, or utility, they can buy the property for its listed purchase price. If they decline this purchase, the

property is auctioned off by the bank to the highest bidder, including the player who declined to buy.

Hasbro, 2020, p. 2

The problem is that players tend to ignore the rules and play by their own "house rules". In a study made by the manufacturers (Leddy, 2014), Hasbro found that 68% of Americans who play *Monopoly* had never read the rules. If the game still lasts too long for some people, Hasbro also includes instructions for a short game within the official rules.

Another criticism is that there is too much luck in the game with Heron (2019) suggesting that the decisions that the players make are reactionary rather than strategic, or what Burgun (2014) would describe as more output randomness than input randomness. However, Kaulfield (2011) argues that it is exactly the type of randomness that younger children like, which would help explain *Monopoly*'s appeal to young families.

As a serious game, *Monopoly* has more adaptations than any other board game, and even as a standalone game, it has been used to help teach subjects such as probability (Gazdula & Farr, 2020) and poverty and inequality (Ansoms & Geenen, 2012), the latter being the game's original intention.

THE MECHANICS OF *MONOPOLY*

BoardGameGeek lists the mechanics of *Monopoly* as follows: Auction/Bidding, Auction: English, Income, Loans, Lose a Turn, Ownership, Player Elimination, Roll/Dice Rolling, Set Collection, Stock Holding, Track Movement, and Trading.

For the sake of this deconstruction, the focus will be on the mechanics as identified in the data gathering stage, that is, the Auction, Player Elimination, Dice Rolling, Set Collection, and Trading.

THE DYNAMICS OF *MONOPOLY*

The dynamics, according to Hunicke et al. (2004), are influenced by the mechanics, so what decisions does the player have to make during each mechanic stage, and more importantly, can any of these decisions be considered strategic? To understand this more clearly, Burgun's (2014) definition of input randomness (strategic) and output randomness (luck) will be assigned to any chance-based mechanism within the game.

Aesthetic experiences are created through the work of dynamics. Things like time pressure and opponent play, for example, create challenges, and similarly with gameplay, we can identify feedback loops that determine how specific states and changes may affect the gameplay (Hunicke et al., 2004).

In *Monopoly*, as the leader becomes richer, they can invest more and the penalties for the poorer players increase. Just like in real life, the rich become richer, and the poor get poorer, colloquially known as the *Monopoly Death Spiral*.

We can imagine ways to alter *Monopoly* using our understanding of aesthetics, dynamics, and mechanics, such as rewarding players who are behind to keep them within a reasonable distance of the leaders or making progress more difficult for rich players. However, the downside of this may be in the prolonging of the game time.

THE AESTHETICS OF *MONOPOLY*

The aesthetics of *Monopoly*, as according to the MDA model (Hunicke et al., 2004), are as follows:

Fantasy – You are bankrupting your friends and family – but not really. Furthermore, the themed versions of *Monopoly* may add to the feeling of being immersed in an imaginary world.

Challenge – It is hard to think of a board game that does not include challenge. Challenges are determined by the objective and the barriers that prevent the player from achieving it (Denisova et al., 2017). Due to the high degree of output randomness, the challenge in *Monopoly* largely comes from the collection of sets and their subsequent development.

Fellowship – Much has been made about the negative aspects of trying to bankrupt and eliminate your fellow players, but some other competitive board games can be equally cutthroat. Ultimately, it's still a game that stimulates discussion between the players.

Submission – This aesthetic particularly comes into its own when you enter either the winning or losing stage of the game. You know you are going to win/lose, but the rules dictate that you must see this through to the end, hoping for the miracle they do not support.

CONCLUSION

Monopoly is a classic game that appeals to a wide, but especially younger audience. As with any game, it is not perfect and the reliance on luck would not appeal to strategists. However, the manufacturers have taken reasonable steps to improve the game without deviating from the fundamental gameplay:

- By adapting the auction mechanic to reduce game time.
- Through introduction of house rules, decided upon by the public (Leddy, 2014).
- By introducing more skilled options for tournament *Monopoly*.
- By bringing out new versions that include "catch the leader" mechanics.
- Through the introduction of themed variants to appeal to a more diverse demographic.

Monopoly has become a gaming institution (Pickles, 2022), and any major change to the rules would be considered a violation. This was evidenced in the aforementioned updating of the rules to include "house rules", an initiative soon dropped following complaints from *Monopoly* traditionalists.

Chess is similar in that there are thousands of variations of *Chess*, and statistically some of those versions must be better than the official version; but whilst you can buy Lord of Rings and Star Wars themed *Chess* sets, it is unlikely that the official version of the rules will ever undergo any significant change.

Even though *Monopoly* will continue to remain one of the bestselling board games of all time, it would be reasonable to suggest that if it were to be released for the first time into the board game arena today, then it would be less successful. Game designers are aware of more mechanics and have learned new and ingenious ways to leverage them to engage players. In deconstructing *Monopoly*, we have learned:

> **The Balance of Input and Output Randomness** – The biggest takeaway would be if randomness is a part of the game, then to build in more opportunities for strategic input randomness. This allows players to make meaningful decisions and not to have them taken away in the roll of some dice. Some output randomness works well, such as the damage dealt to an enemy in a combat game – it would seem less realistic if the damage from a sword, for example, was always a set number. Dice rolling to move is especially irksome to players and has been eliminated most modern games. Simply moving to a space (as in worker placement, for example), or via interconnected lines, such as in *Pandemic* are more common methods of movement. There are many games that could be improved by eliminating the dice roll to move mechanic, but how would this work in *Monopoly*? The whole point of building sets and houses is because there is a chance that other players could land on these properties, so rolling to move must stay. A better approach might be to provide players with an opportunity to mitigate the damage, such as we see in games of combat where players can purchase armour, for example.
>
> **Player Elimination** – The second takeaway would be in avoiding the death spiral and ultimate elimination. It is not a fun experience for players who know that they are going to lose halfway through a game, playing the remainder of a game in gradual decline. Player elimination is common in games for fun, but in educational games, this mechanic should generally be avoided. If it must be included in a game, player elimination works well when the eliminated players are still presented with meaningful tasks that contribute in some way to the outcome of the game. We see this in *Among Us*, the digital and virtual phenomena that allows murdered players to still perform the tasks that are necessary for their team to win. The social deception game *Blood on the Clocktower* has recently used this mechanic to significant effect to create a legacy version of Mafia.
>
> **Game Length** – Most modern board games are designed to last a set amount of time within a pre-defined range that is stated on the box. Conversely, many *Monopoly* games are abandoned due to either time constraints or sheer exhaustion, and a winner is usually declared through some metric or another. There is nothing in the rules that accounts for this situation,

though there are optional short game (60–90 minutes) rules included. One of the problems is in the number of players; four players are optimum, but for games of five or six players, the chances of obtaining a *Monopoly* naturally (a set of cards of the same colour) are dramatically reduced. You then must enter the world of auctions, bluffing, counterbluffing, and sabotage. Your opponents can prevent you from winning, and they know this. So, there are potentially two problems here: (1) an indeterminate length of play, and (2) the players' ability to affect this.

Most modern board games account for this; if you are playing with this number of players, use this rule; if you are playing with that number, use a different rule. This may alleviate the problem, but not solve it. Let us look at the auction, which in *Monopoly* is the English type that you see in auction rooms. This type of auction is one of the most open to sabotage from other players and can also make for a frustrating experience. Other auction types are available, and the one that I would suggest which creates the most strategy and excitement is the sealed bid approach, in which players secretly make a bid, all bids are revealed simultaneously, and the high bidder wins.

Game deconstruction is a useful method that game designers use to understand how games work. As you can see from the *Monopoly* example, the method, which is loosely based around the MDA framework, can take you in many directions depending upon what you discover.

In the next sections, we are going to jump back to game reviews, which are another useful method of understanding more about how games work.

GAME REVIEWS

Reviews of anything tend to be more subjective than objective; for example, a particular movie reviewed on the Internet Movie Database (IMDB) may contain one-star and ten-star reviews in equal measure. Whether you are reviewing a movie, vacation, book, or game, you will relay an opinion based on your experience.

Zagal et al. (2009) found that the game reviewer often included first-person accounts of their experience with the game in question. Sometimes, these personal narratives recount interesting actions carried out by the player. However, more often, they relayed the emotions that the reviewer felt both during and after playing the game.

Examples of personal experience in game reviews include the following:

- Narrative Storytelling (to create interest), for example:

   Welcome to the zombie apocalypse, the near future, somewhere cold. We are glad you have joined our band of survivors. We are currently being led by a pirate and a guy who thinks he's Santa.

- Objective Information (based on facts)

   In Dead of Winter, you are battling both the cold and zombies in a meta-cooperative psychological survival game.

- Subjective Opinion (based on or influenced by personal feelings, tastes, or opinions):

> The gameplay in Dead of Winter logically ties in with the overall theme. But regularly risking death just to take out the trash feels incongruous. It would not happen.

You will also provide a subjective rating based upon your experience, though this rating may contribute to a more objective average in cases such as with IMDB movies, and yes, there are people out there who consider *The Godfather* to be a terrible movie. While debates persist about their quality or significance, there's no denying that game reviews have a definite impact on how individuals perceive, comprehend, and discuss games. Moreover, game reviews frequently take precedence over alternative modes of journalistic discussion regarding games, including news coverage, investigative reporting, and commentary (deFreitas & Maharg, 2011).

GAME REVIEW TIPS

The following tips on writing game reviews are adapted from Ramirez (2019) and Lee et al. (2010), and assume that there are no specific publication restraints for the review in question.

1. **Judge the game for what it is.**
   If you are reviewing an Escape Room, do not complain about how you can only play it once. Write your review based on reasonable expectations.
2. **Do not base your review on somebody else's review of the same game.**
   There is a space for game reviews as sources of information and inspiration; the problem is that those reviews can be skewed by economic interests (Walker, 2013). Furthermore, reviews on mainstream games are abundant, and a quick Internet search will find any number of reviews from opinionated posters (Fernández-Vara, 2019). These reviews relay a sense of how good or bad a game is, but the goal of writing a review is not to rewrite popular opinion but to form your own.
3. **Play the game for several hours to feel its atmosphere.**
   Before you begin to write your review, you will need to play the game. Even if it is a game that is familiar to you. Make notes as you play and think about the themes on which you will be assessing the game on. There are many game evaluation sheets that you can use to guide you through this process.
4. **Compose a short thesis.**
   Prior to commencing your writing, it's crucial to possess a clear understanding of the overarching message you intend to convey. Formulating a concise thesis statement, which encapsulates the central point of your review, will aid in maintaining focus and preventing the review from deviating off-topic. This could be as simple as stating, "I thoroughly enjoyed this game", or as complex as "This game would appeal to players who like

strategy and conflict". Think to yourself: If I were telling friends and family about this game, what would I want their main takeaway to be?
5. **Divide your review into logical parts.**
    When writing a serious review, it may be advisable to write a standard review and then the serious review, to clearly differentiate your opinions based on intention of play.

The standard review generally takes the following form:

1. The hook.
2. Central ideas of the game.
3. Outline of the game advantages.
4. Suggestions as to what features could be improved.
5. Comparison of the game to other games falling into the same category.
6. Summary of likes and dislikes.

THE HOOK

Whether you are writing a review for a game (Lin et al., 2019), or a scholarly book review for publication (Lee et al., 2010), it is recommended that from the outset, the review must capture the reader's attention. A "hook" constitutes a sentence designed to seize your audience's attention and spark their curiosity, ideally encouraging them to engage with your review instead of swiftly scrolling past or moving on. Your hook might encompass a captivating or thought-provoking assertion, or a clever acknowledgment of the gameplay, such as:

> Welcome to the Dead of Winter, have you got what it takes to survive both flesh eating zombies and frostbite inducing arctic conditions? Holed up in your colony you take on the role of a survivor in this thematic and semi-cooperative game. Whether you base your decisions and choices on what is best for yourself, or for the group, do you have what it takes to survive the Dead of Winter…

DESCRIBE THE CENTRAL IDEAS OF THE GAME

The central ideas are what the game is all about. This could include the game objectives (academic and non-academic), and other ideas that are not included within the objectives that are more abstract. For example:

- Making connections is one of the central ideas of the game.
- The central idea of the game is to understand binomial distribution.
- The central idea of the game is that players must harness the "powers of imagination".
- The core concept of the game revolves around observing the future of the global economy from the perspective of young individuals, facilitating discussions about potential global challenges society might encounter in the year 2039 (Murtazoyev, 2009).

OUTLINE THE GAME ADVANTAGES

Whilst playing the game, pay attention to the quality and accessibility of the components, how the game feels, whether it is balanced, and other criteria that will help you to evaluate the game. Remember, players may decide whether to spend time on this game, or not, based on your critique. Even small details can help the reader to understand whether they want to buy this game.

As we tend to play games with likeminded people, at the end of the game, ask the opinions of your fellow gamers, and if they like or do not like something, ask them why. Both professional and amateur reviews include "our group" comments in abundance, such as:

> Whilst the interaction between the unique players goals and the global goals seemed promising, no one in our group ended up enjoying them, as they neither worked cohesively, nor as an interesting challenge.

Whilst it is important to assess the game on a variety of features, there may be something about this game that makes it stand out from the crowd. This could be a style, feature or set of mechanics, or something more personal such as:

> Personally, I love the crossroads cards as they allow me to make meaningful decisions based upon my circumstances. Occasionally the cards featured one of our characters, and that is when the fun really notched up a level.

SUGGEST WHAT FEATURES COULD BE IMPROVED

In the 2010 movie, Tron: Legacy, Jeff Bridges' character suggests that there is no such thing as perfection when he says, "The thing about perfection is that it is unknowable. It is impossible, but it is also right in front of us all the time" (Kosinski, 2010, 1:50). So, with that said, anything can be improved on. Of course, anyone who scored a perfect mark on a test or a perfect score in a quiz would have reasonable grounds to disagree, but discounting these anomalies, the saying holds true. Even the game *Chess*, which is often touted as the perfect game, has spawned thousands of variants (Beasley, 2007), with each iteration improving.

The tabletop industry is saturated with games and arguably, each of them could still be improved upon. Is there anything you dislike about the game you are reviewing? Make a list of any suggestions that you may have regarding improving the game, its components, or its mechanics. If you mention some negative aspects, then be specific, explaining why you think that this or that option requires improvements.

COMPARE THE GAME TO OTHER GAMES FALLING INTO THE SAME CATEGORY

If you review games, then you must have played many, or at least some, games, and you will be able to draw comparisons between those and the game you are reviewing. By compiling an analysis of the key features, you will be able to use the advanced search on BoardGameGeek to find similar games. The search criteria are extensive, and you will be able to filter combinations of features such as:

- Category (Animals, Puzzle, Farming, Educational, etc.)
- Mechanic (Acting, Action, Dice Rolling, Simulation, etc.)
- Sub-Domain (Abstract, Strategy, Party, Thematic, etc.)

Furthermore, the results will be returned to a customisable table.

Remember, all your opinions should be grounded. For example, if you were suggesting that a game was lacking in originality, you might write: "Comparing this game to Gloomhaven is like comparing Carcassonne to Carcassonne with all the expansions and add-ons you can find".

SUMMARISE LIKES AND DISLIKES

Reviews tend to include a combination of likes and dislikes; however, occasionally a game comes along that is so good that the reviewer cannot find anything bad to say about it, and it may not include any dislikes. That said, if the review is critical, try to find at least one positive to include. For example, consider the following summary of the game *Dead of Winter* that attempts to balance the positives and negatives of the game:

HITS

- Stunning artwork and quality components.
- The crossroads cards were logically written and thematic. Including the player characters within these scenarios created an additional twist.
- The semi-cooperative nature of the game enabled multiple strategies throughout the game.
- The game felt balanced and player decisions impacted upon game outcomes.

MISSES

- Taking out the trash seemed an unnecessary and illogical risk.
- Characters are often stuck in one place aligned with their particular skill set.
- Not a particularly original game, but a strong contender within this genre.

CHECK YOUR WRITING

Reviews are a reflection of yourself, and readers may not consider your viewpoint with gravitas if your spelling is erratic or if you repetitively employ a term such as "seriously" within a single sentence.

Avoid vague words and phrases like "The game was bad" or "It looked nice". Instead, provide specific details like, "On the negative side, the encounter cards, over time, lost their thematic luster and became superfluous" or "The game includes the Golden Geek award, winning the 'stunning artwork' category".

REVIEWING A SERIOUS GAME

In his thesis and subsequent work on the quality of games and game design, Fabricatore et al. (2002) suggests that answer to this question lies in the quality of the gameplay, and when playing a game, players seek challenge, mastery, and reward, all packed in entailing and motivating activities.

However, serious games need more than that, such as relevance, relatedness, and purpose:

- **Relevance** to the needs of the individual.
- **Relatedness** to the concept or subject being taught.
- **Purpose** to the goals of the learner/teacher.

Furthermore, a supplementary benefit to playing games for learning is in the connectivism that players achieve through social constructivism principles (Vygotsky, 1997). Single-player games, for example, would have little opportunity for social constructivism, whereas collaborative games would have greater opportunities.

Therefore, any review of a serious game would need to account for the relatedness and relevance of the game's ability to meet the learning objectives. Furthermore, the educational aspect of games would have to be reviewed by a suitably qualified candidate, and ideally a student or teacher currently or recently engaged in the subject matter.

SUMMARY

We deconstruct things to find out how they work and why they work. When we deconstruct games, what we are really trying to do is find out why they are fun to play. As game designers, this is important as it helps us in our understanding for creating our own games. Furthermore, whether it is our own invention or not, we deconstruct games to find out why they do not work. Game reviews are in effect a deconstruction without a formal framework.

Ultimately, figure out what experience you want your players to have and design your game to meet those experiences. It all sounds like common sense; for example, if you are designing a party game, then you could not include a worker placement mechanic ... or could you?

EXERCISE

The taxonomy of game pleasures suggests that the feelings that playing a game evokes can be described as a combination of the following aesthetics:

1. Sensation
2. Fantasy
3. Narrative
4. Challenge
5. Fellowship
6. Discovery
7. Expression
8. Submission

For example, playing *Apples to Apples* might include fellowship, expression, and challenge.

Now consider the top three games that you enjoy playing and compile a short list of the games' aesthetics, taken from the list above.

Is there a pattern? Do you have a preferred aesthetic?

9 Technology

Dr Devon Allcoat

WHY TECHNOLOGY?

In his critique on the decline of social capital in American culture, Putnam (2000) suggests that the pervasiveness of digital games is the source of the decline in tabletop gaming. However, since Putnam's (2000) critique, there has instead been a revolution of tabletop gaming (Trammell, 2019), and we are now said to be living in the "Golden Age" of tabletop gaming (Konieczny, 2019), with the global market value expected to increase by over 3 billion dollars during 2021–2026 (TechNavio, 2022).

The phrase "tabletop games" encompasses a wide variety of games, including board games, card games, miniature games, dice games, pen and paper games, and more. What all these games share is that they are typically played on a table, or a similar surface. Considering that, you may wonder why there is a technology chapter in this book; after all, this book is about tabletop game design, not video game design.

There is a concept that technology is a core cultural part of being human (e.g. Evans, 1998; Hunkin, 2008; McLain et al., 2019). Just as various aspects of human culture develop over time, our technology is constantly developing (Figure 9.1). New technologies of various types are constantly being integrated into our everyday lives. Similarly, new technologies are being incorporated into tabletop games.

FIGURE 9.1 Humans and technology.

DOI: 10.1201/9781003319511-9

DEFINITIONS

What exactly constitutes "technology"? One definition of "technology" by the Oxford English Dictionary is "The branch of knowledge dealing with the mechanical arts and applied sciences; the study of this" and the Cambridge Dictionary says that it is "(the study and knowledge of) the practical, especially industrial, use of scientific discoveries". The Britannica article "Technology" opens: "technology, the application of scientific knowledge to the practical aims of human life or, as it is sometimes phrased, to the change and manipulation of the human environment" (The Editors of Encyclopaedia Britannica, 2022). These definitions are probably substantially broader than what individuals typically consider when they think of the word "technology".

There are a lot of background technologies and processes involved in the making of tabletop games. The supply chain (the network of all the resources involved in creating and distributing the product) involves a myriad of technologies the designer may never have to deal with directly, such as moulding processes, machines that create dice, industrial printers for cards and boards, and the technologies involved in shipping and distribution. However, this chapter will focus specifically on computer technology that can be used as part of the design process, or integrated with the final product, rather than using the broader definitions of the word.

Until recently, traditional tabletop games that incorporated digital elements were sufficiently rare not to require their own classification. A variety of terms have started appearing, including "digital tabletop games" (Bakker et al., 2007), "augmented tabletop games" (Kosa & Spronck, 2018), "computer-augmented games" (Lundgren & Björk, 2003), and "hybrid games" (Kankainen & Paavilainen, 2019). Just as with the term "serious games", these terms have not been used consistently and can be quite ambiguous. Hybrid games, for example, was a term initially coined by Henzinger et al. (1999) to describe a branch of mathematical game theory, but it is also commonly used to describe genre crossing digital games (Champion, 2009). Furthermore, whilst hybrid games are commonly viewed as a combination of digital and physical elements in a single product, viewing them this way can act as a limiting factor when designing and analysing them (Kankainen et al., 2017).

Nevertheless, in recent years, the term "hybrid" as a way to describe any tabletop game that has digital/virtual elements has gained traction (Kankainen, 2020; Kankainen & Paavilainen, 2019; Kankainen et al., 2017; Oliveira et al., 2020; Rogerson et al., 2021), and has become a more standard label for this genre of game. For that reason, the term "hybrid games" will be used in this publication to denote any traditional tabletop game that includes digital, virtual, or electronic augmentation.

Similarly, the term "augmented tabletop games" now most often refers to tabletop games that include augmented reality (AR), and "digital tabletop games" tends to be synonymous with digitised tabletop games such as those found on digital simulators and sandboxes, such as *Tabletopia*, *Tabletop Simulator*, and *Board Game Arena*.

A BRIEF HISTORY OF TECHNOLOGY IN TABLETOP GAMES

Early uses of technology for gaming include chess engines. The term "chess engine", as with many of the terms we discuss in this chapter, has evolved over time. Chess has such a significant history; it can easily take up an entire book by itself but, simply put, chess engines have evolved from computerised opponents to tools for analysis. These have ranged from the *Mechanical Turk*, an 18th-century machine (thought to be autonomous, but later revealed to be manned) and *El Ajedrecista* (truly autonomous, from 1912) to chess computing, including *Deep Blue* and *AlphaZero*. Other older examples of technology-enhanced games are those which included digital components to produce an effect, such as movement or a noise, when a circuit is completed. A well-known example of this genre of game is *Operation* (Glass & Spinello, 1965).

An early example of a digitised tabletop game is *Stop Thief* (Robert Doyle, 1979) where electronic components were used to randomise events and to hide and reveal information. The game included bulky components, an electronic Crime Scanner resembling an old telephone, and would issue a sound at the start of every turn that provided information as to where the thief would be. Interestingly, an updated version called *Stop Thief* was crowdfunded by Restoration Games in March 2017, swapping the Crime Scanner for a smartphone app. The hybrid element in *Stop Thief* is not tied to a specific technology, but to the experience that the technology offers (Kankainen et al., 2017).

Games have also made use of equipment potentially already owned by the player, rather than a custom digital component, in order to provide this hybrid functionality. An early example of this is *Mel Allen's Baseball Game* (RCA Victor, 1959), which utilised a vinyl record with multiple audio grooves for gameplay narrative (voiced by sports commentator Mel Allen), whilst the record cover was used as a game board.

Similarly, VHS-games such as *Nightmare*, popular during the 1980s, is another example of an early hybrid game. The video in *Nightmare* presents narrative, content, and programmed events, and also utilises a timer (Rogerson et al., 2020). Similar to the game *Stop Thief*, later versions of *Nightmare* were adapted to incorporate more modern technology – the DVD.

During the 1980s, as board gamers turned their attention to computers, the theme of utilising equipment already owned by the players to create hybrid games continued, as owners of *ZX Spectrum* could play *Assault Of The Ogroids* (Chalk, 1987), which was a computer-moderated solo board game published in the May 1987 issue of the *Sinclair User* magazine. This included a digital component that created randomisation as well as inventory management and tracking functions (Rogerson & Gibbs, 2020).

Building on this history of board games which use electrical or digital components, modern board games incorporate digital tools and applications (Figure 9.2) to deliver content in novel ways (Rogerson et al., 2021). In this chapter, we explore how digital tools can be used to enhance or supplement tabletop board games, and how these enhancements might add benefits to a serious hybrid board game.

FIGURE 9.2 Companion apps.

DIGITAL CONVERSION

Digital conversion, turning a physical game into a digital one, can have its advantages. Digital versions of traditional tabletop games have resulted in a market of coexistence and choice, rather than one of redundancy and replacement, with some games available in both physical and digital formats. So far, the rise of digital games has not resulted in traditional board games disappearing, and this may be because traditional physical games evoke different emotions and social interactions (Fang et al., 2016). Players enjoy traditional tabletop games because of the tangible experience, face-to-face social interaction, and the chance to disconnect from online media technologies (Rogerson et al., 2018; Woods, 2019).

Many tabletop games are also available as digital apps. The likes of *Carcassonne, Root, Wingspan, Magic: The Gathering, Everdell, Ticket to Ride, Terraforming Mars,* and many more are available to download on mobile app stores and on PCs. Some games, such as *Catan*, are also available on gaming consoles like the Switch, and virtual reality (VR) headsets.

Whilst they're often made available on both mobile and PC platforms, and sometimes on other devices, games are not necessarily equally suited across different types of devices. Simpler games, where not much information needs to be present on the screen at any given time, can be great on phone apps. Larger, more complex games can be best suited to console or computer applications, which have larger screens, so they can present more information at once. Which of these, if any, are more suitable depends on a number of factors, including the complexity of the game, the size of the gameboard, and how much needs to be visible on screen. It is also worth considering the prevalence of tablets that use mobile app stores. The different input methods of touch screen versus mouse and keyboard are also important. The computing power needed can also be a consideration, although with mobile devices becoming more and more powerful, this is becoming less of a concern.

The majority of the elements of a physical game can be replicated digitally. However, some games have had rules changed from the physical version to the digital version, or have essentially created spin-off games. For example, if you compare *The Lord of the Rings: The Card Game* (a physical card game) with *The Lord of the Rings: Adventure Card Game* (a digital game), you will find major differences. These have the same card titles and illustrations, but the gameplay is very different. The physical version of the game has a playtime of approximately 90 minutes, whereas the digital version of the game runs at around 10–20 minutes. *Plague Inc.* was originally a real-time strategy simulation single-player video game. *Plague Inc.: The Board Game* is a co-op board game for 1–4 players.

Sometimes, there are actions that are possible in the digital version that are not in the physical version. For example, *Dobble* (also known as *Spot It!*) has very simple gameplay as a physical card game; you simply need to find matching symbols. The digital app *Spot It! Duel* adds a number of unique gameplay elements, such as differently styled "Dobbles" that you can collect, with their own powers, such as freezing an opponent.

Computer opponents, including artificial intelligence (AI) opponents, are also potentially a useful addition, just as they have been since the early automated chess opponents. Games which could previously only be played with multiple players can employ a computer opponent in order to allow individuals, not just groups, to play. This helps to increase the potential target audience.

BENEFITS AND CHALLENGES OF DIGITALISATION

BENEFITS

A game creator needs to ask themselves is it worth going down the digitalisation route? There are some notable benefits to digitalisation that are useful to consider when answering this question.

BENEFITS TO SELLERS

- **Production.** A digital version of a game, once it has been created, is likely to need maintenance and updates. However, unlike a physical game, there is, for example, no upfront investment in production facilities, there are no ongoing manufacturing costs for multiple prints runs, and it does away with the risk of production errors and wastage.
- **Logistics.** Similarly, without a physical product, the costs of distribution and warehousing throughout the supply chain can be negated, as can delivery failures and potential liability for import duties (but not all taxes).
- **Market.** The digital market has some variation to the physical market. If you offer both physical and digital options, you are able to access an expanded market. This can be through reaching customers on other platforms (e.g. *Steam*), enabling single-player experiences through computer opponents, having different accessibility requirements, etc.
- **The Environment and Sustainability.** Digital games can be more environmentally friendly and sustainable since they do not consume physical resources in both the manufacturing and distribution processes.

It is clear that there are benefits for the game creator to either sell a purely digital game, or by offering both digital and physical options. The digitalisation of a game also has benefits for the end user, and these consumer benefits can lead to an expanded market for the seller.

BENEFITS TO CONSUMERS

- **Storage.** Just as the seller does not need physical storage space for digital games, so too is this the case for the consumers. Physical tabletop games take up space, require storage solutions such as shelving, and require tables with a large enough surface area to fit the game on, as well as physical space to accommodate all the players. Digital games do not have the same limitations.
- **Accessibility.** The accessibility of a digital game can be very different to that of a physical one. There is a significant amount of accessibility software available for computers, and it is possible to build in specific options to the program. These include adjustable text size, colours, support for screen readers, etc. Also, there are no small physical pieces to manipulate, allowing it to be enjoyed by those with a range of physical abilities, and also those using additional accessibility equipment. Digital gaming also allows participants to play together irrespective of location or even language.
- **Price.** The price point for digital games is typically much lower than for their physical counterparts. For example, phone apps currently (as of 2023) commonly range from approximately £1.69 to £7.99. A £3.99 phone app is often the same game as a £24.99 physical game. PC-based tabletop games are typically in the £11 to £16 price range, whilst a physical version of the games may be as much as £60. Thus, digital versions of games are more affordable to more consumers.
- **Setup and Gameplay.** Unlike a physical game, which could have complex setup requirements that take a significant amount of time and space, a digital game can automatically do this, potentially saving time and frustration for the players. Most digital versions, unless they are in a digital sandbox, also manage the rules, turn order, and scoring, leaving the players more time to focus on their actions. This also helps playability, as it requires less cognitive load (Cavicchini & Mariani, 2019).

CHALLENGES

If there were no challenges to digitalisation, then it would be the obvious route to pursue. However, for a variety of reasons, not all physical board games exist in a digital version.

Software

Specific software may be needed to create a digital game. This is discussed in more detail later in the chapter when looking at technology for design. Most software is not free, and may require an ongoing licence, or have a high purchase cost. It is also important to think about the software output. Do you want an executable file? Is a host platform such as *Steam* going to be used? If it is desirable to host on multiple platforms, the game may need to be developed independently for each platform, and may require unique software for each.

Hardware

Purchasing software outright, or a licence to use software, is not sufficient; there is also a need for hardware to run it on. How much processing power does the software require? How many people will be working simultaneously on its development, and therefore, how many devices do you need? Also, consideration needs to be given to the hardware requirements on the consumers' end. How accessible is the technology required to run the game? Are all, or at least most, of the target audience likely to have access to that technology? Do you need to get representative devices to test the game on, to make sure it is working as it should be, and if yes, where would they be obtained from? Thought needs to be put into what makes your game popular. As an example, if the most positive feedback you've received during playtesting is about miniatures, then by going digital that strength would be lost.

Skills and Competencies

Do you have access to the skills and competencies needed to create a digital version of the game? These include skills such as programming, 3D modelling, visual design, and sound engineering. Without these, there would be a need to obtain external support. Generally, this would mean outsourcing either the entire project or various aspects of it, which can be costly.

Lifespan and Obsolescence

There are a number of questions related to lifespan and obsolescence that are relevant to (i) how long your digital game will last, and (ii) how much resource is required to keep it up and running.

- How often will the game need updating?
- Is it necessary to have a permanent team to run support for the application?
- How long will players continue to use it?
- Can it be played if there is not a large active online player base?
- Will the platform/s used update and change?
- Will the platforms always be available?
- Will the hardware become redundant?
- Will the chosen platform/s support new hardware?
- How much computing power does it require to run your game?
- How compatible is your game to multiple devices?

HYBRID GAMES

Contrary to Putnam's predictions, tabletop gaming is very much connected to digital culture (Kankainen, 2020). A simulated digital tabletop game experience may not be the only time to opt to integrate computer technology as part of the final product. Games can also use a combination of standard board game mechanics, processes, and components, whilst also incorporating technology to augment the users' experience. There is an emerging trend of hybrid board games (Kankainen & Paavilainen, 2019), as well as a wealth of online activities (Figure 9.3) supporting the play of offline tabletop games (Rogerson et al., 2016).

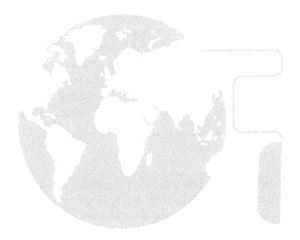

FIGURE 9.3   Online gameplay.

COMPANION APPS

Companion apps for phones and tablets are one way that games can streamline or add to a game experience. Smartphones are a near-ubiquitous technology that the majority of individuals in the developed world have access to and carry around, and so it makes sense to utilise this technology. Indeed, the inclusion of phone apps has become a go-to methodology when creating technology-enhanced board games.

Games like *Unlock* and *Exit* rely on companion apps that take care of timekeeping, are used to store codes that the player has worked out, can be asked for hints, and occasionally deploy AR or other technology to reveal hidden card details or additional puzzles. *One Night Werewolf* uses a companion app to narrate the gameplay and to instruct players when and what actions to take. The app also utilises atmospheric sound effects and music. *World of Yo-Ho* uses a companion app to turn a phone into a game piece, acting as a ship in-game, whilst the app for *Flamme Rouge* handles the complex scoring for the game when in tournament mode.

INTERNET-SUPPORTED GAMES

Whilst there are single-player games, many games are a social experience, requiring interaction with others. It is not, however, always possible to get everyone together in the same room. Internet-supported games can supply a live action experience to consumers at home on their computers. There are a variety of available live online interactive experiences, such as escape rooms, mystery "whodunnit" games, and live interactive theatre.

AUGMENTED REALITY

AR uses technology to simulate digital objects and overlay them onto the physical environment. This is usually done via a smartphone or tablet application. AR is useful when utilising 3D digital models to enhance or "augment" the gaming experience. Unlike industry, where AR is sometimes used to provide on-site/in situ training, the use of AR in tabletop games is currently fairly rare, with only a few games featuring AR. Examples of those that do, include *Tilt 5, Hologrid: Monster Battle, Oracles,* and *Amelia's Secret.* The latter is an immersive short horror-themed Escape Game in AR that is supported by a free companion app. Once players have set up the room by placing all game cards in their indicated locations, using their smartphone, tablet, or AR glasses, they then scan each AR marker to display the 3D objects in the room.

VIRTUAL REALITY

VR also uses technology to simulate a digital experience. Unlike AR, VR creates a fully digital environment, which visually replaces the actual physical environment. Typically, this is done using a headset which blocks out your view of the room (Figure 9.4), making the wearer fully immersed in the digital environment.

FIGURE 9.4   Virtual reality.

There are currently more tabletop game experiences in VR than in AR. As examples, *Tabletop Simulator* supports VR, and there are games with dedicated VR software, such as *Catan VR. Chronicles of Crime* uses VR in a hybrid way, to add to the experience; players simply put the VR glasses onto their mobile device to immerse themselves in the game world and search for clues. In educational games, VR tends to be used more in simulations where immersive VR has the potential to offer inspiring learning experiences that increase self-efficacy (i.e., confidence) and interest (Makransky et al., 2020).

BENEFITS AND CHALLENGES OF HYBRID GAMES

Based on the results of their survey into digitised games, Kosa and Spronck (2018) suggested 11 separate themes for both the negative and positive attitudes of players towards hybrid tabletop games (see Table 9.1).

There is clear alignment between the negative and positive attitudes found by Kosa and Spronck (2018) to the benefits and challenges regarding digitalisation discussed earlier in this chapter. This suggests that hybrid games have similar attributes to purely digital ones, with the same outputs of using technology for either modality.

TABLE 9.1

Attitudes of Players towards Hybrid Games

Negative Attitudes	Positive Attitudes
Obsolescence/incompatibility of technology – 17%	Streamlines the rules/bookkeeping – 9%
Presence of electronics/screens – 12%	Feels the same as a traditional game – 8%
Video game imitation/failed design – 8%	Enhances enjoyment/experience/fun – 7%
Problems with the app – 6%	Different no. of players/coop option – 7%
Lack of tactility/physicality – 5%	Decreases tediousness – 5%
Not the future – 4%	Secret/hidden information – 5%
Loss of design clarity – 4%	Multimedia effects – 4%
Not a standalone game – 4%	Randomisation – 4%
May divert the industry – 3%	Help setting up the game – 4%
Cardboard loses meaning – 2%	Online updating – 3%
Do not have the technology – 1%	AI, dynamic difficulty adjustment – 3%

Source: Data from Kosa and Spronck (2018).

The Hybrid Digital Board Game Model

Until recently, there was little guidance or analysis regarding the potential benefits of creating hybrid games. It may seem obvious, for example, that music can add atmosphere, or that informing the players when they need to take actions can streamline the gameplay. However, despite disparity in the approaches to incorporating digital tools with otherwise non-digital board games, Rogerson et al. (2021) attempted to classify the different roles that these tools play in supporting gameplay.

The model proposed by Rogerson et al. (2021) comprises eight domains, which reflect the 41 functions of digital elements in hybrid games. Figure 9.5 shows an overview of these domains, which are then discussed in more detail.

FIGURE 9.5   The hybrid digital board game model (Rogerson et al., 2021).

Timing

The timing domain incorporates functions associated with timing and scheduling of gameplay, such as countdowns in escape rooms, or sequenced game events in games such as *Werewolf*. This can help keep players attention focused on their actions, not divided by manual tracking of these elements. This can help keep players attention focused on their actions, not divided by manual tracking of these elements.

Randomising

Randomisation is a key benefit of hybrid technology, both for designers and players. The digital randomiser can take care of dice rolling and generating random events.

Housekeeping

Significant "housekeeping" is often required to play a board game (Xu et al., 2011). This domain describes how the digital element in a hybrid game can take responsibility for managing the gameplay, such as generating the board configuration, controlling the AI, tracking in game resources, or updating the game with new content.

Informing

Both players and designers benefit from the use of digital tools for controlling the flow of information, both to and between players. This domain will know secret information, inform the players about a situation or setting, and help communication with and between players. In serious games, this domain could inform players of specific goals and objectives, and provide links to additional information.

Storytelling

Digital tools can can be used to represent or amplify a game's theme and story, thereby increasing the sense of immersion. In this domain, the digital elements may include background effects, play scripted events, customise playing pieces or characters, and allow visualisation of in-game elements. A key element of storytelling in hybrid games is to balance any interaction limitations imposed by the physical medium on one hand, with the flexibility of story content enabled by the digital medium on the other (Davenport & Mazalek, 2004).

Remembering

Digital tools can be useful for recording players' progress and actions. This provides a form of "digital remembering" of game states and events that extends across a playing session, or even multiple sessions. This domain enables the players' progress to be saved and to produce shareable artefacts and unlock achievements.

Calculating

This domain primarily covers ways to use the app to overcome tasks that are "tedious" or long-winded to undertake, such as calculating scores, resolving outcomes, deciding winners and losers, and determining whether players have completed a task.

Teaching

This domain is concerned with providing setup instructions and teaching the rules of the game, and it can assist via prompts or hints, and answer specific questions raised by the players.

TECHNOLOGY FOR DESIGN

Although we have focused predominantly on technology that is part of the final product, it is also useful to consider technology that can be used for the design process (Figure 9.6). Technology for design is not necessarily a major part of the final product itself, but can help to improve the design process.

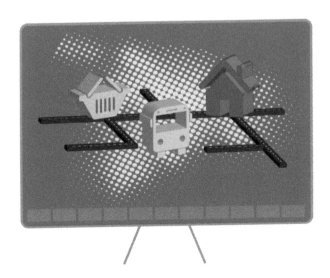

FIGURE 9.6   Design software.

TABLE 9.2

Technologies Used for the Design Process

The Technology	What It Can Do
Computer-aided design (CAD)	We can use CAD to create 3D art for digital games, and models for custom playing pieces.
Computer-aided manufacture (CAM)	CAM allows us to use computer numerical control (CNC) machines to turn digital models into real-world objects.
Laser cutting	Laser cutting is good for 2D designs, allowing for high analogue detail and a luxury feel.
3D Printing	3D printing is excellent for rapid prototyping and custom batches of models, allowing for high levels of design flexibility.
The Internet	The internet has a host of available shared resources (including Creative Commons), purchasable art assets, game development communities, and a pool of around 3 billion eager playtesters!
Authoring tools *(e.g. Adobe Captivate, Articulate 360)*	Authoring tools are particularly useful for building learning and training content.
Productivity software *(e.g. Office 365 Apps)*	Productivity software can help you easily store data and organise your information.
Development software/game engines	Software such as *Unity Game Maker*, *Unreal Engine*, *RPG Maker*, and *Adventure Game Studio*.

Table 9.2 summarises hardware and software that can improve the efficiency of the design process, the quality of the product, and can make more personalised and customised options available and generally support the game design and development processes.

SUMMARY

In this chapter, we have looked at how technology is used with tabletop gaming, including definitions, benefits and challenges, and types of technology. When considering the options of digitalisation and hybridisation, it is important to consider not only these benefits and challenges, but also how and where the game will be used. Remember to ask, "Who are the target audience?" to understand if going digital is appropriate. We can see that there are reasons to utilise digital technology, both in the design process and as a part of the final product, as it can be beneficial for the developers, the sellers, the consumers, and even for educational purposes.

10 Visual Design

Kim Watts

WHAT IS "VISUAL DESIGN"?

To understand how to visually design, we need to look at and understand what both aspects of the words mean. They are defined in the Cambridge English Dictionary as follows:

> **Visual:** Something such as a picture, photograph, or piece of film used to give a particular effect or to explain something. (https://dictionary.cambridge.org/dictionary/english/visual)
>
> **Design:** To make or draw plans for something. (https://dictionary.cambridge.org/dictionary/english/design)

Visual design, therefore, is the act of drawing plans for something that is intended to be seen and explained. In the design world, this is known as visual communication, the practice of displaying often large, complex amounts of information in a way that can be easily absorbed and communicated to the viewer on several different levels. It shouldn't be confused with graphic design, but we'll discuss this more later in the chapter.

Subliminal messages are being delivered to us in the form of visual communication all day, every day (Günay, 2021). Everything we see is, in one way or another, communicating to us, whether that be in obvious forms such as charts and graphs, presentations, the headline news, or maybe more subtle (yet just as, if not even more powerful) forms such as social media content, marketing, branding, TV idents, book covers, packaging and explainer videos, to name just a few. Everything we see is subconsciously feeding us different messages; the new pair of trainers you have your eye on give you an indication of their quality by the way they look, how they are advertised, and the brand they are associated with. The branding of the coffee shop you are walking past signals the quality, cost, and standard of service. The book shop or library you visited at the weekend bombards your visual sense with an array of messages about genres and themes, target audience, and level of comprehension. Which one jumped out at you? What was it saying? Did the colours used suggest what the book is about? For example, a visually dark design would be more suited to a crime, or horror novel. Whereas a colourful, happy design would convey a more light-hearted message such as that of a children's book, positive well-being, or perhaps an opportunity to escape to a fictitious, happy other world.

A prerequisite of effective knowledge absorption through visual communication is of course that of visual literacy, which can be defined as "the ability to interpret images as well as to generate images for communicating ideas and concepts"

DOI: 10.1201/9781003319511-10

(Stokes, 2001, p. 10). John Berger, one of the world's most influential art critics, famously said, "Seeing comes before word. The child looks and recognises before it can speak" (Berger, 1972, cited in Bell et al. 2021, p. 1).

In summary, visual communication has the power to tell us things about the subject before we engage in any other way; before we have read the title, identified the author, or discovered the genre. It can be thought of as a "universal language" as it can evoke similar feelings and emotions no matter where in the world you come from or the verbal language you speak (Günay, 2021). When we think of it like that, it's clear to see just how important and powerful visual communication can be. We will, throughout this chapter, explore more of these ideas, but let's start with visual communication in relation to game design.

RAPID IDEA DEVELOPMENT

By the time you are starting to think about the look and feel of your game, you will already have a great idea and most likely have started to build a picture in your mind as to how you want it to look. Before you begin to visualise anything on a computer, it's best to scribble all your ideas down on paper as this will allow you to work both fast and smart. Move straight to a digital platform and you'll find yourself focusing on perfecting individual components which, in turn, often distracts our attention from the real task in hand, and we can then easily end up down various rabbit holes with a disjointed view of our objective. Get down as many ideas as you can – even the bad ones, as these help the good ones to jump out! You don't have to be an artist; this process is all about getting what's in your head down on paper. There hasn't been any significant research to suggest that the longer you spend coming up with ideas, the better ideas you will have (de Soto, 2015), so using rapid idea development techniques can often be much more effective. As the American inventor Thomas Edison reportedly once said, "To have a great idea, have lots of them!". What follows are a few simple suggestions to get your ideas out of your head, down on paper, and those creative juices flowing.

REMOVE ASSUMPTIONS

We can often become restrained with our creative thinking processes when we feel tied to a specific "must". Try to lose all mental restrictions and assumptions; for example, just because you are creating a tabletop board game does it *really* need a board? And if it does need a board, does it need to be a standard shape? Try thinking out of the box and be as wild as possible… you can always reign your ideas in at a later date.

FORCED RELATIONSHIPS CAN MAKE YOU AN "ACCIDENTAL GENIUS!"

Steve Jobs, the founder of Apple, once said, "Creativity is just connecting things" (Wolf, 1996, p. 163). And in many ways, that's very true; often, the most creative ideas come when unconnected things are put together. If you haven't heard of it already, I'd recommend looking at the Japanese art of Chindogu, a late 90s craze that focused on creating silly and useless gadgets to solve every day simple problems such as a pair of mini umbrellas for your shoes or a set of dusters to attach to your cats' feet! Although the content may not be directly relevant to game design, the concept of idea generation is admirable. Other methods of accidental genius idea development would be to open a book on a random page; the first word you see becomes the starting point for your next idea. Although it sounds simple, it really can work!

VISUALISATION

A more controlled form of idea generation can come from sourcing a range of visuals for your particular area, to spark ideas. This is a key tool used in other areas of design such as interior, fashion, and architecture, where the designer collates images and samples of things they like and creates a mood board to inspire new ideas for their own thinking. Once you have a series of images, you may notice a pattern appearing which will allow you to group your findings in a particular way which, in turn, may divert your thinking into new routes. Also, it's not just about looking at the things you like, but just as important to look at the things you don't like. If you know what you don't like or what you don't want your game to look and feel like, you'll soon start to identify more of the things you do like. This method (known as "reverse thinking") is discussed in more detail in the following section. Keep in mind that mood boards are a useful reference tool throughout the entire process and not just the beginning, for example, if you wish to communicate your ideas to a graphic designer.

REVERSE THINKING

Can you look at your objective from the opposite way around? For example, changing your mindset from "I want to create a board game" to "I don't want to create a board game" and then thinking of all the things you "don't want to do"? In a roundabout way, this process can force you to think about your objective in a completely different way. The reverse thinking process is used widely to solve various problems. Think of airports, for example; they are often extremely big, requiring lots of passengers to walk for long distances to get to where they need to be. The reverse thinking process could have been used here when introducing the "moving walkway" so it's the floor that moves rather than the person. By flipping the problem upside down, a solution was found to several problems. "Moving walkways are effective way to get passengers from one location to another whilst also obtaining crowd control" (Sayegh et al., 2019, para. 1).

THE FIVE WS: WHO, WHAT, WHERE, WHEN, AND WHY

Answering each of the Ws can help us to question our idea in more detail; who are we designing the game for? What's our target audience? When would this group of people play the game? If they are students, for example, would they play in a classroom setting or if they are on the go, does the game need to be easily portable? If it needs to be portable, what size would it need to be and how much space would I have to play with when designing how it looks? At this point, it's a good idea to start mapping your questions in the form of a mind map; this will allow you to see your objective as a whole and start making connections, highlighting the important aspects, and narrowing down on the key elements. You'll then be able to see what might work and what might not. Without even realising it, you'll start making decisions on scale, weight, composition, and structure; these will lead to thoughts on the colours you use, the style of font you select, and so on. As previously mentioned, it's easy to lose sight of your original idea and go off on a tangent. Keep focused. Keep reminding yourself of the theme of your game and keep questioning – does this communicate the right message? A good way to keep on track is to limit the amount of time you spend mocking up your ideas. For example, give yourself 30 minutes to scribble down on paper all your thoughts and ideas. After a break, come back with some fresh eyes, select the strongest ideas, and take those to develop further. Aim to break these down into individual components such as the title (what "type" of font do you feel would work? What would the colour be? Where should this sit on the game itself? Is it the first thing you want players to see? Do the colours/style match the genre? And so on. (See Figure 10.1.)

FIGURE 10.1   Rapid idea development.

SO, WHAT SHOULD THE DESIGN OF MY GAME DO?

Effective use of visual communication should provide players with significant knowledge about the game before they read anything, and this is where the power of visual communication comes into its own. Let's take the previous suggestion of reverse thinking; sometimes, we can only really appreciate the importance of something when it's not there. For example, a London Underground tube map without any colour – the colours are used to indicate the different tube lines, and without the colours, we would have to look much harder to work out which line is which! (See Figures 10.2 and 10.3.)

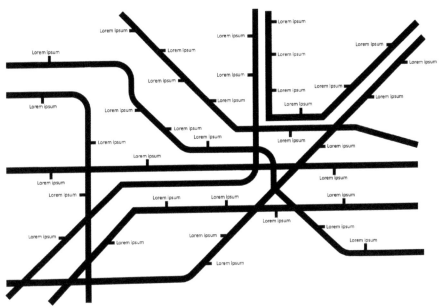

FIGURE 10.2   Tube map without colour.

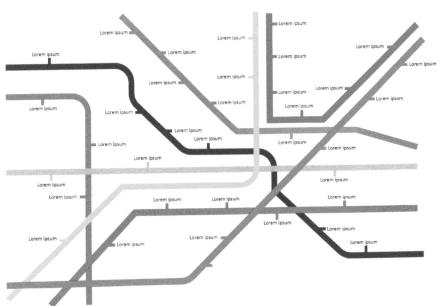

FIGURE 10.3   Tube map with colour.

Think of a warning sign without any **iconography.** We might be able to decipher the importance of the sign based on its **colour**, **shape**, and physical location but without a symbolic instruction, it wouldn't be able to tell us much! (See Figures 10.4 and 10.5.)

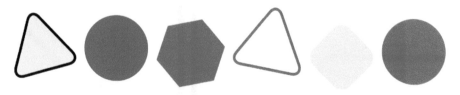

FIGURE 10.4   Warning sign without iconography.

FIGURE 10.5   Warning sign with iconography.

How about an eye test without any **contrast** in size? (See Figures 10.6 and 10.7.)

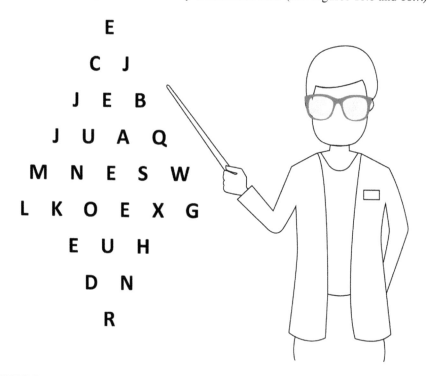

FIGURE 10.6   Eye test without contrast.

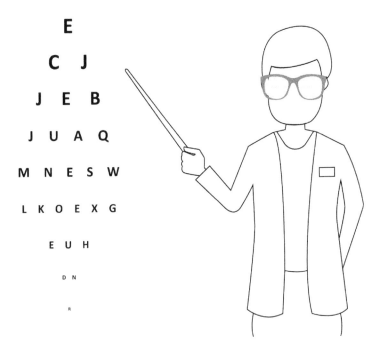

FIGURE 10.7   Eye test with contrast.

All the previously mentioned designed elements can be taken from the visual communicators essential toolkit as shown in Figure 10.8.

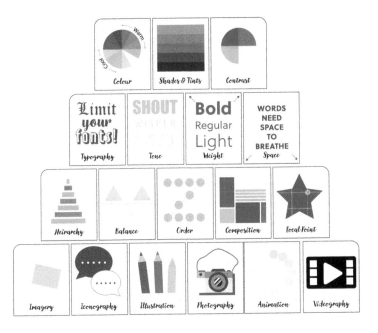

FIGURE 10.8   Visual communicator's toolkit.

If we look at the toolkit above, we can see that **colour**, **typography**, **shape**, **hierarchy**, **iconography**, **order**, and **space** have all been utilised in the design of the card in Figure 10.9.

FIGURE 10.9   Playing card.

The colour green is used in a variety of aspects from the corner, the segments of the central graphic, and also used to highlight key features in the iconography. It may indicate a team, or a specific group of cards. The number in the top left-hand corner must also be important as it's clearly defined, and is where our eye would naturally fall due to how most languages are read, which we are taught to read from a very young age (Anon, 2005; Reading Direction – Oxford Reference). We can therefore assume that the number is a key component of the game and thus provide the player with another source of **key information**. It's vital to keep reflecting on what you perceive as being "key information" or the important visual elements within your game, as we can easily lose sight of our main objectives when we are in the flow of designing. If the content is clearly presented, it could be a powerful tool for learning (Kalmpourtzis, 2018). If, however, the presentation of content is confusing (for example, too many visual messages at once or displayed in a non-logical way), causing a percentage of cognitive overload in the working memory, the learning will be negatively impacted (Centre for Education Statistics & Evaluation, 2017).

TELL A STORY

A bit like a book, **a board game should always tell a story** and, in general, they tend to have a start (does your design indicate in some way where or how the player starts?), a middle (how do you know that there is still more to play before a winner is identified?), and an end (what tells us the game is complete?). Again, like a book, the visual design of a game helps to immerse the players into the narrative with successful use of imagery, style, and storytelling, and is referred to as "visual" storytelling. However, as we previously discussed, for the imagery used to aid memory, recall, and learning retention, it should be associated with the written word rather than being used merely for decorative purposes. An eye tracking study by Beymer et al. (2007) discovered that participants who read a piece of text which was situated with a *non-related* image had to reread the content several time, whereas those who read the same piece of text next to a *related* image absorbed the information much quicker.

MEASURE AND TRACK SUCCESS

Humans are competitive creatures; we want to know who is winning, how far ahead the winner is, if we can catch up, etc., and visual elements within a game help us to quickly absorb information that conveys this message. In a card game, for example, the more cards a player has *could* suggest that they are either winning or losing depending on the nature of the game. Maybe it's communicated by how far around the board a player is, or how many coins or counters they own?

EASILY UNDERSTAND GAMEPLAY THROUGH SIMPLE, CLEAR, AND CONCISE COMMUNICATION

Let's take a game such as *Colour Brain*, for example, by Big Potato Games. The box is white with the title and sub-title *Colour Brain. Crafty Questions. Colorful Answers*. Although I haven't played the game, I'm led to believe that it's fun, energetic, easy to play, and most likely aimed at families. Why do I think this? Well, the font is relaxed with rounded edges to provide a friendly feel, the colours used on the title encompasses all the colours of the rainbow, the sub-title is simple and clear ... all these aspects lead me to the above assumption. The complexity of a game may be reflected in the visuals, style, and layout chosen.

ABLE TO IDENTIFY THE INTENDED GENRE

Let's look at Wingspan by Stonemaier Games, a game which includes 170 beautifully illustrated cards. Each card displays the bird in discussion, known name, scientific name, size, and geographical location to name just a few features. The design of both the box and the cards therefore suggests that this is an educational game intended to inspire and raise awareness. The game was designed by Elizabeth Hargreave in 2019 and was inspired by her visits to Lake Artemesia near her home in Maryland (Beckwith, 2019). This is a great example of how we can take inspiration from anywhere. If you find yourself stuck for ideas, try doing something different; it can be as simple as talking to someone new, walking a different way to work, watching a different TV programme – inspiration really is all around us.

SHOUT OUT TO YOUR TARGET AUDIENCE

For design of any means to be successful, it must speak out to its target audience as well as fulfilling your own vision. If you want players to like your games, you need to Empathise with them (see Chapter 4), and provide them with an emotional connection, and you do that by understanding your players; what they like and don't like, what they find interesting, etc. (Kalmpourtzis, 2018). You may also wish to consider the country in which the game will be published, keeping in mind religion, laws, and other ethnic beliefs. Stepping into the shoes of your customer allows you to see ideas from their perspective; you must put aside your own desires at this point. "In 1954, when Disneyland Park was being constructed, Walt Disney would frequently walk around the park inspecting the progress. Often, he would be seen to walk for a distance, stop, and suddenly crouch to the ground… His explanation was simple: How else could he know what Disneyland would look like to children?" (Schell, 2008, p. 99). Also, identifying your target audience early on will help you to narrow down the type of game you would like to create, putting you on the right track from the start. In essence, the "design" or "visual communication" can help to spark interest, build emotional connections, explain ideas and concepts, and increase understanding with the overall aim of increasing learning retention (Figure 10.10.).

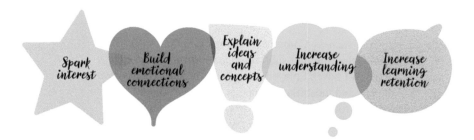

FIGURE 10.10   What your design should do.

GRAPHIC DESIGN

Graphic design is defined by the Cambridge Dictionary as follows:

- "The art of designing pictures and texts for books, magazines, advertising etc."

Graphic design shouldn't be confused with visual communication. Although associated, graphic design is just one form of the latter, as shown in Figure 10.11.

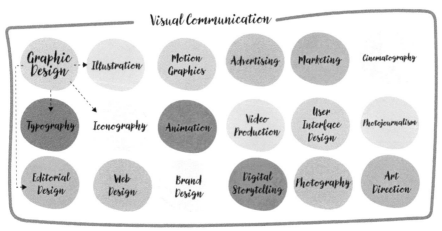

FIGURE 10.11   Graphic design in relation to visual communication.

It is the process of combining 2D text, images, and colour to create a visual form of communication in an aesthetically pleasing way. A bit like a puzzle, graphic design is the art of making different elements work and fit together. Done right, it will create the feeling you want your game to have (Schell, 2008) and should encompass the following.

COLOUR

"Colour is one of the most powerful tools for visual communication" (Fanguy, 2020, para. 1). It is all around us. In nature, warning colourisation communicates to a predator that another creature is poisonous; in healthcare settings, soothing cool colours such as pale blues and greens are used to foster a relaxing environment to encourage rest and therefore faster healing, and packaged foods we buy use the traffic light labelling system, which tells us if a product is high, medium, or low in fats, sugars, and salts. Scientists estimate that there are over 10,000,000 colours that the human eye can see (Mukamal, 2017). Objects, however, do not obtain these colours; they reflect wavelengths of light that our eyes see and are then interpreted by our brain (St Clair, K. 2016). Therefore, the colour one person sees may look different to the next person. Colour theory is a book in itself, but let's focus of the important things to remember when using colours in the design of your game.

The Colour Wheel

The colour wheel, originally invented by Sir Isaac Newton in the mid-1600s (Munsell, n.d.), is an illustrative representation of primary (red, yellow, blue), secondary (orange, green, purple), and tertiary colours. All colours are derived from the primary colours, secondary are direct mixes of primary, and tertiary are created when mixing one primary with one secondary, as shown in Figure 10.12.

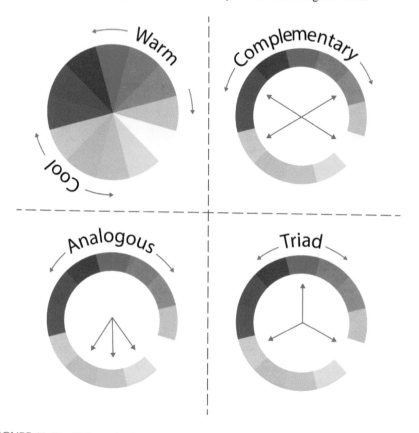

FIGURE 10.12 Colour wheel.

The colour wheel is an important tool for any designer, as from it we can identify "complementary colours" – which appear on opposite sides of the colour wheel creating a striking contrast when used together, "analogous colours" – which appear next to each other on the wheel and typically occur in nature, and "triad" – three different colours taken from equal distances and in a triangle form, which like complementary colours create a strong contrast. A colour scheme is the term designers use to group colours they have selected for a particular design. As a rule, limiting the number of colours in your scheme will result in a harmonic balance, encouraging them to work together rather than clashing against each other. Creating balance doesn't have to be limiting though; for example, if you selected three key colours, you would then introduce various shades and tints to add depth, strength, and diversity (see Figure 10.13).

100% ←——————————————————————————→ *10%*

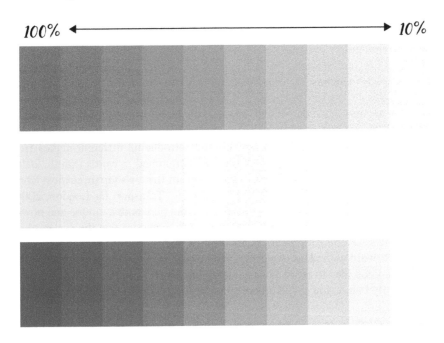

FIGURE 10.13   Colours and tints.

When using colour in software applications, it's extremely important to remember that what you see on screen is not necessarily what you will see in print, even with the best colour calibrated monitor. Ensuring you are using the correct "colour mode" is essential if you want special colours in your artwork. When it comes to modes, colour falls into two different categories: RGB and CMYK (see Figure 10.14). RGB stands for Red, Green, and Blue and is the mode you would choose when designing for onscreen such as a website, video game, or online simulation. CMYK stands for Cyan, Magenta, Yellow, and Black and is the mode you would choose when designing for print using the four-colour process printing method.

CMYK reflects the different coloured plates that are used in print and is the most cost-effective form of digital printing. If you want full control over the colours you are printing, you would choose spot colours such as Pantone (but that's a whole different area, and not relevant for the manufacturing of board games as not only would it be a time-consuming task, but it would also incur excessive costs).

FIGURE 10.14   CMYK/RBG.

STRUCTURE AND LAYOUT

There are numerous useful tricks you can use to get balance within your design and structure (or layout) of the contents, so they work together rather than against each other. The way elements are arranged can make or break a design, and like many aspects of design, the simpler the better. Let's go back to the London Underground tube map; for example, the first edition (as we know it today) was designed by Harry Beck in 1933. He took it upon himself to make sense and clarity by straightening the lines, evening out the content, and introducing different angles from what was a jumbled mess of lines, colours, and crammed in words (Smith, 2016). 73 years later the tube map was shortlisted as one of Britain's top three most iconic design icons (Tube Map Voted a UK Design Icon – Transport for London, 2006). This is a great example of how structure and layout play both a unique and powerful role in visual communication. It's important to recognise that the design phase of the game development process is not a quick one. You will find yourself going back and forward with ideas, concepts, and layouts after rounds of playtesting. It's therefore a good idea to mock your game up and start testing as soon as possible, and certainly before you spend lots of time creating beautiful digital layouts.

GRIDS AND THE RULE OF THIRDS

Photographers use a principle called the "Rule of Thirds", the idea being that you should divide the area your image will occupy (de Soto, 2015) into equally spaced sections consisting of two vertical and two horizontal lines, as shown in Figure 10.15.

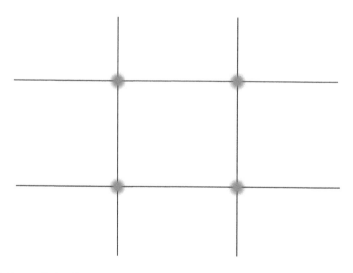

FIGURE 10.15   Rule of thirds.

The rule suggests that positioning main content around the corners of the central square will provide a key focal point. It helps to balance the main aspect and negative space (or "white space" in design terminology) to achieve an effective composition and draw the viewer's eye. The same principle is very useful when thinking about layout and structure in graphic design (Plicanic et al., 2023).

White Space

Possibly one of the most important yet overlooked elements of good design is the use of "white space" (Coates, 2014). White space is exactly what it says; it's the areas within your design that are left blank, sometimes referred to as "negative space". It's the space that allows the main communicating factors of your design to breathe and be seen, and is part of every piece of well-designed visual communication; think of webpages, mobile applications, and billboard designs, for example. Most of the time we don't even notice it, but what we do notice is what it's surrounding – and that's the idea! Often, it can be used to denote quality; think of luxury brands, for example, compared to those at the opposite end of the consumer scale. Which are busy and cluttered, and which are simple and bold? White space helps to show contrast between different elements of a design and in this instance, less is definitely more.

Imagery

Numerous studies have shown that images are more effective than words alone (Paivio & Csapo, 1969, 1973, cited in Weinstein et al., 2019) due to the way our minds dual-code information, and a higher level of knowledge is retained when they work in direct relation to the subject matter or alongside relevant text rather than when used for decorative purposes only (Mayer & Moreno, 2003). An eye tracking study by Beymer et al. (2007) discovered that participants who read a piece of text which was situated with a *non-related* image had to reread the content several times, whereas those who read the same piece of text next to a *related* image absorbed the information much quicker. Research also shows that the use of simple illustrations alongside small amounts of text allows for quicker cognitive absorption than the same text presented without images (Mayer et al., 1996). This is interesting when we think about creating a rule book, for example – have you noticed how much easier it is to understand the rules of a game if pictures support the instructions? In terms of education, visuals are not only easier to process and understand; they're also easier to remember, and this effect is referred to as the Picture Superiority Effect or PSE. Allan Paivio's dual-coding theory suggests that pictures have an advantage over words because they are dual-coded in the human brain, whereas words only generate one code; hence, why it's often easier and quicker to learn through what we see rather than what we read (Paivio & Csapo, 1973). There are various types of visuals you can create for your game including creating illustrations, using stock imagery, or creating and possibly manipulating your own photographs.

ILLUSTRATION

Illustration is the term used when visualising text in an artistic and decorative form. It covers a multitude of disciplines such as line art, where shapes are depicted from bold lines; realism, where objects look true to form; typographic illustration, where type becomes the image; or many other styles such as comic, retro, 3D, and minimalistic (see Figure 10.16). The style you choose will strongly communicate the theme, genre, classification, and intended audience of your game, and so should be carefully considered. Many forms of illustration start by hand and then are taken into a digital environment using vector-based applications such as Adobe Illustrator. Vector illustrations are digital, mathematical formations and are created from lines, shapes, and curves. The major advantage of vector-based illustration is due to the formulas used to create them, illustrations created this way can be scaled up and down to any size without any loss of visual quality or resolution. The logo for your game should be created as a vector illustration. You can start by visualising the idea for your logo by hand and once you are almost happy with it, you can then import it into a vector application to digitally enhance it. You may wish to do this by using a pen tool or a drawing tablet, or simply by manipulating a font you have purchased and available for redistribution.

FIGURE 10.16   Styles of illustration.

STOCK IMAGERY

When looking online, you can easily find a wealth of stock images. These are photographs, graphics, illustrations, icons, and fonts that are instantly available for a fee. Please be vigilant when using any existing images in your own work. Often, these are copyright restricted and even if you have purchased the image, you do need to confirm how you are allowed to use it. For example, a lower fee may allow for use in a blog, but if you are planning to use it in a way that could return a profit (such as a board game), chances are that you will need an extended licence at a much higher price (one that cover commercial use).

PHOTOGRAPHY

To avoid any kind of potential copyright infringement when it comes to using images created by another designer or photographer, for example, you may want to create visuals using your own photographs, allowing you to obtain full copyright ownership. These can form the basis of an illustration, for example, by using a manipulation tool such as Adobe Photoshop. If you don't have access to the Adobe suite of tools, a quick web search for "photo manipulation tools" will return a variety of sources to try.

In Figure 10.17, I have used Adobe Photoshop to manipulate a photograph I took last summer. I have started by using the pen tool to cut the shape out from the background (you could photograph your object against a plain background to make this step easier), then applied a cartoon-style effect manipulating the setting until happy with my result, then finally placing it on a different background.

FIGURE 10.17   Manipulating your own photos.

This process was extremely easy; it took around 5 minutes, and best of all, I own all the copyrights and so I can now use this image in any way I wish. Thinking ahead, planning, and shooting your own photos may take a little more time but gives you cost-effective flexibility in the long run. Converting your own photos into cartoon-style illustrations provides endless opportunities, plus you can then import them back into a vector application to convert them to a vector graphic which allows for further editing such as changing colours, line thickness, shape, and form. As mentioned earlier, you don't have to be an artist; you just have to think creatively – there is always a way!

ICONOGRAPHY

Iconography is the term used to describe visual symbols that convey individual meanings. Ideally, they are created in vector-based applications to allow for digital editing and scaling. Although designed to be small, they are powerful pieces of visual communication; they are language-independent and work exceptionally well when indicating categories, themes, or actions in board game designs, especially on smaller items such as cards where space is limited. When it comes to designing a series of icons, keep it simple. The more detail, the less powerful it will be when printed to size. It's also important to limit the amount of colour you use; one or two variations are great, but any more than that and your icon becomes an illustration (Wolf, n.d.). (See Figure 10.18.)

FIGURE 10.18   Iconography.

TYPOGRAPHY

When it comes to fonts, less is *always* more. Aim to select one primary font which should be used for most of the text, and a secondary font which can be used for supporting text. In this case, this may be the title; you may select a fancy font that would work well for your logo but wouldn't necessarily lend itself well to the font used in the rulebook, for example. There are numerous places to source fonts; some are free but may require attribution, others are paid for, others may be part of a subscription such as Adobe Creative Cloud. Websites such as Google Fonts allow you to input a line of text to see how it will look in various fonts; it's worth investing some time looking at different options as the style of the font does say a lot about your entire design. Have you heard the saying "Never judge a book by its cover?"; well where fonts are concerned, that's exactly what we do. Along with colour, it's the one thing that ties everything else together as it's part of the logo, cards, board, box, rulebook, etc., so, it's worth getting them right. Once you have selected a few you think you like, the next thing is to use the font with the name of your game. Does it work? (See Figure 10.19).

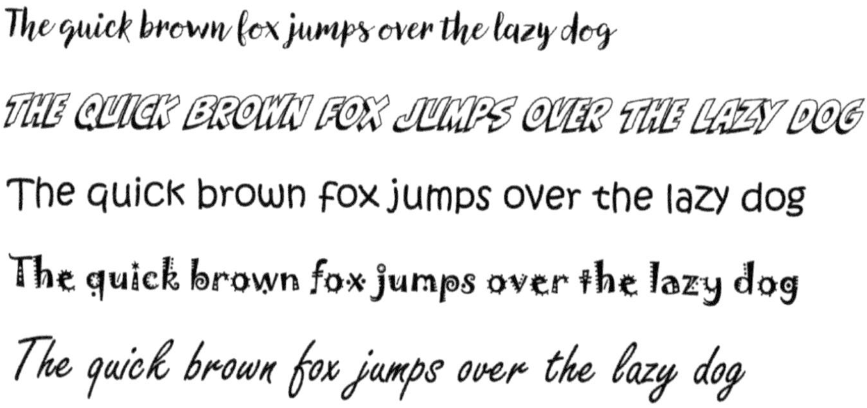

The quick brown fox jumps over the lazy dog

THE QUICK BROWN FOX JUMPS OVER THE LAZY DOG

The quick brown fox jumps over the lazy dog

The quick brown fox jumps over the lazy dog

The quick brown fox jumps over the lazy dog

FIGURE 10.19   Fonts and styles.

Please remember to check copyright information related to any image, graphic, or font you have sourced online which has been created by another individual.

SUMMARY

Throughout this chapter, we have identified what visual design is and looked at ways you can design your game to ensure that it communicates the right message to the viewer. Visuals are, as we have identified, not only easier to process and understand (Mayer, 1999), but if a serious game is designed well, it also has the potential to captivate the learner playing the game (Din & Gibson, 2019), which in return will embed knowledge for deeper learning retention and the transfer of knowledge to apply in new situations (Mayer, 1999). It's particularly important for educational games to capture the attention of players (or learners), especially in a classroom environment where the participant has been directed to play the game rather than have chosen to play it themselves (Ferreira de Almeida & dos Santos Machado, 2021). Equally, to retain and embed knowledge (Mayer, 1999), learners need to enjoy what they are engaging with, and successful use of visual communication is probably one of the biggest hooks. For any type of game, the use of appropriate colours, fonts, imagery, and other forms of visual design discussed in this chapter, are pivotal to communicating key information to your audience.

11 Prototyping and Playtesting

Dr Devon Allcoat

SYSTEMS ENGINEERING

Game design, as we have seen, is interdisciplinary in nature. Consequently, it makes sense to use an interdisciplinary approach to manage the process. Although systems engineering is being discussed in this chapter on playtesting, in reality, systems engineering is fundamental throughout the entire life-cycle of the design process. It helps to identify requirements, manage interfaces, and control risks. It is about how to build the right system, as well as how to build the system right.

SYSTEMS

A system is an organised connected group of "things". These are linked, making one larger system that works in unison, achieving something the individual parts cannot achieve alone. For example, think about the human respiratory system, which comprises various organs and other parts of the body that work together so that you can breathe. A game is ultimately a system. The visuals, physical components, rules and instructions, and any other parts, work together to create the experience that is the game.

Similarly, designing a game can also be considered a system. It connects not just the parts of the game itself, but also everything that goes into its constituent parts and its creation. Think of this in terms of the individuals involved; it brings together the artist, the graphic designer, the writer, etc., all of whom contribute to the "system". Alternatively, consider the stages that have to be completed in order to create a fully functioning game: the concept, the prototyping, the playtesting, manufacturing, distribution, etc. All of the above are elements in the holistic (all-encompassing) view of the product and the process.

The holistic picture can demonstrate that there is a system of systems. "A system of systems arises when a set of needs are met through a combination of several systems" (DeLaurentis & Crossley, 2005, p. 86). Think again about the example of our respiratory system. It is not all that is required to make our bodies work; we have a variety of other systems that are essential for us to live, think, and move (i.e. to function normally).

SYSTEMS THINKING

Systems thinking draws from various fields. The primary purpose of systems thinking is to look at the holistic picture, not just specific parts or components. That means looking at how the whole thing works together, and the relationships involved (Figure 11.1). Often when we look at solving a problem, one approach or method is to use reductionism,

DOI: 10.1201/9781003319511-11

i.e., splitting it up into smaller parts. This can be useful for some challenges, but it relies on the idea that the relationships between the elements do not matter (or do not exist), or that the solution will still make sense when looked at in the context of the bigger picture. Systems thinking instead challenges this approach, encouraging a holistic approach by considering and balancing all the elements and how they are intertwined.

Most people naturally do this, even if they do not call it systems thinking. In previous chapters, we've discussed having cohesive mechanics, mechanics that match the theme, complimentary art style, and appropriate components. All of these fit into the holistic systems thinking approach, and the relationships between each of these elements make up your game.

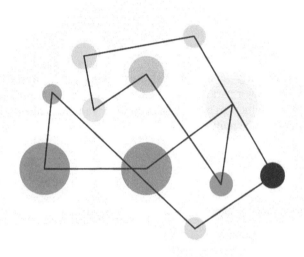

FIGURE 11.1   Systems thinking.

Why are we talking about this for prototyping and playtesting? Well, simply put, your game needs to work together as a whole system, not just as a collection of elements. If you asked one person for feedback about the art, and a different person for feedback about the mechanics, and someone else about the theme, it could result in individual reviews that would not necessarily translate when all of those elements are combined. For example, if presented with just the artwork, feedback that "the cartoon-style art looks great" could, when presented with the complete product, become "the cartoon-style art doesn't really fit with the serious content of the game, or the target audience for four-hour game length strategy games".

So, does that mean you should only be prototyping and playtesting when you have every single element of your game prepared? Well, no. Prototyping and playtesting should be conducted at various stages of the game design process. Equally, once the process of continuous testing and improvement has been completed, it is essential to test the system/game as a whole or as a "final" product. This is to ensure that all the different elements work together successfully.

ITERATIVE DESIGN

Iterative design has already been explored, with design thinking (Chapter 4) using the concept of an iterative process. It is likely that during the design process, various iterations of the game will be developed before settling on the final design. Each of these should be prototyped and playtested since this is the most effective way to obtain feedback and to identify what may benefit from being changed for the next iteration.

PROTOTYPING

A prototype is an early version of your product and is used to test the concept or process. This is a major part of the design thinking process. It is like a first draft of an essay, which you then go back to and edit to make improvements. Of course, it is likely that there will be multiple prototype versions.

EARLY PROTOTYPES

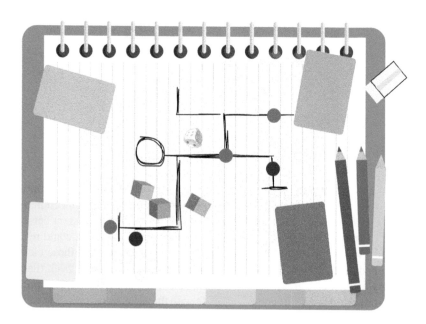

FIGURE 11.2   Early prototype tools.

You can prototype very quickly and very simply for many tabletop concepts. It does not have to be either complex or expensive. For games that do not have a digital component, this can even be done using basic easily attainable materials (Figure 11.2). As examples, the gameboard could be hand drawn, cards can be made by cutting up and writing on paper, and tokens can be made out of paper or standard tokens can be used (purchased specifically or borrowed from other games). This process is easier if a computer and printer are available so that components can be printed rather than done by hand.

3D Printing and Rapid Prototyping

For bespoke or more detailed prototyping, where using pre-existing components is not sufficient, 3D printing can be an ideal alternative. 3D printing is much more accessible than it used to be, being available to hobbyists as a service, or for purchase or rental of equipment. Rapid prototyping is feasible through accessing pre-created models online, or with the use of 3D computer-aided design (CAD) software to design the model or part to be printed. Essentially, with the right skill set and access (either to a printer or by ordering through a third party), 3D models can potentially be created reasonably easily and at a reasonable cost. This means that even with a unique gameplay mechanic that is reliant on a specific component (e.g. unique character pieces), it is still possible to do small-scale production for prototyping and playtesting purposes (Figure 11.3).

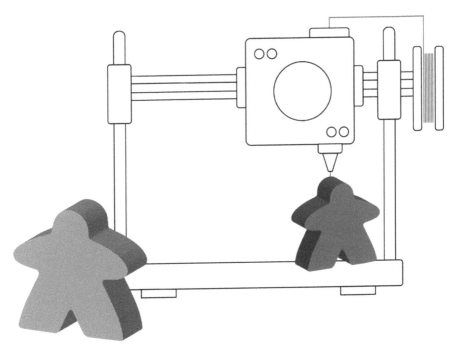

FIGURE 11.3   3D printing.

DIGITAL PROTOTYPES

If components are expensive, or if there is a desire or requirement to share a prototype version of your game with a wider, possibly international, audience, a digital prototype can be extremely useful. However, it would not be relevant to or useful for every type of game, e.g., a digital prototype of a dexterity game would not necessarily generate useful feedback, but there are occasions where even if a game is not intended to be released digitally as a final product, there are advantages of developing a digital prototype to gather valuable feedback. Digital tools have already been discussed elsewhere in this book, and the same software and solutions can be used for digital prototypes.

FINAL PROTOTYPES

Early prototyping for playtesting is typically quite unlike prototyping the final product. Early prototypes are often visually unappealing in exchange for being inexpensive and easy to create. When playtesting a "final" prototype, a more holistic approach needs to be undertaken. More consideration needs to be given to what the actual final components will look and feel like. This will typically require samples to be purchased from various manufacturers. These samples will normally be prototype samples, so they can still be changed if necessary. This might mean adjusting shape, weight, material, colour, etc., of the gameplay pieces, but equally this is just as relevant for the board, the rulebook, and the game packaging (and the storage solution within it). This "final" stage of prototyping and testing is to ensure that at the end of the design process, there is a product that is desirable in all facets. Often, this "final" stage is completed without much consumer feedback, but if there are components that are unique and particularly important to your game, or your ideas, it may be appropriate to seek consumer feedback on the look and feel of these.

TESTING, TESTING, TESTING

ASKING THE RIGHT QUESTIONS

So, you have your prototypes, and it is time for feedback. What questions should be asked, and what type of feedback do you need? Asking the right questions is imperative to getting good feedback. Good feedback does not mean positive or complimentary feedback, but *useful* feedback. Feedback is useful when it helps you to understand the player experience and how it can be improved (Figure 11.4).

About the Player

To get feedback, you would think all that needs to be done is to ask lots of questions about your game. However, it may also be appropriate to ask the players (i.e. the playtesters) some questions about themselves. Specifically, it is useful to know if this is the type of game that they would typically play or not. For example, Playtester 1 could give feedback that the game is far too long and they could not remember the rules, but Playtester 2 may say that it was the perfect length and the right level of complexity. This can be simply down to individual differences, but it could also be linked more specifically to whether or not they are your target audience. Playtester 1 might normally play party games, in which case your strategy game simply does not fit with their preferences or expectations of a game in terms of time taken and complexity. Feedback from your target audience will always be more useful than from someone who would be unlikely to buy or play your game. To understand more about this, it is advisable to ask the playtesters what genres of games they usually play, whether they prefer co-op or competitive games, and what player count they normally play with.

Other useful information to obtain from the testers is their contact details. These should be optional to provide, but are helpful so that they can be invited back to a later round of playtesting, or to ask follow-up questions once feedback has been analysed and possible changes identified as a result of this. It could also be that these are used to inform them about when the game is being released, or available via crowdfunding. If they participated in the final round of playtesting you could also perhaps ask their consent to use their feedback for marketing purposes.

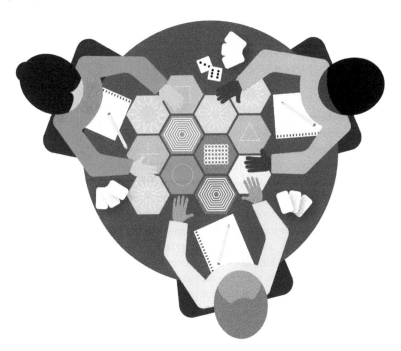

FIGURE 11.4   Playtesters.

About the Game

If someone is asked the simple question of "did you like the game?", it is likely that a simple response will be given, and often feedback of this kind is not useful. Instead, you should ask questions about specific aspects of the game. This will not only help direct the playtester to what it is useful to talk about, but also help you to understand if there are specific areas which are lacking, whilst others are strong, thereby identifying what areas to focus on. Questions that may be of interest include the following topics:

- **Enjoyment**: did the playtester enjoy playing the game? (This could be because it was fun, or because it was interesting, or because it created tension, etc.)
- **Accessibility**: were there any aspects of the game that were not accessible, or were more difficult for them to interact with?
- **Mechanics**: which mechanics did they like? Which mechanics did they not like?
- **Cohesion**: did everything work well together, or does anything seem out of place or incongruent?
- **Engagement**: were they fully engaged with the game? Or were they distracted or bored at any stage?
- **Energy**: did the game have the right energy levels/tension throughout? Or were there lulls, or a point at which there was a clear winner and so energy levels of the other players dropped? This can be linked to engagement.
- **Artistic**: do they like the visuals of the game? Do they like the theme of the game? Do they like the "voice" of the game?

About the Rules

Often, when playtesting, the rules will be explained to the playtesters and the rulebook is not used. This means that feedback on the rulebook is lacking, but testing of the rulebook is essential and should not be forgotten. One of the best methods of testing the rulebook is to playtest it with someone who has never played the game before. Ask them to play the game purely based on the rules as they understand them from the rulebook and without any verbal explanations. If they get stuck on an element of the game whilst playing, they should refer to the rulebook for answers. They can then be observed to see if they are interpreting the rules as intended. This process will indicate whether the rulebook is clearly written (e.g. do they interpret it correctly?), how easy and quick it is to find relevant information in it (how long does it take them to find answers for themselves?), and if anything is missing (is there anything they could not find the answer to themselves?). Ideally, this exercise should be repeated with more than one group of people.

About the Learning

For a game which aims to teach and educate, it is important to find out what players have actually learnt from playing it. The best way to do this depends entirely on the subject, but ultimately what needs to be understood is whether the intended learning outcomes have been met by the game. You could directly share these learning outcomes and ask the playtesters if they felt they learnt about them. Or you can more generally ask what the players felt they learnt from playing the game, and then crosscheck these to see if they line up with your expected outcomes. Whichever approach you take, this is an important step for serious games, to ensure that they are fulfilling their objective.

About the Marketing

In the later stages of the design process, you may even have some potential marketing materials that you want feedback on. For example, do they think that the blurb accurately reflects the gameplay experience? Would the visuals of the marketing catch their eye? Where would they typically look for information about upcoming releases? Which sources do they trust pre-release reviews from? If you're crowdfunding, you could ask questions like what sort of stretch goals would they like to see? How much would they be willing to spend on this game? What would give them the confidence that this will be fulfilled? What extras would they be interested in?

Whilst these questions are not necessarily required for the main design process, they can be extremely useful for successful development and launch of a product.

QUESTIONNAIRE DESIGN

Clearly, there are numerous areas that can be explored in a questionnaire, but it is also important to remember the human component. How long will your feedback form take to fill out versus how long people are prepared to spend doing it? It is best not to overwhelm people with too many questions, or to take up huge amounts of their time (especially if they're doing it as a favour). Everything should be made as simple and as quick to fill out as possible. For example, don't ask them to write out every single game genre they play. Consider what questions can be answered with just a tick box, or could be designed so that playtesters only need to circle a number or text option. Chapter 13 also provides relevant guidance on questionnaire design.

Qualitative feedback is important, and this option should not be dismissed – often, it is helpful to have an explanation of why they feel how they feel. Giving feedback should not be a chore for the playtester and for it to be more accessible, multiple options could be deigned (Figure 11.5), such as a paper-based version, a web-based version, and a verbal option (i.e. they talk and you take notes or record it). The visual accessibility concerns discussed in Chapter 5 should also be considered when designing a questionnaire; for example, are the text font, size, and colours appropriate?

FIGURE 11.5   Questionnaire design.

FINDING PLAYTESTERS

There are lots of ways to find playtesters, and which you use will depend on a few variables, including resources. It is certainly possible to recruit and pay playtesters or pay to have your game hosted at an event or location. However, this is not always necessary, particularly not for every stage of playtesting, you can think about what and who is readily available to you. An obvious first step would be to ask friends and family. They may not be your target audience, but for the very first iteration, it can be a useful starting place. However, it should be kept in mind that they may have a tendency towards positive feedback, rather than useful feedback. There are also plenty of tabletop hobby groups. You can recruit people from these through local meet-ups, social media, online posts, etc. A local board game café may also be willing to host, and similarly, some tabletop game events may allow the gathering of feedback on your prototypes. With a digital prototype, playtesters can be sourced worldwide. When you get closer to your final design, you should aim to playtest specifically with your target audience. For a serious game, this could mean having students or teachers playtest it or, if it is business-oriented, people who work in that industry.

REPLAY VALUE

Replay value is not necessary for all games. However, if you want your game to have a replay value, this is something that should be tested for. This is quite straightforward to do, but requires significant resources, particularly time and playtesters. It requires having a group play the game multiple times, ideally not in one sitting but spread over different occasions.

BALANCE

Testing for balance (Chapter 6) typically requires a higher volume of playtesting. As many combinations and scenarios as feasible should be tested. This can be very time-consuming, and potentially even tedious. For balance testing, it is generally a good idea to use a structured approach. Ideally, to be as efficient as possible, keep track of which combinations and scenarios you have already tested. Through balance testing, you may find that the game needs to be "tweaked" for player fairness, e.g., individual player powers, factions in the game, or even the difficulty of the game itself. This structured approach can also help to reveal any unusual combinations of cards or actions that may interact with each other in a way that does not fit with the usual rules, which need to be addressed in the rulebook.

SUMMARY

In this chapter, we looked at various options and stages of prototyping your game so that you can playtest it. It is likely that you will go through multiple iterations of prototypes, and different tools, techniques, and materials will be used to create these. Once you have your prototype, you then need to playtest your game, and we looked at how to do this, from finding playtesters, to making sure that the right questions are asked. Questions need to be carefully considered in order to get relevant and useful feedback that can be applied to your game design. Ideally, you will also have multiple rounds of playtesting, securing as many opinions and perspectives as possible. Playtesting is key to a well-designed game, so remember: playtest, playtest, playtest.

EXERCISE

Choose any game you like. Try playing the game, pretending you are a play-tester and then write what feedback you would give after playing, assuming that you were asked the generic question, "What did you think about the game?". Next, try writing some questions for playtesters, then answer those. Alternatively (or additionally), ask friends or family to play a game with you, then answer first the generic question, followed by your specific playtester questionnaire.

- How did the feedback compare when answering one generic question versus answering multiple specific questions?
- Did you feel you had enough information from the questions you asked?
- What changes would you make to the questions asked?

12 Taking Your Game to Market

Chris Evans

INTRODUCTION

You've made a board game! You have had the prototype made, it looks amazing, your friends love it, and it only took a few weeks to be manufactured and delivered to your door; this board game business could not be easier, you think. So, what next? If you think your game is good enough, then you may want to consider manufacturing and selling in bulk, perhaps looking at somewhere between 100 and 1,000 games. At this point, it would be worth you taking a step back and reassessing your options, and the first consideration should be whether your game is actually good enough to sell.

Mike Gray, Senior Director of Product Design for Hasbro, currently the biggest games manufacturer in the world, explains the problem:

> A big problem is when you fall in love with your own idea, so you no longer have an objective view of it. You've been hearing all this praise from your friends, but none of its objective. Novices will design a game for themselves – something they want to play. That's fine, but if you want to make money you have to sell a lot of them. So there had better be a lot of "you" around to buy them.
>
> *The Game Inventor's Guidebook, Tinsman, 2008, p. 28*

It is possible to make money designing and selling board games, and many people do, but to make any meaningful profits, you are going to have to create successful games on a large scale. That does not mean that small production runs cannot make any money, or conversely, selling 10,000 copies will make enough money to give up the day job. If you are in it to make money, then you are either going to have to design a game that is popular enough to sell in large numbers, or you are going to have to find a way to increase your profit margin.

There are effectively two routes to market; self-publishing, and through a publishing company, and both of those routes have mechanisms in place that help you assess the quality, and ultimately the saleability, of your game. With self-publishing, you have crowdfunding which comes with backers. The number of backers you receive will give you an indication of the game's potential, but really that is only an indication, and you may still be one negative review away from failure; that is, the game must still be good. Publishers, however, tend to work more closely with you in refining your game for the mass market. For publishers, your game is an investment, and their expertise and experience will help you to refine aspects of your game that need

DOI: 10.1201/9781003319511-12

improvement. The problem with this approach is not so much working with publishers; it is in getting them to work with you.

In this chapter, the pros and cons of both approaches will be explored, as well as what comes before, and after, the publishing process. Furthermore, we will explore various themes, including the importance of effectively communicating your personal narrative and promoting your own identity alongside your product. We will delve into the intricacies of conveying your story to captivate your audience and highlight the unique qualities that set you apart. Additionally, we will examine the various options available to you, the associated costs, the legal considerations, and the logistical aspects that are integral to the overall process. Along the way, the nuances of creating games for learning will also be explored, and how those distinctions may impact upon the decisions that you make when taking your game to market.

TELLING YOUR STORY

Imagine that you are explaining your game to a friend. What would you tell them? What might they ask you? How would you demonstrate to them how amazing your game is going to be? As a game designer, you are not just selling your games, but you are selling yourself, too. Your project page is your chance to tell people that story: who you are, what game you are going to make, and why you are going to make it. This is your story, and imagine that this friend of yours, to whom you are telling this story, is a potential backer. This is your primary goal when telling your story, turning friends, or followers, into backers.

Your story begins at the time you first conceived of the idea of the game. Start writing things down, taking photos, gathering information. Looking through successful board game projects is another effective way to see what kinds of information backers will expect, and later in this chapter, we will do just that. So, what should you write about, and where should you write it? Facebook would be a good place to start, though your own website or Blog may work better for you depending upon your preferences. Ultimately though, this is the same information that, when cherry-picked, will form your crowdfunding project page. By the time you launch, you should be exploiting all appropriate social media, so you may as well start now.

Your story will be about you; introduce yourself, and any similar work you have done (show some examples!). Tell people who are you and what are you planning to make; the more information the better: sketches, samples, prototypes; it all helps backers get as excited as you are.

Explain where the game came from. For a serious game, throw in some learning objectives if you like, but keep words brief. Explain how you got the idea, and how much you have accomplished so far. Sharing the project's history helps others understand the kind of work you do, and how you go about it.

Include a plan, a schedule, and a timeline (graphical if possible). Make content themed, if appropriate, in accordance with your game's theme, fonts, and style. Create a clear, specific timeline for what backers might expect. Include projected budgets, broken down to let people know you have thought things through and have a workable plan.

People buy from people, and being passionate (but not overly emotive) about your game should help your cause.

Much of your story can be conveyed with words, but looking through the most successful Kickstarter projects pages will reveal that information is mostly conveyed with images and videos, and at the top of the project page is the main image – which is the first thing people will see. Take a look at the various banners. This is the visual that will shape the identity of your game. While it doesn't necessarily have to match your box design imagery, maintaining consistency without sacrificing quality is advisable.

Ideally, you will also have a compelling video. Some projects feature this at the top of their page; this is the best way to introduce yourself, and to give people a closer look at what you are working on. When looking through the introductory videos on Kickstarter, you will find that there is quite a variety; some feature the designer and explain their concept and game, some just show the game itself, some have commissioned artists, and others have been created with software packages such as Premiere or After Effects and play out like a short movie. The length of the video is generally between 30 and 90 seconds long. Captions, subtitles, and translations help more people understand what you have to say and get involved with your project (whatever their language or hearing level).

Whichever approach you decide to take, you should tell your story and start to build up your follower base, preferably sooner than later. If you do not use social media, then now is the time to start. According to Frydrych et al. (2014), crowdfunding success is based less on platform-specific functions, and primarily associated with the creation of a convincing narrative. Storytelling has more to do with the creative and retrospective reconstruction and sharing of facts and events (Tindale, 2017), which in organisational contexts is often associated with sense-making processes.

TARGETING YOUR TARGET AUDIENCE

By this stage, you should know your target audience, and if this is a game designed for learning, then you might assume that your target audience will be students of the target age and subject, as well as any educational staff who would be interested in buying your game. The problem with this approach is that you would be unlikely to sell many games. Your target players may not be the same as the potential customers (those who are actually purchasing the game). For serious games, your customers are often educators or businesses, not the students or staff who are playing the game. This is one of the reasons that there's little appetite for developing serious games – outside of a small niche circle, they are unmarketable. Games made for fun, however, have a huge market, but one that is saturated. Nevertheless, people and companies make, market, and sell serious games, and make a living out of it, so how do they do it?

PUBLISHING OPTIONS

Many designers just enjoy the creative hobby of designing a game, creating a few prototypes for friends and family, and stopping there. However, the question you need to ask yourself is, would you rather be a designer, a publisher, or both? Which leads nicely to one of the most frequent questions that will arise when publishing a board game, that is, whether to self-publish or go through a publishing company.

TABLE 12.1

Summary of Pros and Cons of the Two Main Publishing Options

	Pros	Cons
Self-publishing a board game	• All profits directly to the creator (100% of Retail) • More creative control • Quality control	• Low customer awareness • Lack of market knowledge • Logistics and legalities • No guaranteed profit
Using a game publisher	• Larger client base • Upfront or royalty payments • Industry knowledge	• Less money in your pocket (3–5% of retail) • Highly selective • Less creative influence

This process of selling to the end customers marks final stage of creating a board game, but it can also be both confusing and time-consuming. The forthcoming sections of this chapter will explore both options. Each option comes with advantages and disadvantages, as summarised in Table 12.1.

PUBLISHING THROUGH A PUBLISHER

The easy path to getting your game made and sold is through a publisher, that is, if you can convince them that your game is a viable prospect for them. In the next section, we will explore the pros and cons of using a publisher, before diving into the murky world of self-publishing.

SELLING YOUR DESIGN

If you plan to sell your design, you will need to find a publisher who might be interested. For educational games, this can be more challenging, but it really depends upon your game. Timing is important, and seeking out a publisher too early is one of the most common mistakes that inexperienced game designers make (Slack, 2020). First impressions count, and you will need to ensure that you have evidence of rigorous playtesting and blind playtesting; that is, it can be played without you being present. Furthermore, the playtesting will inevitably lead to changes having to be made to your game, and once those changes have been made, then you are back to playtesting.

If you are successful at persuading a publisher to invest in your game, you will sign a contract, work with them in finalising your game, and they will typically do the rest. You will eventually start to receive a share of the profits for every copy of your game that they sell. The amount you get will depend on the deal you strike with the publisher, but for a first-time game designer, it is usually around 2–3% of the wholesale cost, which is typically about 40% of the retail price. So, at 2%, for example, a game that sells for £30 will make you (£30 * 40% * 2%) = 24p.

Even if you sell 10,000 copies, you will only make £1,200 (though at least you will likely receive that money upfront). This does not mean that in this example the publishers would be making a profit of £117,600, however. As we will explore later in this chapter, the costs of creating a game, marketing it, and getting it to the customer, eat into any profit margin. Furthermore, the publisher will also have to deal with any associated risks, such as nobody buying the game.

WHAT PUBLISHERS ARE LOOKING FOR

It does not matter whether you choose to publish through a standard board game publisher or a specialised educational board game publisher; the criteria are often similar. They want a game that will sell sufficient quantities. Typically, if publishers are looking for new games, then they will have some evaluation criteria and an online form for you to complete.

Evaluation Criteria

1. **Conceptually Unique**: Something that stands out from the crowd.
2. **Themed and Visually Appealing**: They do not necessarily need to see the final artwork, miniatures, or custom dice, but they will need to feel immersed into the world that you are presenting to your gamers.
3. **Fully Developed**: The game must be complete. Furthermore, publishers do not use tabletop simulators or print and play versions.
4. **Clear Rules**: Simple, clear, and effective, without grammatical errors.
5. **Playtested, Playable, and Polished**: A good litmus test that you can use is the blind playtest method (gamers can easily play without any intervention from the creator).
6. **Game Design Flexibility**: Publishers do not just make (through manufacturers) and market your game; they will work with you to increase its market viability. Furthermore, most publishing houses have experienced producers, artists, writers, and designers on staff that are familiar with their customers and brand.

Submitting Your Game Online

Submitting through an online form is the most common method of having your game seen by publishers. The questions vary, but generally follow a style that allows them to filter out unsuitable candidates at the earliest opportunity. It is a cutthroat process.

The following checklist will help you to prepare, which you will need to do well in advance of potentially meeting with the publishing company:

- Playtest your game at least ten times (include the completed playtest forms).
- Blind playtest your game at least five times (include the playtest forms).
- Try to feature at least one unique mechanic, or twist on an existing mechanic.
- Present players with a thematic, visually appealing way of choosing what they do on their turn.
- Optionally, include one or more unique components for players to interact with.
- Test if players can start playing the game within 5 minutes of beginning the rules explanation (this is often, but not always a question publishers ask).

Furthermore, publishers will seek deeper insights into your narrative, including your comprehensive understanding of your own game. The subsequent criteria are indicative of what a publisher might expect you to furnish, either through their online submission form, or through a face-to-face meeting.

- Select an appropriate game title and potential tagline.
- Develop a compelling game pitch. To create an effective pitch, draw inspiration from successful crowdfunding platforms like Kickstarter, where designers present their concepts to the public.
- Craft a concise gameplay video. Consider producing a brief video, akin to a Kickstarter presentation (around 90 seconds), focusing not only on your product but also on your personal presence, as you're not only selling the game but also your vision. Publishers might offer some guidance in this regard.
- Identify player engagement factors. Playtesting can help to gather data on how your game sparks players' imagination and captivates their interest.
- Communicate fundamental game details: player count, duration, target audience. Clearly articulate essential game attributes, such as the number of players it accommodates, the typical game length, and the intended age group.
- For serious games, clarify educational objectives. If your game carries educational value, elaborate on the learning outcomes it delivers and how players can achieve them through gameplay.
- Share your publishing history. Publishers often inquire about your experience.
- Provide game rules and in-action photos. Include comprehensive game rules and photographs that depict the game being enjoyed in context. You can employ creative settings like a board game café, or a classroom if it has educational elements.

Finally, submit the form and you should expect to hear from the publishers within a month or two (time varies from publisher to publisher). If they like your pitch, they will require more information and you will be asked to provide them with a prototype.

SELF-PUBLISHING YOUR GAME

The profits you will receive through a publishing company can be pennies, so maybe if you publish the game yourself, you would be able to keep more of the profits, right?

While it is possible to make more money publishing your game, it takes a lot of work, a fair amount of industry knowledge, and a whole lot of risk. For those who have never managed a financial project, it can be a daunting task. To produce your game, you will need to work with manufacturers and shippers, who are always paid in advance. Crowdfunding companies can help with upfront costs, but come with their own set of problems, including taking a small percentage of your campaign total. Furthermore, all marketing, customer complaints, web design, barcoding, translating, packaging, and more, will have to be organised (or done) by you.

Established publishers have customer loyalty, credibility, and a large marketing budget. A self-publisher, however, often lacks all three of these attributes, making it difficult to establish themselves in the market. Furthermore, the legalities and logistics associated with importing stock from overseas can be off-putting. You can use local manufacturing companies to create your games, but they will often cost significantly more than some overseas options. In the next sections of this chapter, we will examine the hurdles that a designer must overcome in self-publishing their own game.

ASSESS THE COMPETITION ON KICKSTARTER

In the last decade, crowdfunding has become a popular form of fundraising that helped thousands of early stage entrepreneurs and ordinary people to realise their business idea (Mollick, 2014), and when you are self-publishing, you will no doubt become one of those entrepreneurs. Initially at least, it would be advisable to conduct some market research on existing Kickstarter games and, in particular, analysing some of the better campaigns first. *Frosthaven* received a staggering $13 million dollars in donations, the highest financial contributions to a crowdfunded board game to date, from a goal of $500,000 and 83,193 backers.

Frosthaven's Kickstarter page is a great place to begin harvesting information as to why this game fared so well, notwithstanding the main reason being the success of its predecessor, *Gloomhaven*. *Frosthaven's* Kickstarter page does a remarkable job at telling their story and selling the game, and while it can be daunting for a first-time designer to compete in this same arena, it can also inspire you and provide a direction of travel. Let us examine the key features:

- **Key Video Presentation**: A brief, captivating animation under 2 minutes, serving as the focal point, introducing the game, characters, storyline, and core concept.
- **Narrative Visuals**: A collection of image-rich pages that delve into the game's narrative, highlighting new characters to engage and inform their audience.
- **Pledge Breakdown**: A visually appealing counterpart to the adjacent column, illustrating precisely what backers will receive for their financial support.
- **Game Mechanics and Innovations**: A section outlining the rules and innovative concepts, and introducing novel elements like buildings, seasons, and puzzles.
- **Tabletop Simulator Experience**: Access the game virtually on Tabletop Simulator for a trial run before making a purchase.
- **Daily Enigmas**: Puzzles updated regularly to entice continuing engagement.
- **Preview Clips**: Professionally crafted videos designed to best showcase the game.
- **Designer's Live Q&A**: Forge a personal connection through a live session where the designer addresses queries, recognizing the human aspect of purchasing.
- **Professional Video Critiques**: Gain insights into expert reviewers' opinions.
- **Gloomhaven Affirmations**: Explore additional offerings by featuring reviews for Gloomhaven, potentially inspiring interest in other products.
- **Interactive Walkthroughs**: Gain an understanding of gameplay dynamics through playthrough demonstrations.
- **Shipment Insights**: Estimated delivery times for potential investors.
- **Developer Profile**: Informative content about the company leading the project.
- **Character Avatars**: Obtain free downloadable avatars featuring game characters.

- **Newsletter Subscription Link**: Stay updated with the latest product information by signing up for the newsletter.
- **Social Media Hub**: Access their various social media platforms, including popular ones, to stay connected and informed.

In reference to this last point, the makers of *Frosthaven* use Twitter, Facebook, Instagram, Reddit, BoardGameGeek, and their own website *Cephalofair*. I would recommend anyone serious about embarking upon a social media board game campaign to check out all these sites to better understand how they are used, and thus how they might work for you.

EDUCATIONAL COMPETITORS

No matter how unique your game, comparable products will exist. At the time of writing, there were 9,000 educational games listed on BoardGameGeek, though a lack of keywords may prevent you finding a definitive list of comparable products. Instead, further analysis of educational board games on Kickstarter will at least help you to understand more about how your competitors are marketing themselves. Figure 12.1 shows a selection of recent educational board game Kickstarter bids who asked for an average of $6,636 and received an average of $11,668 in return.

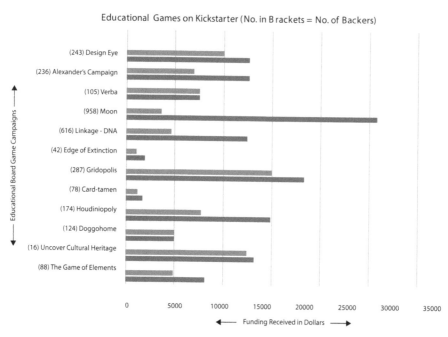

FIGURE 12.1 Recent educational games on Kickstarter with values adjusted for US dollars (Kickstarter, 2023).

In return for their investment, backers received copies of the game, bonus packs of cards or other stretch goals, but also many of the products featured discounted educational packs, print, and play versions, and lesson plans.

DOWNSIDES TO CROWDFUNDING

To those with a creative disposition, setting up a crowdfunding campaign can be a rewarding experience. However, there are potential downsides to crowdfunding:

1. **The costs of campaign development**

    Launching campaigns on Kickstarter can cost anything from nothing to more than £10,000. Like presidential campaigns, the more money that you spend, the more successful you are likely to be, and that is regardless of the marketability of the product. For example, an incredibly slick video that does not feature the game at all (they exist) can be enough to reach your campaign goals. However, there is no guarantee of success. A good Kickstarter campaign will have videos, great art, reviews from top reviewers (you will need to send them copies of the prototype and hope they will review it), a webpage, and a few months of social media advertisements to grow your following. Even if you do all of these, your campaign might not be successful.

2. **Not reaching your goal**

    Kickstarter uses an all-or-nothing funding model. If your project does not reach its goal, then funds do not get collected, and no money changes hands. Your funding period can be set to any time up to 60 days, though statistically, shorter projects tend to have the higher success rates. Your funding goal can be less than you need to fulfil your pledges, but it's recommended that you set it at the minimum amount you need to manufacture your products and fulfil your rewards. At this stage, you should have a reasonable idea of the costs, so write down every expense and total everything up. This will give an indication of what your goal should be. Goals for games on Kickstarter range from £50 through to hundreds of thousands of pounds.

3. **Fulfilling pledges**

    The first thing to remember that this is not free money, and unless you are offering incentives such as creating characters in a game for your backers (see Alex's story below), all this money will likely be spent on fulfilling pledges. You will need a resilient well-thought-out plan in place for how you are going to achieve this, before even embarking on any Kickstarter campaign.

4. **The lack of analytical data**

    Kickstarter differs from other websites and online retailers such as Amazon in that you will have no access to user demographics. On the face of it, this does not sound like a terrible thing, but by making it difficult to target specific market, there will be an impact on potential future sales. With educational games, the lack of statistical data can be even more problematic with regard to the potential for case studies, testimonials, and other feedback.

EDUCATIONAL BOARD GAME COMPANIES

Many start up their own companies, and success stories often follow a similar arc, where their hobbies become their full-time jobs:

- Educators who play board games adapted them for their classes.
- They then created their own educational board game.

- Next, they had some prototypes made, and pitched these to colleagues in other institutions.
- This was followed by setting up an e-commerce company and starting to sell their games online.
- Finally, they left their jobs, and now work full time designing, making, and selling games.

People who set up their own gaming companies arrive at that place for a myriad of reasons, but for oftentimes, this is the approach that companies specialising in serious games take. One such company is Genius Games, famous for science board games and card games such as *Cytosis*, *Virulence*, and *Ecosystem*, but also specialising in Maths and History games, with an educational target of primary through to tertiary level. Genius Games focus on the fun element when creating games, that is, they create games that can be enjoyed by regular gamers as well as students. The company sells direct from their website, but also through Amazon and Kickstarter. Genius Games' products are available at prices that are comparable to their regular game counterparts. For example, *Ecosystem,* a card game, retails at around £15. They also have a strong social network presence that keeps customers updated on new products.

ALEX'S STORY: A KICKSTARTER CASE STUDY

To finish off this section on crowdfunding we will shift focus and explore the trials and tribulations of going down this route, through the real-life experiences of Alex Dixon, and Jack Dixon, Kickstarter entrepreneurs.

"We are Jack and Alex Dixon, the writer and editor on Adventuring with Pride. When we were first starting out with Adventuring with Pride, we had no clue what we were doing! Jack had the idea to make a tabletop RPG book based around representation of LGBT+ characters, and I said that I would help him edit and put it together. Most importantly, neither of us had ever brought a product to market, let alone gone through the Kickstarter process!

Once Jack had written a first draft of one of the adventures, we showed it to some friends to get some feedback... and then more feedback... and finally we got to something that was ready to be shared publicly. We got some nice artworks commissioned and put together a Kickstarter page for the first book. Do put effort into that first impression; every penny spent on making your product more appealing and eye-catching is a pound that someone will be willing to spend on it. Something that you quickly learn about bringing a product to market is this: everything takes longer than you'd think. We went through the first approvals process, then another, and set up a separate bank account to keep the taxman happy, and so on. Eventually it was ready to go live, and we ran a quite successful campaign, going several times over our initial target amount.

The next thing to do was to finish writing up the book. As part of the campaign, we offered people the opportunity to include their own characters, which was a great way to get people to buy into the project (literally) but didn't make for an easy editing process! It took about 4 months to go from 'people have paid money for this' to 'we're now ready to share it with them'. That is a really strange period, where you feel the weight of their money and expectations, but don't feel pressured to rush a product out – it is worth taking the time to get it right and put your best foot forward. It's also worth soliciting as much feedback as possible during this time, either from backers or from other people, to make sure that any unexpected problems are ironed out before going to production.

After the creative phase was over, it's time to start getting the product made. How and where you go with production really depends on margins and your user base. Our business was books, which are a common thing to order from abroad. Even so, we found that it worked out best to have everything produced domestically. This meant we were able to avoid any hidden fees, conveyance charges, or import taxes, at the cost of paying a much higher unit price. It also meant our production loop was much shorter: we could get an updated proof copy in only a couple of days, and we could be assured of quality with local consumer protections. We also had no idea how long it would take to do the shipping itself! Not only do you have to coordinate everything, buy shipping labels, and sort out customs declarations, but it is even an effort to find good boxes that will get the products there in one piece! Shipping was all done from the UK, which did mean some unfortunate import fees for some backers, but this is now expected by most backers, and we did not receive any negative feedback about this. Overall, it took another three months from the start of production until the physical product arrived to backers, even with our short feedback loop.

Make sure to tailor your process to your market and to your product. Smaller markets will appreciate the personal touch and a high-quality product, and you can command a higher price; something with wider market appeal will have smaller margins, but you can afford to mass produce. Since the first Kickstarter, we have adjusted our processes to account for an increase in backing from the community, but we still follow the same broad strategy, and it continues to work for us. At time of writing, Adventuring with Pride has three entries in the series and has won multiple awards, so we must be doing something right!" (Dixon & Dixon, 2023)

PRINT AND PLAY

Using a publisher and self-publishing are the two main options available to you as a game designer, but there is a third option that has become more popular in recent years, especially if you are creating a card game, or a game that is rules-based such as a role-playing game. With print and play, you are effectively passing the responsibility of manufacturing on to the customer.

Using this method, it is best to assume that you will not necessarily make much of a profit on your game as the margins for print and play games are small, especially if you have many varied components to your design.

SUSTAINABILITY

A further consideration in the creation and delivery of games is in the environmental impact that your decisions will have on the planet. While plastic miniatures, for example, make your game look nicer, they will increase the costs, both financially and environmentally. Furthermore, it may increase your profit margin to manufacture and ship your games out of China, but local suppliers or even print and play options will have less of an environmental impact.

COSTS OF MAKING A BOARD GAME

Before you start looking at how much money you can make from producing a board game, you first need to understand what expenses you will need to lay out to create the game. If you are not in the business of providing an end-to-end solution for the production and delivery of your game, you will need to work out how that is going to be achieved. By this stage, you should have a prototype that has undergone significant playtesting and has subsequently been refined to a point where it's good to go. We will also assume that you have commissioned or created the necessary art for your game, and all the associated documentation such as rules, player sheets, and so forth have been created. You now have two options: sell your design to a production company, or produce it yourself. In this chapter, we will explore both options.

How Much Should I Sell My Game For?

The short answer: it depends.

Board games generally retail at between £20 and £50, whereas card games can be around half of that price. Business games however can cost much more. For example, Northgate Training Activities, a company that has built up a reputation for excellence, sells its games to the education and business industries for between £300 and £1,000, but let us assume that this is not the market that you are currently in.

If you are publishing the game yourself, you may choose to ship products from overseas. If you are trying to establish a foothold in the market, or you are fulfilling a small commitment on Kickstarter, small batch manufacturing may be a safe interim approach while you test the market reaction to your product, but with your production, shipping, and marketing costs, you can easily end up losing money on every sale if you don't price it correctly. A typical margin that you should be looking for is the total of your production and shipping costs, multiplied by five (called X5), where shipping means shipping to your warehouse, for example, an Amazon warehouse, or your garage for a smaller order, if you have the space. So, by that logic, your £40 prototype should retail at £200! You are not going to sell many at that price, so you are going to have to find someone who will make your product for up to one tenth of the price that your prototype cost you.

This is how game companies operate; their goal is to make enough money to produce new games, spend it on marketing campaigns, fund logistics planning, reprint the current game if it does well, etc.

The reason that games manufacturing companies calculate around X5 (or a similar model) is to offset other unfactored costs, rather than to make a huge profit. It's possible for some companies to fluctuate to X6 or X7. Some estimated costs that could wipe out any profit include:

GAME RETAIL PRICE	**£25.00**
Landed cost (cost of shipping the product to your warehouse)	£5.00
Logistics (warehousing shipping to customers)	£5.00
Marketing	£5.00
Development budget (future reprints/new titles)	£5.00
Payroll (employee salaries – including your own)	£5.00

It's possible to get a better deal when working in bulk. For example, the landed cost is improved if you order by the container rather than by the pallet. Small publishers (you) should keep these financial rules in mind if they produce a small number of games. Any game manufactured in quantities below 2,000 units will encounter challenges in generating sufficient profit to adhere to the X5 benchmark.

Finally, it is important to remember that your game should have a price that is comparable to other games in the same market. It is this market that will decide if the price you put for your game is worth it.

Social Media Leverage

According to Li et al. (2021), we have witnessed the development of intensified interactions between firms and their customers through social media usage over the last decade.

All the games that you play, and the companies that manufacture these games, will have some presence on social media. How are games companies using these social media sites, which sites do they use, and how many followers do they have? What is unique or compelling about their products, and how are they promoting and exploiting those features?

Using social media platforms like Facebook, Instagram, Twitter, and even BoardGameGeek, can be effective for promoting tabletop games. These platforms provide a way to reach a large audience and engage with potential customers who are interested in tabletop gaming. If this is your first game, then you will likely use a crowdfunding site. In this book, we talk specifically about Kickstarter, but there are other crowdfunding sites such as GameFound, Indiegogo, and Verkami as well.

At the time of writing, Facebook is currently the top social media platform by number of users, followed by Instagram and TikTok. When it comes to social media you need to go with the zeitgeist, to keep up with the quickly fluctuating changes. If everyone is using TikTok, for example, and its platform is analogous with your marketing campaign, then use TikTok.

CONFERENCES

Both established and first-time publishers can often be found at games conferences armed with copies of their new games. Conferences are not only good for selling and marketing your game, but also for the connections that you will make and the inspiration that you will find during your time there. The UK Games Expo at the NEC is the largest in the UK, but there are many others, such as Essen Spiel in Germany, and Gen Con is the USA. Furthermore, educational conferences may be a good place to market your educational game, or even better, a game-based learning conference. With these events, its always recommended that you research all your options beforehand, which includes, if possible, attending the conference as a member of the public before you decide.

GETTING YOUR GAME MADE

There are many manufacturers of games to choose from, including domestic options in many countries. When creating prototypes, we recommend using companies that turn around quality product in a relatively brief period of time. Short runs may also be manufactured by these companies, for example, to fulfil crowdfunding pledges, and there are economies of scale to be gained for larger batch sizes. However, as your numbers increase, as will the rationale for sourcing suppliers from overseas, which may offer cheaper production costs.

GETTING YOUR GAME MADE OVERSEAS

When bulk buying, shipping from overseas can dramatically reduce your overall costs and therefore the next several sections will provide some basic information, designed to act as a guide rather than a set of rules, about sourcing product overseas. Should you decide to go down this route then you will need to carry out much deeper research into the pros, cons, and legalities of doing this.

HOW DO I SOURCE A MANUFACTURER?

There are many countries that you can ship from, with the most popular being China, Germany, and countries in Eastern Europe. China is currently typically the cheapest, and has many options, but the delivery can take 30 days or more. The level of service varies; you could find a cheap manufacturer on made-in-china.com, or go with a more customer-focused company.

CONTAINERS OR PALLETS?

When you are shipping out of China, you will have some decisions to make, and these decisions could be more complex depending on which manufacturing company you choose to work with. Some companies will include all the shipping requirements as an option in their costing model, while others expect the customer to arrange this. Large retailers tend to use whole containers. The other options would be to buy space in a shared container, where you are paying by the pallet.

Air or Sea?

Though shipping by air is much faster (7 days, rather than 30 or more), you will be charged by weight, and the cost can come out up to five times higher.

Import Duty

Import duty rules will differ from country to country. In the UK, for example, you will be contacted by Royal Mail (or your courier) if you need to pay import duty on goods from China, and told how to pay. You will usually be given three weeks to pay any charges, before they return the parcel. You may be charged VAT or excise duty on it. You will also need to pay customs duty on goods from China if they are worth more than a certain value. Information on tariffs can be found on the government website (GOV.UK, 2023). When crowdfunding, it is important to be upfront about these charges, and who is responsible for paying them. You can arrange to pay these in advance, and incorporate the costs into the price you set, or you could make the backers aware that they will be responsible for these costs, and provide an estimate.

Current Problems with Shipping

At the time of writing, manufacturing in general has been experiencing problems with shipping products across the globe, in terms of rising costs and longer delays. Caused by factors such as COVID-19 – which has affected every industry globally (Xu et al., 2022), Brexit – which has negatively impacted upon shipping to the UK from Europe (Bailey & Rajic, 2022), and the war in Ukraine – and its impacts on global supply chains (Ngoc et al., 2022). Now, as you are reading this, all these issues may no longer be a problem, and the world may be a better place. Certainly, we can already see that the supply chains are already recovering from the impact of COVID-19. The important takeaway here is that when dealing with third parties, we are dealing with uncertainty, and this uncertainty is exacerbated the more remote those third parties become.

In an interview with *Time* magazine (McCluskey, 2020), Maggie Clayton, the director of sales and marketing for *Greater Than Games*, contextualises the issues that the industry is facing:

> We have had a container of our most popular game sitting in China since May of this year. We have taken pre-orders for it, so all that product is technically sold—except for the fact that we do not have the games or the money yet. So, we are in this weird situation where there's high demand for our products because of the increase in people playing games during the pandemic, but we just cannot get the product over here.

Maggie Clayton
Greater Than Games, Interview with Time Magazine (2020)

SALES OUTLETS

If you are self-publishing, then you will also be responsible for selling your game and delivering it too – depending upon which approach you take. In this section, we will look at some of the more popular options available to you to sell your game.

Through Your Crowdfunding Site

Assuming that your campaign is successful, you will already have a number of sales via your backer's pledges. Furthermore, you can add an "Order Here" button to your crowdfunding project page, which could link to options to buy the game such as Amazon, your website, or another retail outlet.

Your Own Website

Game makers might also use some resources to create their own e-commerce website. There are many ways you can do this, and services such as WordPress or Shopify streamline the process, while giving your game a direct channel to attract customers. This site can act as your hub, and include links to your social media sites, as well as online retail sites such as Amazon. Furthermore, your website can also provide customer engagement options such as newsletters and blogs which will help you to engage with visitors, and provide customer data to improve future advertising. The data analytics from the website will provide information of people who are visiting your site, and this, in turn, will enable you to target specific demographics, increasing opportunities for sales.

Online Marketplaces

It is estimated that by 2025, world online shopping in global e-commerce markets could exceed $7 trillion, accounting for almost one-quarter (23.6%) of all consumer spending on earth (Pool, 2023). Most of us in the UK are aware of marketplace websites such as Amazon and Etsy, but are there others we can use? Who are the other big players around the world? Which are the best places to sell our niche products?

Amazon is currently the biggest global online retailer. For that reason, the focus for the next section will be on Amazon, though other online marketplaces are also used by game publishers.

Amazon

Amazon is a popular means of selling board games, including educational board games. Furthermore, they will provide storage and other logistics, whether you decide to manufacture and ship in bulk from overseas, or in smaller quantities from a domestic seller. Amazon take away much of the pain of shipping product from abroad, but this does come at a cost. Expenditures such as warehousing, shipping, commission fees, and advertising can be expensive. Another option is Amazon Marketplace, where product is either fulfilled by the seller (you), or fulfilled by Amazon. In the first instance, goods are kept in your own inventory, and shipping and customer service are handled by yourself. Goods fulfilled by Amazon, however, are stored in Amazon's fulfilment centres, and shipping and customer service are handled by Amazon.

Amazon currently charges 15% commission on each sale made via its site along, with various shipping and warehousing fees. While this is not uncommon and financially manageable for most game makers, an area of greater concern is the advertising that is required to make your games more noticeable to customers. This is by no means compulsory, but without doing this, your game could become lost. The price of advertising alone could potentially overshadow the profits of your game, so make sure to do your research and figure out a firm financial budget before selling with Amazon. Additionally, search engine optimisation can help you to be found on any platform.

Another key component to remember when using Amazon is promoting product awareness. As mentioned earlier, by creating your own website and social media presence, you can reach a much larger audience and generate a buzz about your game. But Amazon, being the dominant online retailer, is where someone might go to purchase your game, as the transaction feels more secure and credible rather than buying on a low-ranking website. So, again, it is important to examine and estimate where your game may fall into the spectrum of the online marketing ecosystem and how you can take full advantage of all opportunities which could generate sales.

It should be noted that these methods of advertising are not unique to Amazon, and other online marketplaces also operate with similar advertising models.

BOARD GAME DISTRIBUTORS

Many self-publishers choose to reach out to private board game distributors that sell specifically to the gaming community, either online or through physical stores connected to the distributor. This can be a convenient way to gain access to skills, competencies, and experience that you don't have otherwise. Do note that distributers that sell educational games are rare and, of those, many only sell the games that they themselves have created. Agreements between a game developer and a distributor vary, so depending upon their distribution model, other costs, including warehousing and shipping, could be part of the distribution agreement.

The sales outlets discussed are just some of the more popular ones. It is recommended that you thoroughly research all available selling options so that your marketing budget can be utilised effectively.

SUMMARY

Taking your game to market can be a tricky, time-consuming, and ultimately financially unrewarding business. However, there are success stories out there, and success is not only measured in financial terms (though hopefully you at least break even). Broadly speaking, there are two paths to publishing your game: going through a publisher and self-publishing. Both approaches take time and effort, though self-publishing considerably more so. If you want to be a successful game designer, then you will need to weigh up the pros and cons and choose what works best for you.

EXERCISE

Have a look at the campaign pages of some tabletop games on Kickstarter.

Think about which ones you might consider backing.

Why would you back them? The obvious answer would be because you like the look of the game, but consider other incentives or elements that may influence your decision:

- Attractiveness of a particular pledge.
- Quality of the video/imagery.
- Awards and/or reviews.
- Quality of the overall page.
- The story behind the game.
- Anything else.

13 Evaluating and Writing about Your Serious Game

Dr Lauren Schrock

This chapter is dedicated to students, educators, developers, and hobbyists interested in designing research to evaluate a serious game and using academic writing to discuss a serious game with an academic audience. This is significant, as learning how to research and write academically may enable you to contribute to educational scholarship, reach new audiences, develop your reputation as an expert, and produce high-quality assignments.

DESIGNING RESEARCH TO EVALUATE YOUR SERIOUS GAME

Researching your serious game is a serious activity. In contrast to playtesting, in which you may have previously tested the playability of a game, such as the extent players are able to follow the rules and sequences to complete the game (see Chapter 11), excellently designed research to evaluate a serious game can transform education due to the collection of data about players' learning and engagement. To make this contribution, it is necessary to know how to create a research question, select a research method, and maintain research ethics to evaluate a serious game.

CREATING A RESEARCH QUESTION

Before you conduct your evaluation of a serious game, it is important for you to design a research question. To design a research question, you will need to identify what you want to find out during your evaluation of a serious game. For instance, you may want to research constructive alignment, which is the way intended learning outcomes of the game are achieved through playing the game (see Chapter 2). Or you may wish to investigate the quality of play, such as the level of enjoyment or player interaction that influences a person's engagement in learning. A useful research question will be specific (White, 2017); hence, it may contain reference to your serious game, the research participants, and the "serious" topic of the game. Note that a research question starts with a question word, such as the sample research questions that appear in Table 13.1. Therefore, devoting time and reflection to the design of a research question is beneficial to helping you set the direction of your evaluation.

DOI: 10.1201/9781003319511-13

TABLE 13.1

Example Research Questions about Serious Games

- What are the challenges to implementing a serious game in a university seminar?
- What are the benefits to playing an online serious game in a virtual learning environment?
- How can my serious game improve university students' understanding about sustainability?
- How can my serious game be used to assess university students' critical thinking?

SELECTING A RESEARCH METHOD

Once you have created your research question, you will need to select and justify an appropriate research method that will enable you to answer your research question. Research methods are typically classified as qualitative or quantitative depending on the type of data you aim to collect: *qualitative methods* seek to collect non-numerical data, whereas *quantitative methods* collect numerical data (Saunders et al., 2019). Within these categories, there are several methods for data collection you may select, such as a qualitative focus group or a quantitative survey. You can learn more about qualitative and quantitative methods for data collection by accessing textbooks and online resources that teach the design of research (Figure 13.1).

FIGURE 13.1   Thinking about research.

You may be wondering whether it is more appropriate to use a qualitative or quantitative method. It's important to note that there is not one best method for conducting an evaluation of a serious game. Rather, the decision to apply one method over another may be based on the answer you seek with your research question as well as practical considerations, such as the quantity and quality of participants, time, and resources available to conduct your research. You may also choose to combine or mix methods (Bryman, 2008). To help you decide on a research method, reflect on the questions in Table 13.2. Being able to answer these questions will help you to explain your research plan and justify why you have designed your research a certain way.

TABLE 13.2

Questions for Designing Your Method for Data Collection about Your Serious Game

Who: think about your participants

- Who are your potential participants? For instance, are they university students, teachers, developers, or experts?
- How many participants are needed to conduct your research?
- How many participants are available to participate?
- How will you contact your potential participants?
- How experienced are your participants, have they participated in research before?
- What existing knowledge are you expecting your participants to have? For instance, do participants require a certain level of knowledge about a subject in order to play the game and understand data collection questions?
- What experience are you expecting your participants to have prior to participating? For instance, are participants are expected to be new to board games or professional gamers?

What: think about the data you want to collect

- What do you want to know from a participant?
- How do you want a participant to communicate their response? For instance, do you prefer to analyse ratings, or verbal reflections?
- Why do you prefer to collect qualitative or quantitative data? How do you plan to analyse this data?
- How will collecting qualitative or quantitative data help you to avoid challenges when conducting your research?

Where: think about resources available to you

- Where can you conduct your data collection? For instance, can it occur virtually, in-person, or a hybrid of both?
- What tools/software do you have available to collect and analyse your data?
- What resources do participants have available to them to participate in data collection? For instance, can participants access a computer and stable internet connection if the data collection is to occur online?

When: think about planning and time management

- When will your participants be available to participate?
- How much time do participants have to participate?
- How much time do you have to collect your data?
- How much time do you have to analyse your data?
- Will you be able to collect data before, during, and/or after participants play the serious game?

TABLE 13.3
Example Research Evaluations of Serious Games

Scenario 1: Quantitative evaluation of students' memorisation of definitions of key concepts
Chen is an app designer who produced a game testing students' memorisation of different definitions for
key concepts. To evaluate whether the students' recollection of the definitions improved due to playing
the serious game, Chen created an individual survey for participants to complete before and after
playing. The same survey was distributed to individuals both pre- and post-game play, and contained
closed questions in which students were asked to identify the correct definition for each concept. The
survey used the same definitions and concepts presented in the serious game. By comparing individual
results of the survey, Chen was able to evaluate the constructive alignment of the serious game.

To evaluate the quality of playing the game, Chen introduced scaled questions in the post-game survey,
such as:

To what extent do you agree with the following statements?
I enjoyed playing this game.
Strongly Agree – Agree – Neither Agree or Disagree – Disagree – Strongly Disagree
I would recommend this game to a friend.
Strongly Agree – Agree – Neither Agree or Disagree – Disagree – Strongly Disagree

Scenario 2: Qualitative evaluation of students' application of accountancy calculations
Bo is a teacher who created a game that allows postgraduate students to calculate and balance several
fictional company accounts. To assess whether students improved their ability to use various
accountancy calculations after playing the game, Bo conducts several focus groups with students.
During a focus group, Bo asked the students about their learning and the quality of their gaming
experience by asking open questions, such as:

How would you describe your experience of playing this serious game?
How does your experience playing this serious game compare to the serious game you played last week
in class?

A key consideration to the design of your research is to identify what data you need
to collect to answer your research question. For instance, you may want to gather data
that can evidence whether the learning outcomes of the game and the quality of the
gaming experience have been met. To collect this data, you will need to design questions for data collection, such as those presented in the scenarios in Table 13.3. There
are several types of data collection questions you may choose to design: an *open question* allows a participant to freely give their response (such as an open text box) or a
closed question in which a participant selects from response options that are already
provided (such as a multiple-choice question) (Walliman, 2022). You may decide to
collect qualitative data through open questions, quantitative data with closed questions, or a mix of qualitative and quantitative data by using both open and closed questions. As you create your data collection questions, you will also want to consider how
many questions to create as this will influence the amount of time required by individuals to participate. This is important since asking too many questions can exhaust
your participants, thus undermining the quality of the data you wish to collect.

When designing questions for data collection, there are several problems to avoid
when asking about a serious game. For example, to ensure participants understand the
question and can answer accurately, you need to design each question so it focuses on

TABLE 13.4

Avoid Poorly Designed Questions When Collecting Data

Avoid questions that ask about more than one item

Poorly designed question: Do you agree that this serious game is fun and educational? Yes or No

When responding to this question, it is not clear if a participant may agree that the serious game is fun, yet not educational, or vice versa. Therefore, a way to resolve this and clarify the data you collect is to separate both items into unique data collection questions:

Do you agree that this serious game is fun? Yes or No

Do you agree that this serious game is educational? Yes or No

Avoid questions that use undefined acronyms or technical jargon

Poorly designed question 1: How has this serious game improved your understanding of RMs?

Poorly designed question 2: How does this serious game develop your academic integrity?

In the first question, it is not clear what "RMs" stands for, therefore making it difficult for a participant to respond appropriately. In the second question, a participant may lack knowledge about what "academic integrity" means, though they may understand "referencing of sources". Therefore, it is important to be aware of the experiences, background knowledge, and language of your participants to design questions that they can answer. Hence, to help a participant understand the question so they can respond authentically, ensure acronyms and jargon are clarified:

Improved question 1. How has this serious game improved your understanding of Research Methods?

Improved question 2. How does this serious game develop your referencing of sources?

Avoid closed question responses that do not account for all potential answers

Poorly designed question responses: How many hours did it take for you to finish playing this game?

Less than one hour – One to two hours – Two to three hours

A participant may be unable to answer this question correctly if they took more than three hours to complete the game as this option does not exist. Hence when designing questions it is equally important to consider the response options available to participants when answering as poorly designed options can impact the quality of data you collect. For example, a participant who took more than three hours to complete the game may select "Two to three hours" when this is inaccurate; this can negatively influence the quality of your research findings.

one unique item, avoids undefined acronyms and technical jargon, and includes all possible responses (Bryman, 2016). View the poorly designed questions for data collection in Table 13.4, then reflect on how you can create data collection questions that help you achieve a rigorous evaluation of a serious game by avoiding these problems. A good way to check the quality of your questions and response options prior to data collection is to test the questions and response options with a friend, classmate, teacher, colleague, or expert to see if they can understand and answer the questions without guidance from you. This feedback is helpful for improving your data collection questions. Taking the time to design and test your data collection questions can help you to avoid collecting poor data that can undermine the evaluation.

Once you have collected your data, you will need to analyse it. To analyse qualitative or quantitative data, you will need to employ an analysis technique, such as thematic analysis or descriptive statistics. As data analysis is too extensive a topic to cover in this chapter, you can learn more about analysing data by consulting a textbook or resource on research methods, and reviewing examples of research in conference papers and academic articles.

Maintaining Research Ethics

Encompassing your research evaluation of a serious game is research ethics. Research ethics are guiding principles that ensure the safety, integrity, and confidentiality of participants involved in data collection, and yourself (Resnik, 2018). Due to the importance of research ethics to protect those involved in the research, whether this be participants, yourself, other researchers, or the organisations involved in the research, it is necessary to consider research ethics at three stages of your evaluation: before, during, and after.

Before you start data collection, you will need to plan how you will avoid ethical risk. For example, you will need to create a template for a participant consent form that details to participants what their participation in the study involves, how their data will be used and stored, and how you will protect their anonymity and confidentiality (Figure 13.2). Due to the importance of research ethics and avoiding harm and risk to humans, you will likely need to obtain ethical approval to conduct your research before you can evaluate the serious game. This ethical approval may be granted from an institutional review board, an independent ethics committee, or a university's ethics committee. To ensure that you are receiving the necessary ethical approval, it is important to seek guidance from a classmate, colleague, or expert. If you are conducting your evaluation as an independent researcher that is not affiliated with an academic institution, then you may contact a nearby university for advice on obtaining ethical approval.

FIGURE 13.2   Approved research ethics.

During your data collection, you need to prioritise research ethics in your conduct and oversight of the evaluation. For instance, you will need to protect participants from risks of harm, such as avoiding physical danger, mental distress, or damage to a participant's well-being. This may be a concern in serious games involving group competition, such as in the example provided in Table 13.5. To help you prepare for

---

TABLE 13.5

Examples of Research Ethics When Evaluating a Serious Game

Informing participants about the research before data collection

Angel created a consent form for the research outlining what participation in the research involves, how the data collected will be used, and how to contact the researcher after the study has been completed should a participant like their data removed. Before the focus group commences, Angel asks each participant to read and sign the consent form. One of the participants says that they find it difficult to understand the consent form, so they are not sure if they feel comfortable participating. What would you advise Angel to do?

Why is this example significant? Researchers need to ensure participants are informed of the research prior to participating, which means participants must be able to understand what participation involves. Furthermore, participant consent must be voluntary. This means participants must not feel forced or coerced into consenting and participating in the study.

Protecting participants from harm during data collection

Yuval is observing a group of players whose comments towards each other become increasingly inflammatory as the game becomes more competitive. Yuval is concerned that the comments will escalate, causing harm to participants' well-being. Yet Yuval is not sure whether to intervene or allow the participants to keep playing. What would you advise Yuval to do?

Why is this example significant? Researchers have a commitment to protecting the safety of all participants, including the prevention of risk or harm to their mental and physical health and well-being.

Protecting participants' confidentiality after data collection

Chidi has conducted a focus group with participants after observing their play of the serious game. To illustrate the game's rules and sequences, Chidi would like to include photos of the participants as they played the game during the research study. The photos include the face of each participant. What would you advise Chidi to do?

Why is this example significant? Researchers need to protect the confidentiality of their participants, which includes avoiding disclosure of a participant's identity.

Protecting loss of data after data collection

Micah has downloaded the results of their survey and saved it to an external USB. In a hurry to leave, Micah accidentally leaves their USB on a shared table. Upon realising the USB is missing, Micah returns and is unable to find the USB. What would you advise Micah to do?

Why is this example significant? Researchers need to secure their data after collection to prevent loss or theft that can compromise participant confidentiality when that data is accessed by unintended individuals or groups.

Protecting research integrity

Madhur previously conducted an evaluation of their serious game without ethical approval from their institution. Now Madhur wishes to publish an academic article using this data, though they are concerned about the lack of ethical approval prior to the data collection. What would you advise Madhur to do?

Why is this example significant? Researchers must adhere to the guidance and policies of their institution when considering the publication of data. It may not be possible for Madhur to use the data they previously collected if the appropriate approvals and participant consent was not obtained.

---

potential risks when conducting research, it is important to imagine possible situations that may arise and plan for how you will resolve these. For example, consider how you will respond to a situation in which a participant says that they do not feel the need to sign a consent form.

After data collection, you must consider how you will protect participant confidentiality and prevent your data from being stolen, lost, or compromised. You can protect participant information by anonymising your data to ensure that it cannot be traced back to identify an individual, group, and/or organisation. In addition to protecting participants, you also need to consider what tools/software you will use to store your data. For instance, you may use a secure email or cloud storage. You may be subject to organisational guidance and national regulations that stipulate how data must be stored, so it is beneficial to seek further information to ensure that you adhere to data storage policies.

Overall, when conducting research to evaluate your serious game, you need to:

- Set the direction of your evaluation through the design of a research question.
- Select an appropriate method for data collection.
- Create data collection questions that focus on one item, avoid acronyms and/or technical jargon, and include all possible responses.
- Follow research ethics throughout the evaluation, including before, during, and after data collection.

USING ACADEMIC WRITING TO DISCUSS YOUR SERIOUS GAME

After completing your research to evaluate your serious game, you may be interested in discussing this research with an academic audience through a conference paper or a journal article. Or you may be a student tasked with writing an assignment on a serious game for your degree. Hence, learning academic writing is beneficial so you can disseminate your research to academic audiences to build your reputation as a respected expert in serious games, as well as produce high-quality pieces of work for submission at a university.

UNDERSTANDING ACADEMIC WRITING

Academic writing is a specific form of communication that values argumentation, evidence, and objectivity (Coleman, 2020). *Argumentation* refers to the creation of a critical point, which is supported by *evidence* such as literature and data, and communicated *objectively* by focusing on the facts. These aspects of academic writing are exemplified in Table 13.6. Note that the techniques of academic writing are distinct from "storytelling" when you present your serious game to a market (see Chapter 12). This is significant as a different communication style is needed for each unique audience.

TABLE 13.6

Examples of Academic Writing about a Serious Game

Argumentation: what you want to say

Identify the point you want to make:

Point 1. There are few serious games on this subject.

Point 2. One of the challenges to creating a serious game is constructive alignment.

Evidence: how you know about what you say

Show support for your point:

Evidence 1. There are few serious games on this subject, such as Game A and Game B. This support uses examples of two games to illustrate how there are few games on this subject.

Evidence 2. One of the challenges to creating a serious game is constructive alignment (Author, Year). This support uses a citation to reference a similar point made by another author. In addition to acting as evidence, citations are also important to maintaining academic integrity.

Objectivity: how you say what you want to say

Focus on the facts by avoiding exaggerations, undefined acronyms, and wordiness:

*Poorly Written Point 1A. There are **extremely** few serious games on this subject.* It is not appropriate to exaggerate when writing academically, so avoid words like "extremely" as it is not necessary to include, since "few" gets the point across that there are not many serious games on this subject.

*Poorly Written Point 1B. There are few **SGs** on this subject.* It is not appropriate to include acronyms without identifying to the reader what they mean the first time the acronym is used. Therefore, ensure acronyms are clarified, such as writing "serious games (SGs)".

*Poorly Written Point 1C. There are **not very many** serious games on this subject.* It is important to write concisely when writing academically as you may be limited in the available word count. Therefore, it is important to write concisely by using as few words as possible to convey the same meaning, such as "not very many" can be replaced with "few".

SEARCHING FOR SOURCES

As you construct an academically written piece, you will need to weave together different evidence. To locate sources of information that can be cited as evidence, such as academic articles or books, it is important to develop a comprehensive search strategy. Table 13.7 provides you with guiding questions to help you search for literature on serious games, and these questions can be adapted to suit your academic writing needs. Planning how you will search for sources will help you to use your time efficiently and effectively when gathering evidence in support of your argument.

TABLE 13.7

Searching for Sources on Serious Games

What academic sources can you access? Consider your local and university libraries where there is likely to be a support librarian who can help you navigate their collection to find sources you need, such as books and academic articles.

What non-academic sources can you access? There are many sources of information that may not be found in a university library, which are nonetheless significant to understanding the current context. For instance, reports, news articles, and magazines can be relevant sources to evidence your argument. Yet be aware of bias, relevance, and reputation when assessing the credibility of non-academic sources to decide whether it can be included.

Can you use Google Scholar? Google Scholar is an online platform enabling you to search for books, articles, conference papers, and abstracts (Google, n.d.). However, a search on Google Scholar may produce an overwhelming number of results; therefore, it is important to search with intention as this will help you to manage your time.

What key words and filters can you apply to improve your search? Implement Boolean Search Terms to help you combine key words to improve your search results, such as:

- "Serious games" will search for sources that contain "serious games" within the text to avoid potentially irrelevant search results.
- "Board games" **AND** "Video games" will search specifically for sources that contain both types of games to narrow your search results.
- "Board games" **NOT** "Video games" will search for sources that contains "board games" and not "video games" to focus your search results.
- "Board games" **OR** "Video games" will search for sources that contain either "board games" or "video games" to increase the number of search results.

Before selecting your key words, it may be helpful to brainstorm a potential list of words that you can continuously remix and combine in various ways to expand the results you collect from your search.

Filter your search by selecting options such as year of publication, language, and type of source (such as peer-reviewed) to further narrow your results. This will help you to obtain sources that are relevant, timely, and of an academic nature, which is significant for justifying the credibility of sources.

Constructing a Paragraph

To construct a piece of academic writing, you will need to be able to produce a paragraph that builds on descriptive and critical analytical writing. *Descriptive writing* demonstrates your understanding of an idea, event, or source, whereas *critical analytical writing* may show your comparison and justification about the ideas, events, and/or sources (Cottrell, 2019). There is an example paragraph illustrating these types of writing in Figure 13.3. Notice that the paragraph includes sources. You will need to develop your paragraphs to include citations to relevant sources in support of your points. This is important as you are expected to create a strong argument when submitting an assignment, conference paper, or journal article.

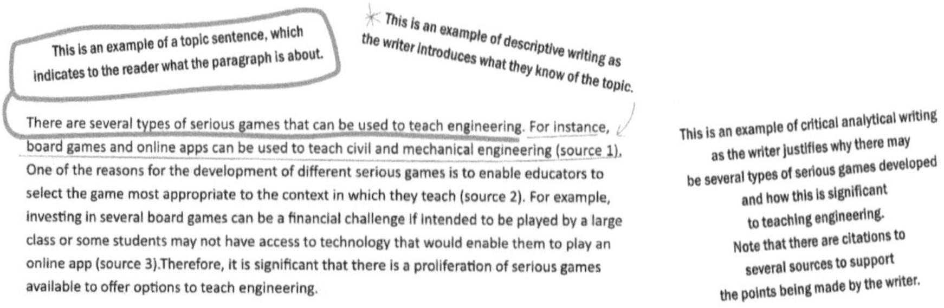

This is an example of a topic sentence, which indicates to the reader what the paragraph is about.

This is an example of descriptive writing as the writer introduces what they know of the topic.

There are several types of serious games that can be used to teach engineering. For instance, board games and online apps can be used to teach civil and mechanical engineering (source 1). One of the reasons for the development of different serious games is to enable educators to select the game most appropriate to the context in which they teach (source 2). For example, investing in several board games can be a financial challenge if intended to be played by a large class or some students may not have access to technology that would enable them to play an online app (source 3).Therefore, it is significant that there is a proliferation of serious games available to offer options to teach engineering.

This is an example of critical analytical writing as the writer justifies why there may be several types of serious games developed and how this is significant to teaching engineering. Note that there are citations to several sources to support the points being made by the writer.

FIGURE 13.3   Example paragraph of academic writing about a serious game.

In summary, when using academic writing to discuss your serious game, you must:

- Create an argument that is supported by evidence and communicated objectively.
- Develop a search strategy to locate sources of evidence.
- Apply descriptive and critical analytical writing to construct a paragraph.

SUMMARY

This chapter has provided you with guidance and examples for designing research to evaluate a serious game, and using academic writing to discuss your serious game with an academic audience. Developing your skills in research and writing will enable you to submit high-quality assignments on serious games at university and build your reputation as an expert in serious games by creating conference papers and journal articles. Research and academic writing are significant steps to sharing how a serious game can make an impact on the way we learn, assess, and teach.

14 Conclusion

Dr Devon Allcoat

CHAPTER REVIEW

Now that we are at the end of this book, let's take a look back at each of the chapters and summarise what they covered.

CHAPTER 1: INTRODUCTION

The opening chapter introduced the main concepts in this book, by exploring what a game is, and explaining the terms "serious games", "simulations", and "meaningful" (as used in the title of this book).

CHAPTER 2: SERIOUS GAMES

This chapter discussed the concept of serious games, which can be used for teaching and learning. It investigated the benefits of serious games, including learner engagement, immediate feedback, and social learning opportunities (both competitive and collaborative). Furthermore, to create an effective and engaging serious game, the principles of constructive alignment were explored, highlighting the value of aligning the serious game with learning outcomes and assessment.

CHAPTER 3: PSYCHOLOGY AND PEDAGOGY

Both psychology and pedagogy (i.e. teaching, education, and learning) were the focus of this chapter. It gave an introduction to a few key psychology theories to consider when thinking about game design, including Bartle's Player Taxonomy (also known as Bartle Player Types) and two motivation theories (self-determination theory and Dan Pink's motivation model). Applying these theories can help a designer to understand their target audience and what motivates them. The chapter also discussed learning theories that can be applied to serious game design. These educational theories help you to understand how people learn, and can be applied to the design of teaching materials, including serious games. Specific theories covered include active learning, social learning theory, constructivism, social constructivism, Kolb's experiential learning cycle, and Bloom's learning domains and taxonomy. These demonstrate the benefits of interactivity, social collaboration, and thoughtful reflection.

CHAPTER 4: DESIGN METHODOLOGY

The "design" in game design was the focus of this chapter, which introduced models and frameworks that assist the designer in creating a game. The conceptual framework for serious games assists the designer in understanding the relationship between the parts that form a serious game (including opportunities for learning, feedback, and reflection), and how they can be used as a framework on which to model your own serious games. The design thinking model is used to describe the interactive, non-linear approach to game design introducing practical examples to provide context and meaning to the key stages of Empathise, Design, Ideate, Prototype, and Test.

CHAPTER 5: ACCESSIBILITY

This chapter covered a wide variety of areas to consider when thinking about accessibility and inclusivity (including colour-blindness, visual accessibility, cognitive abilities, attention, intelligence, memory, emotional accessibility, dexterity and physical capabilities, communication, hearing, and language). Inclusivity, socioeconomic factors, and representation were also discussed. Designing a game that is perfectly accessible to every individual is very unlikely, but this chapter helps readers to design games to be as accessible as possible (within the constraints of the type of game you are creating and what resources are available). Each of the accessibility areas is explained in detail, with recommendations on how to meet a variety of needs and capabilities.

CHAPTER 6: GAME CATEGORIES AND MECHANICS

The key components, categories, and mechanics that define games and serious games were discussed in this chapter. Genres of games and their significance to serious game design were discussed, whereas mechanics were classified in this book by Space, Time, Objects, Actions, and Rules. Certain mechanics provide certain advantages when creating serious games, and the evolution of tabletop games has rendered certain mechanics redundant in the modern tabletop gaming arena. Finally, the individual merits of chance, skill, and game balance were also considered, together with the influence and impact that they bring to games.

CHAPTER 7: NARRATIVE

Narrative, and how it can be incorporated into games, was the focal point of this chapter. The concept of narrative was defined, including related concepts such as story, story arcs, player experience, and basic plots. In addition to tabletop games, both digital games and simulations were explored. Narrative is not a requirement for tabletop games, but they can benefit from both embedded narrative written by the creators and emergent narrative that comes from gameplay and interaction with other players. Narrative can reward the players, provide good pacing and engagement, and help to advance the game. Immersion is also discussed, including a new proposed theory of immersion. Ultimately, whilst narrative is not necessary, it can be a powerful tool, impacting immersion, enjoyment, and emotions.

CHAPTER 8: DECONSTRUCTING A GAME

Deconstruction of games is a common practice both in teaching game design and in the actual design of a game. This chapter reflected on the importance of deconstruction to make sense of a game, understand what makes it work, and how playing it may affect a player. Frameworks and models such as the MDA model can assist in game deconstruction by formalising and standardising the process. Finally, the chapter explored how a game review can also be interpreted as a game deconstruction, and how that review process may feed into our overall understanding of how and why games work or don't work.

CHAPTER 9: TECHNOLOGY

This chapter looked at how technology is used for tabletop gaming, including both digitalisation and hybridisation. Both benefits and challenges were explored, including benefits to both the creators/sellers and the consumers, such as logistics, sustainability, and cost. Challenges examined include software, hardware, and skills and competencies. Specific digital technologies were considered, both for the design process and as a part of the final product. Consumer-facing technologies such as companion apps, augmented reality (AR), and virtual reality (VR) were included, as were design technologies such as design software, 3D modelling and printing, and game engines. The chapter reminds the reader to consider the context and the target audience to better understand if going digital is appropriate.

CHAPTER 10: VISUAL DESIGN

The visual design chapter explained what visual design is, and looked at ways games can be designed to ensure that they accurately communicate key information to the viewer. Visuals are easier to process and understand and, when well-designed, have the potential to capture the attention and engagement of the player. This embeds knowledge for deeper learning retention and allows the transfer of knowledge to apply in new situations. The chapter discusses that it is particularly important for educational games to capture the attention of players (or learners), especially in a classroom environment where the participant has been directed to play the game rather than chose to play it themselves. Equally, to retain and embed knowledge, learners need to enjoy what they are engaging with and successful use of visual communication is probably one of the biggest hooks.

CHAPTER 11: PLAYTESTING

This chapter looked at different stages of game prototyping used to conduct playtesting. Game creation often involves multiple iterations of prototypes, using varying tools, techniques, and materials. Types of prototypes discussed include early pen-and-paper models, 3D printing, rapid prototyping, digital prototypes, and final manufacturing prototypes. How to complete playtesting was described, including how to ask the right questions to get relevant and useful feedback, rather than feedback that is generic, unhelpful, or not clear. The importance of playtesting is reinforced, as it can make the difference between success and failure.

Chapter 12: Taking Your Game to Market

The steps that a game designer may want to take once they have a working game were discussed in this chapter. After you have a working prototype of your game, the next steps to becoming a published game designer were explained, through to the delivery of the product to the customer. The two main approaches to having the game made are either working with a publisher or self-publishing. These topics were explored in some detail, including themes of crowdfunding campaigns with companies such as Kickstarter, marketing a game, and sourcing product in the UK and overseas. Sustainability was also considered.

Chapter 13: Evaluating and Writing about Your Serious Game

This chapter shared advice on how to evaluate and write about serious games, providing guidance and examples for designing research to evaluate a serious game, and using academic writing to discuss your serious game with an academic audience. The first part of the chapter explained how to design research, including developing research questions, choosing a research method, and adhering to research ethics. The second part of the chapter covered academic writing and searching for sources to help you produce a university assignment, conference paper, or journal article. Developing skills in research and writing will enable you to submit high-quality assignments on serious games, and build your reputation as an expert in serious games by creating conference papers and journal articles, enabling communication with an academic audience. Research and academic writing are significant steps to sharing how a serious game can make an impact on the way we learn, assess, and teach.

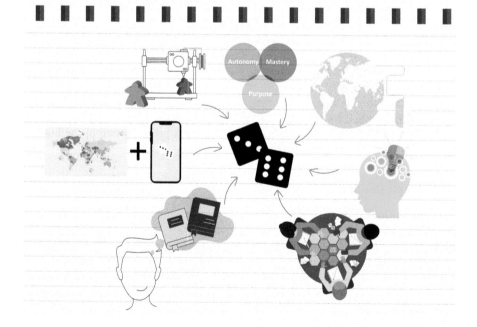

FIGURE 14.1   Bringing it all together.

MAKING MEANINGFUL GAMES

Hopefully, having reached the end of this book, you now understand the best methods, approaches, and techniques to successfully undertake meaningful game design. Whether you want to make a game that is purely for entertainment, a game that has deeper meaning and purpose, or a game that is primarily educational, the principles outlined in this book can be brought together to help you develop a successful game (Figure 14.1). We hope you go forth and create accessible, enjoyable, and well-designed meaningful games.

References

Aben, B., Stapert, S., & Blokland, A. (2012). About the distinction between working memory and short-term memory. *Frontiers in Psychology*, *3*. https://doi.org/10.3389/fpsyg.2012.00301

Abt, C. C. (1970). *Serious games*. University Press of America.

Ahmed, A., & Sutton, M. J. D. (2017). Gamification, serious games, simulations, and immersive learning environments in knowledge management initiatives. *World Journal of Science, Technology and Sustainable Development*, *14*(2/3). https://doi.org/10.1108/wjstsd-02-2017-0005

Aitchison, M., Benke, L., & Sweetser, P. (2021). *Learning to deceive in multi-agent hidden role games. Communications in computer and information science, CCIS (Vol. 1296)*. https://doi.org/10.1007/978-3-030-91779-1_5

Al-Elq, A. H. (2010). Simulation-based medical teaching and learning. *Journal of Family and Community Medicine*, *17*(1). https://doi.org/10.4103/1319-1683.68787

Althoen, S. C., King, L., & Schilling, K. (1993). How long is a game of snakes and ladders? *The Mathematical Gazette*, *77*(478). https://doi.org/10.2307/3619261

Anania, E. C., Keebler, J. R., Anglin, K. M., & Kring, J. P. (2016). Using the cooperative board game pandemic to study teamwork. *Proceedings of the Human Factors and Ergonomics Society*. https://doi.org/10.1177/1541931213601405

Anbarci, N., & Ismail, M. (2022). *AI-powered mechanisms as judges: Breaking ties in chess and beyond*. Cornell University

Anderson, L. W., Krathwohl, D. R., Airasian, P. W., Cruikshank, K. A., Mayer, R. E., Pintrich, P. R., Raths, J., & Wittrock, M. C. (2001). *A taxonomy for learning, teaching, and assessing: A revision of Bloom's taxonomy of educational objectives*. Pearson, Allyn & Bacon.

Ang, S. C. (2006). Rules, gameplay, and narratives in video games. *Simulation and Gaming*, *37*(3). https://doi.org/10.1177/1046878105285604

Anon. (2005). *Reading direction*. Oxford Reference. Retrieved March 8, 2023, from https://www.oxfordreference.com/display/10.1093/oi/authority.20110803100406828

Ansoms, A., & Geenen, S. (2012). Development monopoly: A simulation game on poverty and inequality. *Simulation and Gaming*. https://doi.org/10.1177/1046878112451877

Arthur, P., & Passini, R. (1992). *Wayfinding: People, signs, and architecture*. McGraw-Hill.

Atkinson, R. C., & Shiffrin, R. M. (1968). Human memory: A proposed system and its control processes. In K. W. Spence, & J. T. Spence (Eds.), *The psychology of learning and motivation* (Vol. 2, pp. 89–195). Academic Press.

Audet, D. (2012). Probabilities and expectations in the game of snakes and ladders for two players. *Département de Mathématiques, Collège de Bois-de-Boulogne*.

Avedon, E. M., & Sutton-Smith, B. (1971). Games as structure. In *The study of games* (pp. 401–426).

Azizan, M. T., Mellon, N., Ramli, R. M., & Yusup, S. (2018). Improving teamwork skills and enhancing deep learning via development of board game using cooperative learning method in reaction engineering course. *Education for Chemical Engineers*, *22*. https://doi.org/10.1016/j.ece.2017.10.002

Baddeley, A. D., & Hitch, G. (1974). Working memory. In G. H. Bower (Ed.), *The psychology of learning and motivation: Advances in research and theory* (Vol. 8, pp. 47–89). Academic Press.

Bailey, D., & Rajic, I. (2022). *Manufacturing after Brexit*. UK in a Changing Europe. Retrieved from https://ukandeu.ac.uk/research-papers/manufacturing-after-brexit/

Bakker, S., Vorstenbosch, D., van den Hoven, E., Hollemans, G., & Bergman, T. (2007). Weathergods: Tangible interaction in a digital tabletop game. TEI'07: First International Conference on Tangible and Embedded Interaction.

Baldassarre, C. (2015). 7 hobbies science says will make you smarter. *Entrepreneur*. Available at: https://www.entrepreneur.com/living/7-hobbies-science-says-will-make-you-smarter/306645 (Accessed: 13//03/23)

Bandura, A. (1977). Self-efficacy: Toward a unifying theory of behavioral change. *Psychological Review, 84*(2), 191–215.

Bartle, R. (1996). Hearts, clubs, diamonds and spades: Players who suit MUDs. *Journal of MUD Research, 1*, 19.

Bartolucci, M., Mattioli, F., & Batini, F. (2019). Do board games make people smarter? Two initial exploratory studies. *International Journal of Game-Based Learning, 9*(4). https://doi.org/10.4018/IJGBL.2019100101

Beasley, J. (2007). Games & puzzles publications. In *The classified encyclopedia of chess variants*. J. Beasley.

Becker, K. (2018). *What's the difference between serious games, educational games, and game-based learning? | The Becker Blog.* http://minkhollow.ca/beckerblog/2018/02/03/whats-the-difference-between-serious-games-educational-games-and-game-based-learning/comment-page-1/

Beckwith, R. T. (2019). New board game inspired by Lake Artemesia. Retrieved March 8, 2023, from https://www.hyattsvillewire.com/2019/04/02/wingspan-board-game-elizabeth-hargrave/

Beetham, H., & Sharpe, R. (2013). *Rethinking pedagogy for a digital age: Designing for 21st century learning*. https://doi.org/10.4324/9780203078952

Bell, C., Bach, B., & Krauer, T. (2021). Ways of seeing: peace process data-viz as research practice (June 07, 2021). *Convergence*, Forthcoming 2022, Available at SSRN: https://ssrn.com/abstract=3911096 or http://dx.doi.org/10.2139/ssrn.3911096

Berlinger, Y. (2021, June 14). *Monopoly versions*. https://jergames.blogspot.com/2006/02/monopoly-versions.html

Beymer, D., Orton, P. Z., & Russell, D. M. (2007). An eye tracking study of how pictures influence online reading. In *Lecture notes in computer science (including subseries lecture notes in artificial intelligence and lecture notes in bioinformatics)* (Vol. 4663, pp. 456–460). Springer Verlag. https://doi.org/10.1007/978-3-540-74800-7_41

Biggs, J., & Tang, C. (2011). *Teaching for quality learning at university* (5th ed.). McGraw-Hill Education (UK).

Biggs, J., & Tang, C. (2015). Constructive alignment: An outcomes-based approach to teaching anatomy. In *Teaching anatomy* (pp. 31–38). https://doi.org/10.1007/978-3-319-08930-0_4

Bloom, B. S., Engelhart, M. D., Furst, E. J., Hill, W. H., & Krathwohl, D. R. (1956). *Taxonomy of educational objectives, Handbook I: The cognitive domain*. David McKay Co. Inc.

BoardGameGeek. (2023a, March 11). *BoardgameGeek, subdomains*. https://boardgamegeek.com/advsearch/boardgame

BoardGameGeek. (2023b, March 5). *BoardgameGeek, mechanics*. https://boardgamegeek.com/browse/boardgamemechanic

Bonwell, C. C. (2000). *Active learning: Creating excitement in the classroom*. ASHE-ERIC higher education reports. ERIC Clearinghouse on Higher Education, The George Washington University, Washington, DC.

Booker, C. (2004). *The seven basic plots: Why we tell stories*. Continuum.

Brams, S. J., & Ismail, M. S. (2021). Fairer chess: A reversal of two opening moves in chess creates balance between White and Black. *IEEE Conference on Computational Intelligence and Games, CIG, August*. https://doi.org/10.1109/CoG52621.2021.9619066

Brandreth, G. (1985). *The monopoly omnibus* (1st ed.). Willow Books.

Bransford, J. D., Brown, A. L., & Cocking, R. R. (2000). How people learn: Brain, mind, experience, and school. In *Committee on learning research and educational practice.* https://doi.org/10.1016/0885-2014(91)90049-J

Branson, R. K., Rayner, G. T., Cox, L. J., Furman, J. P., King, F. J., & Hannum, W. H. (1975). Interservice procedures for instructional systems development. Executive summary and model. In TRADOC Pam 350-30, Ft. U.S. Army Training and Doctrine Command. (Vols. 1–5).

Brett, A., & Smith, M. (2003). Overview of the affective domain. *Educational Psychology Interactive*, 1–21. Retrieved from http://edpsycinteractive.org/brilstar/chapters/affectdev.pdf

Browne, C. (2005). *Connection games: Variations on a theme.* CRC Press.

Bruner, J. (2002). The uses of stories. In *Making stories: Law, literature, life* (pp. 3–35). Farrar, Straus and Giroux.

Bryman, A. (2008). Why do researchers integrate/combine/mesh/blend/mix/merge/fuse quantitative and qualitative research. In M. M. Bergman (Ed.), *Mixed methods research: Theories and applications.* SAGE.

Bryman, A. (2016). *Social research methods* (5th ed.). Oxford University Press.

Burgun, K. (2014, October 15). *Randomness and game design.* Retrieved February 11, 2023, from https://www.gamedeveloper.com/design/randomness-and-game-design

Burkey, D. D., & Young, M. F. (2017). Work-in-progress: A "cards against humanity'-style card game for increasing engineering students" awareness of ethical issues in the profession. *ASEE Annual Conference and Exposition, Conference Proceedings, June.*

Caillois, R. (1961). *Man, play and games* (M. Barash, Trans.). Free Press of Glencoe.

Camilleri, M. A., & Camilleri, A. C. (2017). The students' perceptions of digital game-based learning. *Proceedings of the 11th European Conference on Games Based Learning, ECGBL 2017.*

Camp, J. M., & Schnader, A. L. (2010). Using debate to enhance critical thinking in the accounting classroom: The Sarbanes-Oxley Act and U.S. tax policy. *Issues in Accounting Education*, 25(4), 655–675.

Cardinot, A., & Fairfield, J. A. (2019). Game-based learning to engage students with physics and astronomy using a board game. *International Journal of Game-Based Learning*, 9(1). https://doi.org/10.4018/IJGBL.2019010104

Cardona-Rivera, R. E., Zagal, J. P., & Debus, M. S. (2020). GFI: A formal approach to narrative design and game research. *Lecture notes in computer science (including subseries Lecture notes in artificial intelligence and Lecture notes in bioinformatics) (Vol. 12497).* https://doi.org/10.1007/978-3-030-62516-0_13

Carter, C. (2021, February 9). *Magic: The gathering and monopoly had their "biggest year ever" in 2020, Hasbro says.* Retrieved February 10, 2023, from https://www.dicebreaker.com/companies/hasbro/news/magic-the-gahtering-monopoly-record-sales-hasbro-earning-report

Cavicchini, S., & Mariani, I. (2019). Hybrid board game: Possibilities and implications from an interaction design perspective. CEUR Workshop Proceedings, 2480.

Centre for Education Statistics and Evaluation. (2017). Cognitive load theory: Research that teachers really need to understand. *Centre for Education Statistics and Evaluation.* Retrieved March 2, 2023, from https://education.nsw.gov.au/about-us/educational-data/cese/publications/literature-reviews/cognitive-load-theory

Chalk, G. (1987, May). Attack of the Ogroids. *Sinclair User.*

Champion, E. (2009). Roles and worlds in the hybrid RPG game of oblivion. *International Journal of Role-Playing*, 1(1), 37–52.

Chen, S., & Michael, D. (2005). *Serious games: Games that educate, train and inform.* Thompson Course Technology.

Clarke, S., Peel, D. J., Arnab, S., Morini, L., Keegan, H., & Wood, O. (2017). EscapED: A framework for creating educational escape rooms and interactive games to for higher/further education. *International Journal of Serious Games*, 4(3), 73–86. https://doi.org/10.17083/ijsg.v4i3.180

Coates, S. (2014). *White space: An overlooked element of design*. Mahurin Honors College Capstone Experience/Thesis Projects. Paper 442. https://digitalcommons.wku.edu/stu_hon_theses/442

Coleman, H. (2020). *Polish your academic writing*. SAGE.

Colour Blind Awareness. (2022). *About colour blindness*. Retrieved July 18, 2022, from https://www.colourblindawareness.org/colour-blindness/

Consalvo, M., & Paul, C. A. (2020). Introduction: Welcome to the discourse of the real: Constituting the boundaries of games and player. In *Real games*. https://doi.org/10.7551/mitpress/12109.003.0004

Constantinescu, C., Allcoat, D., Van de Mosselaer, N., & Weser, V. (2016). An interdisciplinary approach to studying presence and immersion. [Unpublished manuscript].

Costikyan G. (1994). I have no words & I must design. *Interactive Fantasy*, 2(1), 22–38.

Costikyan, G. (2000). Where stories end and games begin. *Game Developer*, 7, 44–53.

Costikyan, G. (2013). *Uncertainty in games*. MIT Press.

Cottrell, S. (2019) *The study skills handbook* (5th ed.). Red Globe Press.

Creighton, S., & Szymkowiak, A. (2014). The effects of cooperative and competitive games on classroom interaction frequencies. *Procedia - Social and Behavioral Sciences*, 140. https://doi.org/10.1016/j.sbspro.2014.04.402

Csikszentmihalyi, M. (1975). *Beyond boredom and anxiety: Experiencing flow in work and play, The Jossey-Bass behavioral science series*. https://doi.org/10.2307/2065805

Csikszentmihalyi, M. (1990). *Flow - The Psychology of Optimal Experience. 314*. https://doi.org/10.1017/CBO9781107415324.004

Davenport, G., & Mazalek, A. (2004). Dynamics of creativity and technological innovation. *Digital Creativity*, 15(1), 21–31.

de Soto, D. (2015). *Know your onions*. BIS Publishers.

Deci, E. L., & Ryan, R. M. (1985). *Intrinsic motivation and self-determination in human behavior*. Plenum Press. http://dx.doi.org/10.1007/978-1-4899-2271-7

deFreitas, S., & Maharg, P. (2011). *Digital games and learning*. Continuum International Publishing Group.

del Castillo, R. (2017). Gags and games: Wittgenstein and his relation to jokes. In *The philosophy of play as life*. https://doi.org/10.4324/9781315454139

DeLaurentis, D. A., & Crossley, W. A. (2005). A taxonomy-based perspective for systems of systems design methods, in: Conference Proceedings – IEEE International Conference on Systems, Man and Cybernetics. pp. 86–91. https://doi.org/10.1109/icsmc.2005.1571126

den Haan, R. J., & van der Voort, M. C. (2018). On evaluating social learning outcomes of serious games to collaboratively address sustainability problems: A literature review. *Sustainability*, 10(12). https://doi.org/10.3390/su10124529

Denisova, A., Guckelsberger, C., & Zendle, D. (2017). Challenge in digital games: Towards developing a measurement tool. *Conference on Human Factors in Computing Systems – Proceedings, Part F127655*. https://doi.org/10.1145/3027063.3053209

Dietrich, N. (2019). Chem and roll: A roll and write game to illustrate chemical engineering and the contact process. *Journal of Chemical Education*, 96(6). https://doi.org/10.1021/acs.jchemed.8b00742

Din, Z & Gibson, E. (2019). Serious games for learning prevention through design concepts: An experimental study. *Safety Science*, 115, 176–187. https://doi.org/10.1016/j.ssci.2019.02.005.

Dixon, A., & Dixon, J. (2023). *Adventuring with pride*. The Pocket Workshop.

Djaouti, D., Alvarez, J., & Jessel, J. (2009). Classifying serious games: The G/P/S model. *Serious Games Mechanisms and Effects*, *2005*, 10–24. https://doi.org/10.4018/978-1-60960-495-0.ch006

Dorst, K. (2011). The core of "design thinking" and its application. *Design Studies*, *32*(6). https://doi.org/10.1016/j.destud.2011.07.006

Doyle, R. (1979). Stop Thief! *Parker Brothers*.

Duarte, L. C. S. (2015). *Revisiting the MDA framework*. Retrieved February 18, 2023, from https://www.gamedeveloper.com/design/revisiting-the-mda-framework

Dunnigan, J. (2000). *The complete wargames handbook*. Retrieved from https://archive.org/details/CompleteWargamesHandbookDunnigan

Egenfeldt-Nielsen, S. (2011). What makes a good learning game? *ELearn*, *2011*(2). https://doi.org/10.1145/1943208.1943210

Eidle, K., Duncan, M. & Colquitt, J. (2022). *Themes in facilitator guides for medical education games*. Mercer University School of Medicine, Savannah.

Evans, F. (1998). Two legs, thing using and talking: The origins of the creative engineering mind. *AI & Society*, *12*(3), 185–213.

Fabricatore, C., Nussbaum, M., & Rosas, R. (2002). Playability in action videogames: A qualitative design model. *Human-Computer Interaction*, *17*(4). https://doi.org/10.1207/S15327051HCI1704_1

Fang, Y. M., Chen, K. M., & Huang, Y. J. (2016). Emotional reactions of different interface formats: Comparing digital and traditional board games. *Advances in Mechanical Engineering*, *8*(3), 1–8.

Fanguy, W. (2020). *What is colour theory? Meaning and fundamentals*. Retrieved March 27, 2023, from https://xd.adobe.com/ideas/process/ui-design/what-is-color-theory/

Fauziah, A., Apriliaswati, R., & Susilawati, E. (2018). The use of boggle game to improve students vocabulary in writing descriptive text. *Jurnal Pendidikan Dan Pembelajaran*. http://jurnal.untan.ac.id/index.php/jpdpb/article/download/23686/18594

Fernández-Vara, C. V. (2019). *Introduction to game analysis*. https://doi.org/10.4324/9781351140089

Ferreira de Almeida, J. L., & dos Santos Machado, L. (2021). Design requirements for educational serious games with focus on player enjoyment. *Entertainment Computing*, *38*. https://doi.org/10.1016/j.entcom.2021.100413

Fiore, S., Metcalf, D., & McDaniel, R. (2007). Theoretical foundations of experiential learning. In Melvin L. Silberman (Ed.), *The handbook of experiential learning*. John Wiley and Sons.

Frydrych, D., Bock, A. J., Kinder, T., & Koeck, B. (2014). Exploring entrepreneurial legitimacy in reward-based crowdfunding. *Venture Capital*, *16*(3), 3–16.

Gagné, R. M. (1972). Domains of learning. *Interchange*. https://doi.org/10.1007/BF02145939

Gardner, M. (1989). *Mathematical magic show: More puzzles, games, diversions, illusions and other mathematical sleight-of-hand*. Mathematical Association of America.

Gazdula, J., & Farr, R. (2020). Teaching risk and probability: Building the Monopoly® board game into a probability simulator. *Management Teaching Review*, *5*(2). https://doi.org/10.1177/2379298119845090

Gilbert, L., & Gale, V. (2007). *Principles of e-learning systems engineering*. https://doi.org/10.1533/9781780631196

Glass, M., & Spinello, J. (1965). *Operation*. Milton Bradley.

Gobet, F., & Campitelli, G. (2006). Educational benefits of chess instruction: A critical review. In Tim Redman (Ed.), *Chess and education: Selected essays from the Koltanowski conference* (Vol. 44, Issue 115). University of Texas.

Gómez-Maureira, M. A., van Duijn, M., & Rieffe, C. (2022). Mapping the use of video games in research contexts, in: FDG '22: Proceedings of the 17th International Conference on the Foundations of Digital Games, Vol. 4, pp. 1–10. https://doi.org/10.1145/3555858.3555926

Gonzalo-Iglesia, J. L., Lozano-Monterrubio, N., & Prades-Tena, J. (2018). Noneducational board games in university education. Perceptions of students experiencing game-based learning methodologies. *Revista Lusofona De Educacao, 41*(41). https://doi.org/10.24140/issn.1645-7250.rle41.03

Google. (n.d.) About Google Scholar. Retrieved March 27, 2023, from https://scholar.google.co.uk/intl/en/scholar/about.html

GOV.UK. (2023, March 20). *Tariffs on goods imported into the UK.* https://www.gov.uk/guidance/tariffs-on-goods-imported-into-the-uk

Griffin, R. A., & Jackson, N. R. (2011). Privilege monopoly: An opportunity to engage in diversity awareness. *Communication Teacher, 25*(1). https://doi.org/10.1080/17404622.2010.514273

Gruska, J. (2012, September 25). *The importance of going first in Monopoly.* Retrieved from https://monopolynerd.com/

Gruzdev, M. V., Kuznetsova, I. V., Tarkhanova, I. Y., & Kazakova, E. I. (2018). University graduates' soft skills: The employers' opinion. *European Journal of Contemporary Education, 7*(4). https://doi.org/10.13187/ejced.2018.4.690

Guckian, J., Eveson, L., & May, H. (2020). The great escape? The rise of the escape room in medical education. *Future Healthcare Journal, 7*(2). https://doi.org/10.7861/fhj.2020-0032

Günay, M. (2021). Design in visual communication. *Art and Design Review, 09*(02), 109–122. https://doi.org/10.4236/adr.2021.92010

Haggman, A. (2019). *Cyber wargaming: Finding, designing, and playing wargames for cyber security education.* Royal Holloway, University of London.

Halimah, N., & Basri, M. (2017). Fun vocabulary learning in EFL classroom through charades game: Why not? UAD TEFL International Conference, Vol. 1. https://doi.org/10.12928/utic.v1.192.2017

Harp, S. F., & Mayer, R. E. (1997). The role of interest in learning from scientific text and illustrations: On the distinction between emotional interest and cognitive interest. *Journal of Educational Psychology, 89*(1), 92–102. https://doi.org/10.1037/0022-0663.89.1.92

Hasbro. (2020). *Rules of Monopoly.* https://www.officialgamerules.org/monopoly

Hattie, J., & Timperley, H. (2007). The power of feedback. In *Review of educational research* (Vol. 77, Issue 1, pp. 81–112). https://doi.org/10.3102/003465430298487

Heikkilä, V. T., Paasivaara, M., & Lassenius, C. (2016). Teaching university students Kanban with a collaborative board game. *Proceedings – International Conference on Software Engineering.* https://doi.org/10.1145/2889160.2889201

Heinlein, R. A. (1947). Five ways to write speculative fiction. *Nota Do Tradutor, 1*(24), 126–131.

Henzinger, T. A., Horowitz, B., & Majumdar, R. (1999). Rectangular hybrid games. In *Lecture notes in computer science (including subseries Lecture notes in artificial intelligence and Lecture notes in bioinformatics), Proceedings of the 10th International Conference on Concurrency Theory. CONCUR: Concurrency Theory, LNCS,* Vol. 1664, pp. 320–335.

Heron, M. (2016). *Meeple like us – Review of "Under the Boardwalk."* https://Www.Meeplelikeus.Co.Uk/Documentary-under-the-Boardwalk/

Heron, M. (2019, June 19). *Meeple like us – Monopoly Review.* https://www.Meeplelikeus.Co.Uk/Monopoly-1933/

Heron, M. J., Belford, P. H., Reid, H., & Crabb, M. (2018). Meeple centred design: A heuristic toolkit for evaluating the accessibility of tabletop games. *The Computer Games Journal, 7*(2). https://doi.org/10.1007/s40869-018-0057-8

Herrera, F., & Bailenson, J. N. (2021). Virtual reality perspective-taking at scale: Effect of avatar representation, choice, and head movement on prosocial behaviors. *New Media & Society, 23*(8), 2189–2209. https://doi.org/10.1177/1461444821993121

Hershkovitz, S. (2019). Wargame business. *Naval War College Review, 53*(9).

Huizinga, J. (1938/1949). *Homo Ludens: A study of the play-element of culture.* Routledge & Kegan Paul, pp. 1–220 (originally published in Dutch in 1938).

Huizinga, J. (1950). *Homo Ludens: A study of play-element in culture.* Roy Publishers.

Hunicke, R., LeBlanc, M., & Zubek, R. (2004). MDA: A formal approach to game design and game research. Workshop on Challenges in Game AI, pp. 1–4. https://users. cs.northwestern.edu/~hunicke/MDA.pdf

Hunkin, T. (2008). *Technology is what makes us human.* Retrieved from https://www. timhunkin.com/a118_technology_is_human.htm

Illingworth, S., & Wake, P. (2019). Developing science tabletop games: Catan® and global warming. *Journal of Science Communication, 18*(4). https://doi.org/10.22323/2.18040204

Ishak, S. A., Din, R., Othman, N., Gabarre, S., & Hasran, U. A. (2022). Rethinking the ideology of using digital games to increase individual interest in STEM. *Sustainability, 14*(8), 4519. https://doi.org/10.3390/su14084519

Jakada, M. B. *et al.* (2021). When psychological ownership nurtures satisfaction: A tripartite attitude theory and psychological ownership theory perspective. *Rajagiri Management Journal, 16*(3), 193–212. https://doi.org/10.1108/ramj-01-2021-0010

Jennings, F. G. (1967). Jean Piaget: Notes on learning. *Saturday Review, 20*, 81–83.

Johnson, A. (2018, June 26). *13 facts about Monopoly that will surprise you.* Insider.

Johnson, D. W., & Johnson, R. T. (2019). Cooperative learning: The foundation for active learning. In *Active learning – Beyond the future.* https://doi.org/10.5772/intechopen.81086

Jovanovic, M., Starcevic, D., Stavljanin, V., & Minovic, M. (2008). Educational games design issues: Motivation and multimodal interaction. *Lecture notes in computer science (including subseries Lecture notes in artificial intelligence and Lecture notes in bioinformatics)* (Vol. 5288). https://doi.org/10.1007/978-3-540-87781-3_24

Juul, J. (2002). The open and the closed: Game of emergence and games of progression, in: Proceedings of the Computer Game and Digital Cultures.

Juul, J. (2005). Half-real: Introduction. In *Half-Real: Video Games between Real Rules and Fictional Worlds.* https://doi.org/10.1111/j.1399-0012.2012.01647.x

Kalmpourtzis, G. (2018). *Educational game design fundamentals. Educational game design fundamentals.* A K Peters/CRC Press. https://doi.org/10.1201/9781315208794

Kankainen, V. (2020). *Towards a hybrid media ecosystem of tabletop gaming.* DiGRA 2020: The 13th Digital Games Research Association Conference: Play Everywhere, Tampere, Finland.

Kankainen, V., Arjoranta, J., & Nummenmaa, T. (2017). Games as blends: Understanding hybrid games. *Journal of Virtual Reality and Broadcasting, 14*(4). https://doi. org/10.20385/1860-2037/14.2017.4

Kankainen, V., & Paavilainen, J. (2019). Hybrid board game design guidelines. *DiGRA International Conference: Game, Play and the Emerging Ludo-Mix,* Kyoto, Japan.

Kaulfield, J. (2011). Randomness, player choice, and player experience. In *Tabletop: Analog game design,* pp. 24–29. Lulu.com

Keller, J. M. (1987). Development and use of the ARCS model of motivational design. *Journal of Instructional Development, 10*(1932), 2–10. https://doi.org/10.1002/pfi.4160260802

Kelley, D. (1988). *The art of reasoning.* W. W. Norton & Company.

Kickstarter (2023) Available at: https://www.kickstarter.com/discover/advanced?term= educational+BOARD+GAMES&category_id=34&sort=magic&seed=2815407&p age=1 (Accessed 12/03/2023)

Klabbers, J. H. G. (2008). *The Magic Circle: Principles of Gaming & Simulation.* Rotterdam: Sense Publishers.

Kobzeva, N. (2015). Scrabble as a tool for engineering Students' critical thinking skills development. *Procedia - Social and Behavioral Sciences, 182*. https://doi.org/10.1016/j. sbspro.2015.04.791

Kolb, D. (1984). Experiential learning: Experience as the source of learning and development. In *Strategic learning in a knowledge economy*. Prentice Hall. https://doi.org/10.1016/B978-0-7506-7223-8.50017-4

Konieczny, P. (2019). Golden age of tabletop gaming: Creation of the social capital and rise of third spaces for tabletop gaming in the 21st century. *Polish Sociological Review, 206*(2), 199–216.

Kosa, M., & Spronck, P. (2018). What tabletop players think about augmented tabletop games: A content analysis. ACM International Conference Proceeding Series.

Kosinski, J. (Director). (2010) *Tron Legacy* [Film]. Walt Disney Pictures; Sean Bailey Productions

Kramer, W. (2015). What makes a game good? *Game & Puzzle Design, 1*(2), 84–86.

Krathwohl, D. R. (2002). A revision of Bloom's taxonomy: An overview. Theory into Practice. https://doi.org/10.1207/s15430421tip4104_2

Kurt Vonnegut Shape of Stories. (2018). *YouTube.* Retrieved January 30, 2023, from https://www.youtube.com/watch?v=GOGru_4z1Vc&t=157s&ab_channel=EvaCollinsAlonso

Laamarti, F., Eid, M., & El Saddik, A. (2014). An overview of serious games. *International Journal of Computer Games Technology, 2014.* https://doi.org/10.1155/2014/358152

Lai, B., Zhang, H., Liu, M., & Pariani, A. (2022). *Werewolf among us: A multimodal dataset for modeling persuasion behaviors in social deduction games.* arXiv preprint arXiv:2212.08279

Lanicek, J., Pierce, A., Raffaele, D., Rathbone, K., & Westermann, E. (2020). Unusual approaches to teaching the Holocaust. *The Australian Journal of Jewish Studies, 33*, 85–89.

Larkey, P., Kadane, J. B., Austin, R., & Zamir, S. (1997). Skill in games. *Management Science, 43*(5). https://doi.org/10.1287/mnsc.43.5.596

Lazarus, R. (2021, November 4). *Astigmatism: Top 9 FAQs.* Optometrists.org. https://www.optometrists.org/general-practice-optometry/guide-to-eye-health/how-does-the-eye-work/astigmatism-top-9-faqs/

Lazarus, R. S., Deese, J., & Osler, S. F. (1952). The effects of psychological stress upon performance. *Psychological Bulletin, 49*(4), 293–317. https://doi.org/10.1037/h0061145

Lean, J., Moizer, J., Towler, M., & Abbey, C. (2006). Simulations and games: Use and barriers in higher education. *Active Learning in Higher Education, 7*(3), 227–242. https://doi.org/10.1177/1469787406069056

LeBlanc, M. (2000). Formal design tools: Emergent complexity, emergent narrative. *Game Developers Conference.*

LeBlanc, M. (2004). *Mechanics, dynamics, aesthetics: A formal approach to game design.* Lecture at Northwestern University.

LeBlanc, V. R. (2009). The effects of acute stress on performance: Implications for health professions education. *Academic Medicine, 84* (10), 25–33. https://doi.org/10.1097/acm.0b013e3181b37b8f

Leddy, C. (2014, March 25). *Facebook fans to determine world's favorite 'House Rules' to be included in future Monopoly games.* Retrieved from https://newsroom.hasbro.com/news-releases/news-release-details/facebook-fans-determine-worlds-favorite-house-rules-be-included

Lee, A. D., Green, B. N., Johnson, C. D., & Nyquist, J. (2010). How to write a scholarly book review for publication in a peer-reviewed journal: A review of the literature. *Journal of Chiropractic Education, 24*(1). https://doi.org/10.7899/1042-5055-24.1.57

Li, F., Larimo, J., & Leonidou, L. C. (2021). Social media marketing strategy: Definition, conceptualization, taxonomy, validation, and future agenda. *Journal of the Academy of Marketing Science, 49*(1), 51–70.

Lin, D., Bezemer, C. P., Zou, Y., & Hassan, A. E. (2019). An empirical study of game reviews on the Steam platform. *Empirical Software Engineering, 24*(1). https://doi.org/10.1007/s10664-018-9627-4

Lipovsky, M. E., & Brennan, B. A. (2022). *Does playing math games improve students' attitudes towards mathematics?* International Graduate Program for Educators Master's Projects. 11.

Lombardi, B. M. M., & Oblinger, D. G. (2007). Authentic learning for the 21st century : An overview. *Learning, 1,* 2.

Lopes, R. P. (2014). Cabinet - strategy board game for network and system management learning. XIII Simpósio Brasileiro de Jogos e Entretenimento Digital.

Lopez-Pernas, S., Gordillo, A., Barra, E., & Quemada, J. (2019). Examining the use of an educational escape room for teaching programming in a higher education setting. *IEEE Access, 7,* 31723–31737. https://doi.org/10.1109/ACCESS.2019.2902976

Lundgren, S., & Björk, S. (2003). Game mechanics: Describing computer-augmented games in terms of interaction. *Proceedings of Technologies for Interactive Digital Storytelling and Entertainment (TIDSE 2003).*

Luton, W., & Freeman, W. (2021). *Guide: How to deconstruct games better.* Retrieved February 12, 2023, from https://departmentofplay.net/guide-how-to-deconstruct/#:~:text=8%20tips%20for%20effective%20game%20deconstructions%201%20start,failures%20...%208%20deconstruct%20your%20own%20games%20

Makransky, G., Petersen, G. B., & Klingenberg, S. (2020). Can an immersive virtual reality simulation increase students' interest and career aspirations in science? *British Journal of Educational Technology, 51*(6). https://doi.org/10.1111/bjet.12954

Mayer, R. E. (1999). Multimedia aids to problem-solving transfer. *International Journal of Educational Research, 31,* 611–623. https://doi.org/10.1016/S0883-0355(99)00027-0

Mayer, R. E., Bove, W., Bryman, A., Mars, R., & Tapangco, L. (1996). When less is more: Meaningful learning from visual and verbal summaries of science textbook lessons. *Journal of Educational Psychology, 88*(1), 64–73. https://doi.org/10.1037/0022-0663.88.1.64

Mayer, R. E. & Moreno, R. (2003). Nine ways to reduce cognitive load in multimedia learning. *Educational Psychologist.* Retrieved July 10, 2023. Available at: https://www.tandfonline.com/doi/abs/10.1207/S15326985EP3801_6

McCluskey, M. (2020, September 28). The board game business is booming, but the global shipping crisis could be disastrous. *Time.*

McKee, R. (1997). *Story: Substance, structure, style and the principles of screenwriting.* ReganBooks.

McKenzie, R. B., & Lee, D. R. (2019). *In Defense of monopoly: How market power fosters creative production.* University of Michigan Press. https://doi.org/10.5860/choice.46-1012

McLain, M., Irving-Bell, D., Wooff, D., & Morrison-Love, D. (2019). How technology makes us human: Cultural historical roots for design and technology education. *Curriculum Journal, 30*(4), 464–483.

Meeple Like Us. (n.d.) *Meeple Like Us.* Retrieved October 21, 2022, from https://www.meeplelikeus.co.uk/

Merrill, M. D. (2002). First principles of instruction. *Educational Technology Research and Development, 50,* 43–59.

Mewborne, M., & Mitchell, J. T. (2019). Carcassonne: Using a tabletop game to teach geographic concepts. *Geography Teacher, 16*(2). https://doi.org/10.1080/19338341.2019.1579108

Michaelsen, P. (2015). Haretavl – Hare and Hounds as a board game. In *Sport und Spiel bei den Germanen.* https://doi.org/10.1515/9783110338294.197

Minbaeva, D., & Collings, D. G. (2013). Seven myths of global talent management. *International Journal of Human Resource Management, 24*(9). https://doi.org/10.1080/09585192.2013.777539

Mitic, K. (2011, February 16). *MONOPOLY millionaires enables players around the world to "Pass Go" and play with hundreds to thousands of their friends.* https://www.ea.com/en-gb/news/monopoly-millionaires-free-facebook

Mollick, E. (2014). The dynamics of crowdfunding: An exploratory study. *Journal of Business Venturing, 29*(1), 1–16.

Mukamal, R. (2017). *How humans see in color.* Retrieved from https://www.aao.org/eye-health/tips-prevention/how-humans-see-in-color

Munsell, A. (n.d.). *Sir Isaac's influence on the colour wheel.* Retrieved March 29, 2023, from https://munsell.com/color-blog/sir-isaac-newton-color-wheel/

Murtazoyev, F. (2009). *Over 130 people to take part in the "SCO Model-2039" Business Game.* Retrieved January 12, 2023, from https://www.asiaplustj.info/en/news/31/20090512/over-130-people-take-part-sco-model-2039-business-game

Nagal, L. (2021). *Analysis of 'The settlers of Catan' using Markov chains.* Texas Christian University.

Nakao, M. (2019). Special series on "effects of board games on health education and promotion" board games as a promising tool for health promotion: A review of recent literature. *BioPsychoSocial Medicine, 13*(1). https://doi.org/10.1186/s13030-019-0146-3

Newmann, F. (1992). *Student engagement and achievement in American secondary schools* (pp. 2–3). Teachers College Press.

Next Generation. (1997, July). What makes a good game? *Next Generation.*

Ngoc, N. M., Viet, D. T., Tien, N. H., Hiep, P. M., Anh, N. T., Anh, L. D. H., Truong, N. T., Anh, N. S. T., Trung, L. Q., Dung, V. T. P., & Thao, L. T. H. (2022). Russia-Ukraine War and risks to global supply chains. *International Journal of Mechanical Engineering, 7*(6), 633–640.

Nicholson, S. (2015). A recipe for meaningful gamification. In *Gamification in education and business* (pp. 1–710). https://doi.org/10.1007/978-3-319-10208-5_1

Nicholson, S. (2016). Ask why: Creating a better player experience through environmental storytelling and consistency in escape room design. *Meaningful Play, 2016*, 1–17.

O'Donnell, D. (2020) *The six basic plots and the dramatic curve, Medium.* The Writing Cooperative. Retrieved March 30, 2023, from https://writingcooperative.com/the-six-basic-plots-and-the-dramatic-curve-8f310689b091

Olano, M., Sherman, A., Oliva, L., Cox, R., Firestone, D., Kubik, O., Patil, M., Seymour, J., Sohn, I., & Thomas, D. (2014). SecurityEmpire: Development and evaluation of a digital game to promote cybersecurity education. *2014 USENIX Summit on Gaming, Games, and Gamification in Security Education, 3GSE 2014.*

Oliveira, A. P., Sousa, M., Vairinhos, M., & Zagalo, N. (2020). Towards a new hybrid game model: Designing tangible experiences. *2020 IEEE 8th International Conference on Serious Games and Applications for Health, SeGAH 2020.* https://doi.org/10.1109/SeGAH49190.2020.9201838

Oliveri, G. (1997). Mathematics. A science of patterns? *Synthese, 112*(3). https://doi.org/10.1023/A:1004906107430

Orbanes, P. (2002). Everything I know about business I learned from monopoly. *Harvard Business Review, 80*(3), 51.

Orr, D. (1992). *Ecological literacy: Education for a post modern world.* State University of New York.

Paivio, A., & Csapo, K. (1973). Picture superiority in free recall: Imagery or dual coding? *Cognitive Psychology, 5*(2), 176–206.

Parlett, D. (2005). RULES OK or Hoyle in Troubled Waters. *8th Annual Colloquium of Board Game Studies Association.*

Pavlov, I. P. (1897). *The work of the digestive glands.* Griffin.

Peck, J., & Shu, S. B. (2009). The effect of mere touch on perceived ownership. *Journal of Consumer Research, 36*(3), 434–447.

Peck, J., & Shu, S. (2015). From tragedy to benefit of the commons: Increasing shared psychological ownership. *ACR North American Advances, 43*, 40–44.

Peterson, S. N. (2017). Using a modified version of Pictionary to help students review course material. *Journal of Microbiology & Biology Education, 18*(3). https://doi.org/10.1128/jmbe.v18i3.1375

Piaget, J. (1964). Cognitive development in children: Development and learning. *Journal of Research in Science Teaching, 2*(3), 176–186. http://dx.doi.org/10.1002/tea.3660020306

Pickford, H. C., Joy, G., & Roll, K. (2016). Psychological ownership effects and applications. *Mutuality in Business, 2*, 1–19.

Pickles, L. (2022, July 25). *Monopoly Review*. Retrieved March 22, 2023, from https://www.board-game.co.uk/monopoly-review/

Pierce, J. L., Kostova, T., & Dirks, K. T. (2003). The state of psychological ownership: Integrating and extending a century of research. *Review of General Psychology, 7*(1), 84–107. https://doi.org/10.1037/1089-2680.7.1.84

Pink, D. (2009). *Drive: The surprising truth about what motivates us*. Riverhead Books.

Plattner, H., Meinel, C., & Leifer, L. (Eds.). (2012). Design thinking research. Berlin: Springer.

Plicanic, K., Ingersoll, S., Tan, A. L., Goellner, A., Davidson, C., & Boyd, D. (2023). *The Rule of Thirds in Photography: Your Complete Guide*. Retrieved March 27, 2023, from https://www.adobe.com/uk/creativecloud/photography/discover/rule-of-thirds.html

Pool, J. (2023, March 1). *The World's Top Online Marketplaces 2022*. Retrieved February 10, 2023, from https://www.webretailer.com/marketplaces-worldwide/online-marketplaces/

Prensky, M. (2001). Digital game-based learning digital game-based learning by Marc Prensky. *Secretary, May*, 1–6.

Priestley, R., & Lambshead, J. (2016). *Tabletop wargames: A designers' and writers' handbook*. Pen and Sword Books.

Pritchard, D. B. (2007). *The classified encyclopedia of chess variants*. J. Beasley.

Pulsipher, L. (2012). *The fundamental differences between board and card games and how video games tend to combine both functions*. Game Developer.

Putnam, R. D. (2000). *Bowling alone: The collapse and revival of American community*. Simon and Schuster.

Putri, D. M., & Alhusna, A. (2021). Enriching students' vocabulary by using charade game at pre-intermediate level. *Harakat An-Nisa: Jurnal Studi Gender Dan Anak, 6*(1). https://doi.org/10.30631/harakatan-nisa.2021.61.49-54

Rahmah, A., & Astutik, Y. (2020). Charades game: Does it affect students' learning on English vocabulary? *EnJourMe (English Journal of Merdeka): Culture, Language, and Teaching of English, 5*(1). https://doi.org/10.26905/enjourme.v5i1.4258

Ramirez, M. (2019). *https://www.grammarly.com/blog/how-to-write-review/*. Grammarly. Retrieved February 12, 2023.

Ravyse, W. S., Seugnet Blignaut, A., Leendertz, V., & Woolner, A. (2017). Success factors for serious games to enhance learning: A systematic review. *Virtual Reality, 21*(1). https://doi.org/10.1007/s10055-016-0298-4

RCA Victor. (1959). *Mel Allen's Baseball Game*.

Resnik, D. B. (2018). *The ethics of research with human subjects: Protecting people, advancing science, promoting trust*. Springer.

Ribeiro, H. V., Mendes, R. S., Lenzi, E. K., del Castillo-Mussot, M., & Amaral, L. A. N. (2013). Move-by-move dynamics of the advantage in chess matches reveals population-level learning of the game. *PLoS ONE, 8*(1). https://doi.org/10.1371/journal.pone.0054165

Rigoli, F., Rutledge, R. B., Chew, B., Ousdal, O. T., Dayan, P., & Dolan, R. J. (2016). Dopamine increases a value-independent gambling propensity. *Neuropsychopharmacology, 41*(11). https://doi.org/10.1038/npp.2016.68

Riivari, E., Kivijärvi, M., & Lämsä, A. M. (2021). Learning teamwork through a computer game: For the sake of performance or collaborative learning? *Educational Technology Research and Development, 69*(3).

Rogerson, M. J., & Gibbs, M. (2020). The precursors to modern hybrid boardgames. *DiGRA Australia National Conference, QUT*, Brisbane, Australia.

Rogerson, M. J., Gibbs, M., Carter, M., & Alison, F. (2018). Understanding player elimination in boardgames as a form of permadeath. *DiGRA International Conference: The Game is the Message*, Turin, Italy.

Rogerson, M. J., Gibbs, M., & Smith, W. (2016). "I love all the bits": The materiality of boardgames. *Conference on Human Factors in Computing Systems - Proceedings*.

Rogerson, M. J., Sparrow, L. A., & Gibbs, M. R. (2021). Unpacking boardgames with apps: The hybrid digital boardgame model. *Conference on Human Factors in Computing Systems - Proceedings*.

Ryan, R., & Deci, E. (2000). Self-determination theory and the facilitation of intrinsic motivation. *American Psychologist*, *55*(1), 68–78. https://doi.org/10.1037/0003-066X.55.1.68

Sackson, S. (1981). *Card games around the world*. Dover Publications.

Safdari, R., Ghazisaeidi, M., Goodini, A., Mirzaee, M., & Farzi, J. (2016). Electronic game: A key effective technology to promote behavioral change in cancer patients. *Journal of Cancer Research and Therapeutics*, *12*(2). https://doi.org/10.4103/0973-1482.154939

Salen, K., & Zimmerman, E. (2004). *Rules of play: Game design fundamentals*. The MIT Press.

Salen, K., & Zimmerman, E. (2005). Game design and meaningful play. In *Handbook of computer game studies*. The MIT Press.

Samoray, J. (2002). Professor teaches kids through cribbage. *Oakland University Newsletter*.

Saunders, M. N. K., Lewis, P., & Thornhill, A. (2019). *Research methods for business students* (8th ed.). Pearson.

Sayegh, A., Song, H., Seibold, Z., & He, I. (2019). *Moving Walkway*. Retrieved March 17, 2023, from https://airtraveldesign.guide/Moving-Walkway

Schell, J. (2008). *The art of game design: A book of lenses* (pp. 1–489). CRC Press. https://doi.org/10.1201/9780080919171

Schwind, V., Knierim, P., Tasci, C., Franczak, P., Haas, N., & Henze, N. (2017). These are not my hands! Effect of gender on the perception of avatar hands in virtual reality. *Proceedings of the 2017 CHI Conference on Human Factors in Computing Systems*, pp. 1577–1582. https://doi.org/10.1145/3025453.3025602

Shank, M. (2006). Teacher storytelling: A means for creating and learning within a collaborative space. *Teaching and Teacher Education*, *22*(6), 711–721. https://doi.org/10.1016/j.tate.2006.03.002

Shanklin, S. B., & Ehlen, C. R. (2007). Using the monopoly board game as an in-class economic simulation in the introductory financial accounting course. *Journal of College Teaching & Learning (TLC)*. https://doi.org/10.19030/tlc.v4i11.1525

Shizgal, P., & Arvanitogiannis, A. (2003). Gambling on dopamine. *Science*, *299*(5614). https://doi.org/10.1126/science.1083627

Simpson, E. J. (1972). *The classification of educational objectives in the psychomotor domain*. Illinois; Illinois (Urbana)

Singh Dubey, R., Paul, J., & Tewari, V. (2022). The soft skills gap: A bottleneck in the talent supply in emerging economies. *International Journal of Human Resource Management*, *33*(13). https://doi.org/10.1080/09585192.2020.1871399

Sipos, Y., Battisti, B., & Grimm, K. (2008). Achieving transformative sustainability learning: Engaging head, hands and heart. *International Journal of Sustainability in Higher Education*, *9*, 68–86.

Skinner, B. F. (1948). "Superstition" in the pigeon. *Journal of Experimental Psychology*, *38*, 168–172.

Skinner, B. F. (1951). *How to teach animals.* Freeman.

Skinner, B. F. (1953). *Science and human behavior.* The Macmillan Company.

Slack, J. (2020). *The top 10 mistakes new board game designers make: (and how to avoid them) (The board game Designer's guide).* CRC Press.

Smith, D. (2016). *The history of the tube map.* Londonist. Retrieved March 9, 2023, from https://londonist.com/2016/05/the-history-of-the-tube-map

Smith, M. F. (1991). *Prototyping: Adoption, practice and management.* McGraw-Hill.

Sousa, M. (2020). Modern serious board games: Modding games to teach and train civil engineering students. *IEEE Global Engineering Education Conference, EDUCON, April.* https://doi.org/10.1109/EDUCON45650.2020.9125261

St Clair, K. (2016). *The secret lives of colour.* John Murray Publishers.

Steen, L. A. (1988). The science of patterns. *Science, 240*(4852). https://doi.org/10.1126/science.240.4852.611

Stenros, J. (2017). The Game Definition Game: A Review. *Games and Culture, 12*(6), 499–520. https://doi.org/10.1177/1555412016655679

Stokes, S. (2001). Visual literacy in teaching and learning: A literature perspective. https://wcpss.pbworks.com/f/Visual+Literacy.pdf

Suits, B. (1967). What is a game? *Philosophy of Science, 34*(2), 148–156.

Susi, T., Johannesson, M., & Backlund, P. (2007). Serious games – An overview. IKI Technical Reports HS-IKI-TR-07-001, 28. https://www.diva-portal.org/smash/get/diva2:2416/fulltext01.pdf

TechNavio. (2022). *Board Games Market by Distribution Channel, Product, and Geography - Forecast and Analysis 2022-2026.*

The Editors of Encyclopaedia Britannica (2022, August 31). *Technology. Encyclopedia Britannica.* https://www.britannica.com/technology/technology

Thorndike, E. L. (1898). Animal intelligence: An experimental study of the associative processes in animals. *Psychological Monographs: General and Applied, 2*(4), i–109.

Tindale, C. (2017). Narratives and the concept of argument. In Paul Olmos (Ed.), *Narration as argument* (pp. 11–30). Springer.

Tinsman, B. (2008). *The game inventor's guidebook.* Morgan James Publishing.

Trammell, A. (2019). *Analog games and the digital economy.* https://analoggamestudies.org/2019/03/analog-games-and-the-digital-economy/

Transport for London. (2006). *Tube Map voted a UK design icon.* Retrieved March 8, 2023, from https://tfl.gov.uk/info-for/media/press-releases/2006/march/tube-map-voted-a-uk-design-icon

Tyng, C. M., Amin, H. U., Saad, M. N. M., & Malik, A. S. (2017, August 24). The influences of emotion on learning and memory. In *Frontiers in psychology.* Frontiers Media S.A. https://doi.org/10.3389/fpsyg.2017.01454

Varonis, E. M., & Varonis, M. E. (2015). Deconstructing candy crush: What instructional design can learn from game design. *International Journal of Information and Learning Technology, 32*(3). https://doi.org/10.1108/IJILT-09-2014-0019

Vlachopoulos, D., & Makri, A. (2017). The effect of games and simulations on higher education: a systematic literature review. *International Journal of Educational Technology in Higher Education, 14*(1). https://doi.org/10.1186/s41239-017-0062-1

Vörös, A. I. V., & Sárközi, Z. (2017). Physics escape room as an educational tool. *AIP Conference Proceedings, 1916.* https://doi.org/10.1063/1.5017455

Vygotsky, L. S. (1967). Play and its role in the mental development of the child. *Soviet Psychology.* https://doi.org/10.2753/rpo1061-040505036

Vygotsky, L. S. (1978). *Mind and society: The development of higher psychological processes.* Harvard University Press.

Vygotsky, L. S. (1997). *The collected works of LS Vygotsky: Problems of the theory and history of psychology* (Vol. 3). Springer Science & Business Media.

Walk, W., Görlich, D., & Barrett, M. (2017). Design, dynamics, experience (DDE): An advancement of the MDA framework for game design. In *Game dynamics: Best Practices in procedural and dynamic game content generation* (pp. 27–45). https://doi.org/10.1007/978-3-319-53088-8_3

Walker, J. (2013, April 17). *A good discussion of the problematic economic model of certain game review websites.* Retrieved February 12, 2023, from https://botherer.org/2013/04/17/a-response-to-pars-adblockersgames-press-article/

Walliman, N. (2022). *Research methods* (3rd ed.). Routledge.

Wan Norhaidi, W. M. S., Romly, R., & Abdullah, A. N. S. (2019). Lowering anxiety among low proficiency ESL learners using the mafia game. *International Journal of Innovative Technology and Exploring Engineering, 8*(7), 67–73.

Watson, J. B. (1924). *Behaviorism.* People's Institute Publishing Company.

Watson, J. B., & Rayner, R. (1920). Conditioned emotional reactions. *Journal of Experimental Psychology, 3*(1), 1.

Weinstein, Y., Sumeracki, M., & Caviglioli, O. (2019). *Understanding how we learn.* Routledge.

White, P. (2017). *Developing research questions* (2nd ed.). Palgrave.

Winn, B. M. (2011). The design, play, and experience framework. In *Handbook of research on effective electronic gaming in education.* https://doi.org/10.4018/978-1-59904-808-6.ch058

Witter, R. T., & Lyford, A. (2020). Applications of graph theory and probability in the board game ticket to ride. *ACM International Conference Proceeding Series,* pp. 1–4. https://doi.org/10.1145/3402942.3402963

Wolf, B. K. (n.d.). A complete guide to iconography. Retrieved March 29, 2023, from https://www.designsystems.com/iconography-guide/

Wolf, G. (1996, February). Steve Jobs: The Next Insanely Great Thing. The Wired Interview, *Wired, 4*(2), 102–107, 158, 160, 162–163.

Woods, S. (2019). Eurogames: The design, culture and play of modern European board games. *Journal of Chemical Information and Modeling, 53,* 9.

Xin, T. G. (2022). The framework of a game design (MDA framework). *Technical University of Malaysia Malacc.*

Xu, Y., Barba, E., Radu, I., Gandy, M., & MacIntyre, B. (2011). Chores are fun: Understanding social play in board games for digital tabletop game design. Proceedings of DiGRA 2011 Conference: Think Design Play, Vol. 6.

Xu, Y., Li, J. P., Chu, C. C., & Dinca, G. (2022). Impact of COVID-19 on transportation and logistics: A case of China. *Economic Research-Ekonomska Istrazivanja, 35*(1), 2386–2404.

Yoon, B., Rodriguez, L., Faselis, C. J., & Liappis, A. P. (2014). Using a board game to reinforce learning. *Journal of Continuing Education in Nursing, 45*(3). https://doi.org/10.3928/00220124-20140224-14

Yusoff, A., Crowder, R., Gilbert, L., & Wills, G. (2009). A conceptual framework for serious games. *Proceedings - 2009 9th IEEE International Conference on Advanced Learning Technologies, ICALT 2009.* https://doi.org/10.1109/ICALT.2009.19

Zagal, J. P., Ladd, A., & Johnson, T. (2009). Characterizing and understanding game reviews. *FDG 2009 - 4th International Conference on the Foundations of Digital Games, Proceedings.* https://doi.org/10.1145/1536513.1536553

Zeshan, U. (2020). *Serious games in co-creative facilitation.* Ishara Press.

Index

Milton Keynes UK
Ingram Content Group UK Ltd.
UKHW022040141024
449569UK00014B/670